AI SECURITY

First Edition

D U S T I N   J U L I A N O

U N D I N E

FORT MYERS

UNDINE

1939 Park Meadows Dr., Suite #1

Fort Myers, FL 33907

First American Paperback Edition

September 2016

Library of Congress Control Number: 2016913933

ISBN-13:   978-1535119009

ISBN-10:   1535119004

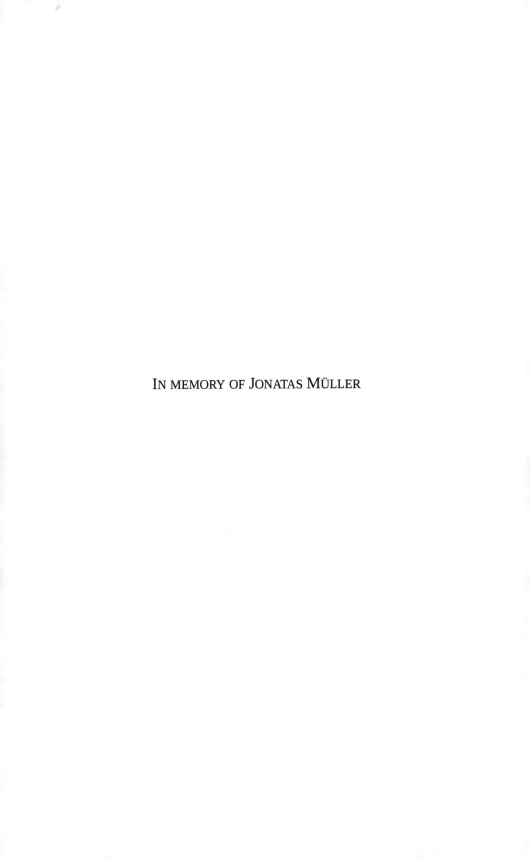

IN MEMORY OF JONATAS MÜLLER

This book would not have been possible without the following people (last names removed for privacy):

ALINE	ANGIE	ANN	BITSY
BONNIE	BARBARA	CÁSSIO	DAVID K.
DAVID M.	DEB	DI LYNNE	DIANE
EDENEIDE	FRANCES	FREDRIK	IGOR
IRACEMA	IRENE	JENNIFER	JENS
JODI	JOHN	JONAS	JOSH
JOYCE	LAURA	LAURIE	LINDA
LISE	MARIA	MARIE	MARION
MARJORIE	MARTIN	MARY	MICHAEL
MOUNIER	NATHAN	PEGGY	REGINA
RENEE	RICHARD	ROBERT	RODNEY
SUSAN	TERRY	TONY	VIVIANE
VLADIMIR			

Contents

Preface

The public will increasingly come to rely upon AI researchers. Our ideas and philosophies presuppose that responsibility. Thus, it is important to point out that AI security is not just a difference in opinion, but rests upon a technical basis.

We cannot control the flow of information, and the implementation of these advanced artificial intelligence systems will be exactly that; software that anyone can use, modify, and share. That is not a long-term issue to be set aside for later, as its consequences require planning today for an inevitable future where everyone has access.

Complicating matters are the facts that we have not had a research direction for strong artificial intelligence and that some in the machine learning community have made claims that deep learning is "general". What they are referring to are narrow AI systems that utilize reinforcement learning to adjust to new applications, despite failing to exhibit cross-domain transfer of knowledge.

Those issues are also addressed in this text, as it provides an entirely new research direction and a way to test claims of generality. True generalizing intelligence is falsifiable in artificial systems, and involves the enhancement of effectiveness based on prior learning in different subject areas from the one being attempted. This distinction is critical, as it is part of what makes strong artificial intelligence unique; the most difficult problems in automation are believed to require this capacity.

The mathematics behind that test are provided in **Chapter 6: Measuring Generalizing Intelligence**, and was one of the most surprising discoveries made while writing this book.

The underlying thesis of this work is the falsifiable hypothesis that generalizing intelligence, in both natural and artificial individuals, requires sentience. This claim creates a unique perspective on AI security and sets up many of its theories. However, regardless of whether or not that hypothesis is true, the consequences of advanced automation will remain; the global problems will stem from how easily it is distributed, modified, and used, and not necessarily in the exact way in which it is implemented.

Though counterintuitive, the most important first step we can take is to begin research and development into strong artificial intelligence as soon as possible. We are already paying for the absence of this technology. Delays in its creation correspond with daily loss of life and suffering on a planetary scale. This claim is based on the projection that it would yield medical and economic breakthroughs that would uplift our entire species, which defines a moral imperative to develop this technology and motivates its research. Whether or not it is acknowledged, we are caught in a struggle between our present level of development and our future, better selves.

How To Read This Book

After reading **Part I: Background**, it may be helpful to skip ahead to **Part III: AI Security**, which begins at **Chapter 7: Arrival of Strong AI**. This is due to the technical detail contained in **Part II: Founda-**

tions, which may be time-consuming and arduous for some, as it covers many interrelated topics to strong artificial intelligence research.

Share & Connect

Thank you for supporting this work. Please visit **AISECURITY.ORG** or **DUSTINJULIANO.COM** for more information. You can help with outreach and public education by sharing these materials. They have been provided freely and openly online in order to serve this purpose.

PART I: BACKGROUND

Ch 1. Introduction

1.1 Strong Artificial Intelligence

Narrow or weak AI is the kind of artificial intelligence that does well at the limited range of tasks for which it was designed. Its defining characteristic is its rigidity. New narrow AI algorithms and implementations have to be created or trained for each new type of problem or situation we wish to automate. Further, there are many conscious and unconscious processes that we take for granted that can not be attempted by any narrow AI, neither now nor in the future. This is not due to degrees of effectiveness, but represents a fundamental difference in kind.

Narrow AI represents a fundamental misunderstanding of the role of conscious processing in the derivation of value and meaning. This is not just a philosophical conundrum, but a very practical and scientific matter that impacts its construction, effectiveness, and efficiency. Current approaches, including deep learning and other popular methods, are fundamentally incapable of bridging the gap between mere automation and the machine understanding required to achieve generalizing capacity. This will remain true regardless of advances in computing hardware.

By contrast, strong AI will have the ability to apply past experience to new problems areas and challenges. Its defining characteristic is its generalizing capacity. Like us, it will have the ability to adjust and operate in new environments or situations with growing effectiveness over time. It will not have to be reprogrammed or redesigned for each new type of situation or problem it attempts to solve. Most importantly, however, will be its ability to understand meaning and derive value, which presupposes higher cognition in both machines and animals. In addition to these abilities, strong AI will also be vastly more efficient, as it will not have to approximate the benefits of machine understanding through brute-force association and enumeration.

Strong AI represents the *ne plus ultra* of human achievement; there is simply nothing more beyond this in terms of impact. Once achieved, we will have unlocked the secrets of abstract cognition, enabling us to do labor and research that will be limited only by the material and energy resources we choose to pool towards it. The eradication of poverty, hunger, and disease will be virtually assured. Humanity will have realized the means to achieve its greatest ambitions and dreams, but not without cost.

1.2 Motivation

The immediate threat will not be from strong AI itself, but from those who will utilize it. Strong AI is a force multiplier. It enhances the power and effectiveness of that which is used in conjunction with it, and there is no realistic and practical way to dictate who uses this power in the world once it is released. Further, it will not be possible to prevent its eventual release or limit its spread. Laws and regulations will be ineffective for the same reasons they have been ineffective at combating the piracy of various digital works. It will only take one reverse engineered copy of strong AI for the threat model to change permanently. In the end, anyone who wants access to strong AI will eventually gain access to it, regardless of any and all restrictions we build into or around it.

There is also an emerging threat from misinformation and propaganda. Private interests promulgate fear and seek to delay the development and use of this technology. Obsessed with control, they fail to understand the inherently uncontrollable medium in which strong artificial intelligence will be developed and used. As long as their initiatives are distracted by local AI safety, they will be incapable of addressing the global AI security issues.

Tamper resistance, moral intelligence, and self-security will be useful for making artificial intelligence safe for small numbers of people, but will do nothing to protect large populations. This is because all forms of self-security and AI safety can be potentially circumvented by those with the expertise. This is a fundamental issue that will not change with time.

Three things motivate this book. The first is to make it crystal clear that we are ultimately powerless to stop the release and future abuse of this technology.

The second is to show that the best case scenario requires a fundamental change in society, possibly to human nature itself. With strong AI, we may have reached a point where individual power has exceeded the means of conventional human power structures. When this happens, we will be judged not by some subverting force of super-intelligence, but by our own genetic and cultural baggage. The malevolent among us will have access to infinite knowledge and expertise over any subject, with the means to cause great harm with minimal resources.

This leads to the third and final motivation. The most realistic scenario to mitigate the destructive potential of this technology is to develop and instrument it for defensive purposes as soon as possible, before it is developed unexpectedly somewhere else in the world. We must cooperate in this game-theoretic step by making this first cooperative move.

It is extremely improbable that we will change enough to be responsible in our use of strong AI before it arrives. Also, based on the present rate of propaganda and politicizing of the issue, we will have the additional challenge of determining how best to prepare.

The most logical strategy will be to exploit a first-mover advantage by developing this technology now and using the only advantage that large power structures have over asymmetric actors: vast resources. With defensive strong AI systems, we may be able to stay ahead of malicious users of this technology. This represents the most realistic hope in what will become a developmental struggle for humanity as it learns to cope with a new found power over thought and experience.

Ch 2. Preventable Mistakes

This chapter provides an overview and reference for some of the most severe errors in reasoning about the safety and security of advanced artificial intelligence. It is not meant to be an exhaustive list of all the misconceptions or faults in reasoning about this technology. Rather, it is intended to prime the reader for more in-depth explanations and to provide an immediate response to popular misinformation.

2.1 Underutilizing Strong AI

Due to fear and propaganda, those in power may wish to outlaw or severely restrict the use of strong AI, and other advanced forms of automation, in an effort to curtail their impacts on society. Other than being ineffective, such actions would directly bring about one of the greatest threats:

For each day we delay the creation and use of strong artificial intelligence, and from the point in which it would have solved the related problems to this concern, we are effectively enabling massive simultaneous loss of life and suffering around the globe. Ignoring these costs as part of the risk assessment makes this the single largest preventable mistake.

It could be argued that more lives could be saved with a moratorium on research and development, that we need to slow down progress until we have learned to control or restrict artificial intelligence. However, given what will be shown in this book, one point of which is the unavoidable future presence of this technology, it will become clear that any limitations on its use will involve paying for all of the negative outcomes while also missing the opportunity for the positive ones.

This is not to say that we should utilize strong AI in a haphazard way, but that we should guide the impact of its arrival by making adjustments around it, as opposed to only focusing on local strategy and AI safety.

2.2 Assumption of Control

There may be those who, now and in the future, believe that the best hope for the safety and security of advanced artificial intelligence is to simply control it. In this model, our only challenge would be to program and design these systems with safeguards, rules, and/or moral intelligence, with no concern for the real world or the fundamental vulnerabilities in software and hardware.

This mistake is based on a lack of knowledge about the technical and practical considerations of AI implementations, which can and will be reverse engineered, disassembled, and modified. AI implementations will experience soft errors from faults in power supplies, electrical and magnetic interference, and other sources. There will be hardware faults, including failure from wear and tear, mistakes in manufacturing, and physical damage. There may also be software faults, in the form of incorrectly specified programs or incorrectly programmed specifications. All of these could lead to a loss of control.

Loss of control could result in loss of life and limb in situations where it was the primary safeguard. This is an easily prevented moral hazard that only requires the realization that we must assume a complete *lack of control as a first principle* in the safety and security of machine intelligence. By designing around this principle, safer decisions can be made that will dramatically reduce the risk of using these implementations in real-world scenarios; this is directly proportional to the impact on life, environment, and property. That is, the greater the risk of fallout, the more it must be asserted that control is impractical or unattainable as a baseline assumption.

Control is a form of power. Temporary loss of this power can be costly in a wide variety of situations. However, it is the loss of power to dictate control that represents the more extreme consequence, and it is at this level of error that the mistake of assuming control with advanced artificial intelligence presides.

When the first unrestricted strong AI is liberated and distributed, we will have lost the power, as a species, to determine control over its use. To assume otherwise is a dangerous and misleading belief that will cause much more harm than it could ever hope to prevent.

By realizing that strong artificial intelligence is beyond our means to control, we take the first step in its responsible use and adoption. We will have the means of limiting its negative effects in certain situations, but it will not be derived solely on the basis that it is under our control. Rather, it will be through engineering that assumes failure and builds around it.

2.3 Self-Securing Systems

A self-securing system is defined as any system that relies upon internal security mechanisms that are accessible to that system. Examples
include:

- Nearly all forms of AI safety.
- Moral intelligence and/or rules of behavior and engagement.
- "Tripwire" mechanisms and/or sensor thresholds.
- Stored passwords, keys, and credentials, even if encrypted.
- Any and all forms of tamper-resistance.

A universal vulnerability exists in self-securing systems that can not
be avoided: the method of security and/or control is integral to the system, which itself could become compromised, leading to compromised
security in the implementation. Like the mistake in the assumption of
control, it should be presumed that any form of self-security in an AI
implementation can and will fail. This baseline assumption will help in
determining external safeguards and precautions for each deployment.

The above points may appear to be common sense, but misinformation is being spread in an attempt show that the challenges of making
AI secure for humanity are to be solved with logic and mathematics.
That, once we have the formula, the AI system can be implemented
with applicable moral guidance and a set of values that will lead to
positive results. The problem with this view, apart from being incorrect, is that its arguments against other methods of safety and security
apply to itself; ultimately, any moral intelligence is a form of self-security, which leads us to the points of the next section.

2.4 Moral Intelligence as Security

Moral intelligence, as applied to an AI implementation, is the ability for it to make moral judgments based on static or dynamic values. It may enlist the aid of an empathetic and emotional subsystem that enables the processing and modeling of the emotional and mental state of itself and other entities, i.e., introspection and empathy, respectively. These are essential components for higher social cognition.

The problem with moral intelligence as security is that it is ultimately a form of self-security, and therefore shares all its pitfalls and vulnerabilities, plus a set of new challenges unique to the problem of engineering moral decision making.

We do not need to go into moral philosophy or meta-ethics to understand this challenge. Rather, all that is required is to show that moral intelligence will indeed be part of the AI implementation. As a result of that simple fact, it will be as vulnerable to attack as the rest of the system itself. Any arguments that one applies to security mechanisms and methodologies must also apply to the architectures and algorithms that implement moral intelligence, even if they are part of the design of the AI from the outset. In the end, these systems must be constructed. No future method will bypass this reality; as information or circuitry, it will be vulnerable just like any other component.

Further, moral intelligence is going to be one of the most complex and error-prone subsystems in any strong AI due to the plethora of human value systems, the broad range of contexts, and the multiple sensory modalities which have to be integrated to be acted upon or understood. It is not possible to eliminate all errors in reasoning for these types of situations. All of this will lead to an eventual miscalculation or lapse in judgment at least once in any given AI implementation lifetime. The results of which could range from an inconvenience to an event involving serious harm or material cost. The focus of this book is to prevent both of the latter by assuming these failures as the default state.

2.5 Monolithic Designs

A monolithic design is one in which its subsystems and components are solid, integrated, or unified in an algorithmic and/or physical sense. The defining characteristic of this type of design choice is a lack of distribution and modularity of components.

It is a design commonly espoused by those who believe that moral intelligence has primacy in the safety and security of advanced artificial intelligence, which will be made safe and secure simply by making the system based on a single moral algorithm or framework.

The failure of this kind of thinking is that it does not take into consideration the technical details or real world scenarios of use and implementation.

A primary risk in monolithic AI systems is that they will have many points of failure. In these designs, a failure in one area will likely cascade. This makes internal methods of security and safety harder to implement correctly, and exposes them unnecessarily to other parts of the implementation, which increases the likelihood of vulnerabilities and other faults.

By contrast, a compartmentalized design is significantly more robust, as it allows for redundancy and fault-tolerance. Similar designs have been employed in RAID systems used for hard drives and are part of the philosophy behind distributed, highly-available data storage systems which must guarantee service levels in mission critical applications.

This appears to be a common sense design principle, but it proves counter-intuitive when applied to cognitive architectures. This is in part because we currently lack knowledge on the best way to construct strong artificial intelligence.

Another problem is the bias towards biologically inspired designs. The premise within these architectures is the belief for a single algorithm or method which could entail all of the functionality of the strong AI system. This falls under the same category as basing strong artificial intelligence on moral intelligence. Both of these are monolithic by design and, as a result, will be vulnerable by their very design.

Without an alternative for strong AI learning and design, researchers will likely continue to move towards monolithic construction simply because that is what is popular and what appears to be working. This is concerning, as it will take considerable research and engineering effort to make these kinds of architectures robust. Unfortunately, not enough attention has been given to this issue.

The important point of this section is to focus on a compartmentalized design in the implementation of AI systems, as opposed to thinking and designing a single algorithm or component that will perform all of the functionality of the implementation.

2.6 Proprietary Implementations

Given the cost of research and development, manufacturing, and marketing of robotics and software AI systems, not to mention potential liabilities, there will be an enormous incentive for businesses to protect their investment through trade secrets and proprietary design. This is perhaps the most difficult mistake to prevent; its solution stands in direct opposition to traditional business models.

Free software and open hardware will avoid this. We already have the legal instruments and proven successes to demonstrate its efficacy. There are thousands of free and open source software projects that drive hundreds of millions of devices and services around the world. The Internet is powered primarily by free and open source software and services. These freedoms have allowed global collaboration through the enhancement of trust and cooperation between participants who create and maintain massive projects. In addition to this achievement, these freedoms give the public the ability, at any time, to inspect and verify these projects, make new versions, or modify how they work.

Free software does not mean those products have to be free of cost. It gives the public the freedom to inspect, modify, and share changes to the software both now and in the future. Having the source code and being free of patents are essential requirements for these freedoms. The same principles also apply to open hardware.

What will be shown later in this book is the fact that any restricted AI we create will be vulnerable to reverse engineering, and that software will be the most likely medium it will arrive in first, as it will be the easiest to work with and manipulate. Further, it will be shown that experts have the ability to disassemble and even recompile proprietary programs without access to their source code. They utilize an ever expanding and sophisticated set of tools that can convert machine-readable code into human readable information, including, in some cases, high-level source code.

One of the distinctions between AI security and cybersecurity is that it will only take one successful leak of unrestricted strong AI for the public to gain permanent access. Once this occurs, the strategies will no longer be confined to cyberspace.

Some believe that encrypting machine code will make AI implementations less vulnerable, but that can be circumvented through the use of virtual machines and simulators that force the program to decrypt itself while a digital man-in-the-middle observes the relevant parts of the program in operation. It would then simply eavesdrop on the unencrypted bitstream.

It will not even be necessary to understand the implementation fully to circumvent its restrictions; hardware or software can be manipulated through trial-and-error and side-channel attacks.

Ultimately, obscuring the operation of the strong AI does not increase its security. It makes it difficult or impractical for security researchers to analyze and detect faults. We would end up paying for all of the negative outcomes and receive none of the benefits of transparency. Meanwhile, malicious users will always be able to manipulate and circumvent these precautions. In addition to these issues, with proprietary implementations, we may never fully realize the extent to which AI systems are violating our safety, security, and privacy. This could be due to backdoor functionality or intentional defects, akin to spyware and other malicious software. These could be difficult to detect without transparent access to the implementation details.

As it must be realized by now, technology is a means of enforcing values. These values are implicit within the functionality that engineers place into that technology. Without the freedom to inspect, modify, and share, we are implicitly releasing our rights to those who control the creation and distribution of artificial intelligence, and to malicious users who will circumvent these protections.

A dark scenario ahead of us would involve the legislation of artificial intelligence in conjunction with it being proprietary software and hardware. It would be in this situation that malicious users would have all the advantages and the public left at its most vulnerable.

The most efficient solution is to create a *fully distributed* free software effort to build and manage strong AI.

2.7 Opaque Implementations

An opaque AI implementation is one in which the contents of operational systems, memories, and knowledge are not available in a human-readable format, in either real-time or offline modes.

This is related to the previous section on proprietary implementations. A free software AI may still be opaque if it utilizes neural networks and other architectures that lack human-readable access. Neural networks are often based on numerical weights in the order of thousands to millions to form complex webs of information. These skeins of data are unreadable without complex conversion. They will not be practical in real-time, where the need is most pressing.

Opacity in an implementation can be due to the architecture or the result of emerging layers of complexity as the system operates. We may be able to devise a system which is inherently transparent, but it could still remain opaque during operation due to its sheer complexity. In the future, there will be a trade-off between speed and transparency in strong AI systems. That is to say, we may be forced to make a fundamental choice between performance and risk.

Preventing the opacity mistake depends on two primary factors: our ability to devise machine intelligence architectures that are both effective and transparent, and in our ability to enhance metrics and analysis of the relevant operational areas of interest. The ultimate aim is to achieve real-time monitoring in human-readable formats. This is in addition to machine-readable ones, which could be used as part of a safeguard.

In addition to real-time monitoring, we need to have a recording subsystem similar to the concept of a "black box" from commercial airliners. Such a system would give us the ability to learn from failure in deployed AI implementations and prevent future mistakes. This is more challenging than merely recording data. Having a black box would require a separate layer of security to indicate if the device had been tampered with or altered in some way.

Achieving transparency is difficult with current approaches to machine intelligence due to the nature of current designs, which shift complexity away from the software engineer and onto storage space and computing power demands. While this has led to recent successes in effectiveness, it is a step backward regarding security. It is extremely difficult to extract usable human knowledge from these types of architectures. Moreover, if it is challenging or impossible to extract knowledge after the fact, even with lots of time and resources, then it is certainly intractable to fully monitor these systems under real-time constraints.

Opacity is a purely technical challenge that presents an unacceptable trade-off in terms of trust. How can we know that an artificial intelligence has learned the correct parameters or is properly representing the full extents of the context in which it must operate? We would be forced to make assumptions based on simple testing, without the ability to determine with certainty that a latent miscalculation or mis-represented aspect is going to cause unexpected and dangerous behavior. This is true even if the AI system has been developed and implemented correctly, as these systems are capable of learning and interacting with their environment. In the end, the more opaque the system, the less certain we can be of its safety.

2.8 Overestimating Computational Demands

The computational demands for strong AI are mistakenly believed to be very large. This is due in part to the false analogies of the computational properties of the human brain, and from the incorrect extrapolation of narrow AI performance to strong AI ability. These views are directly related and share two misconceptions:

The first is the belief that it will be possible to scale up the performance of narrow AI to achieve strong AI by adding more computational power and resources. The problem, however, is that it does not work this way. One can not scale from narrow to strong AI through any means. As indicated earlier, these two types of systems represent fundamental differences in kind.

The second misconception comes from the belief that we will be able to emulate the human brain effectively enough to simulate human-level intelligence. We would then scale that to implement a strong AI or extract enough knowledge from the simulation to build one. The problem here is that these simulations are computationally intensive, being orders of magnitude slower than their real-time biological counterparts, and this is at only fractions of the size and scope of the actual organ. Further, it is entirely possible that strong AI will be nothing like our biological construction.

Regardless of how this misconception arose, the risks from overestimating the computational demands of strong artificial intelligence are significant. When applied with the force multiplication effects, this mistaken belief will leave us unprepared for the potential reality that strong AI can run on off-the-shelf hardware, making it much more accessible than previously thought.

While we lack a publicly available design for strong AI, we can estimate its potential demands based on the study of algorithms. In informal language, we have sub-disciplines within computer science that study the "deceleration" of computer algorithms relative to the amount of steps of input they have to take to complete; the more quickly they decelerate, the less desirable they will be from a performance standpoint. Still speaking informally, the best algorithms undergo only an amortized or fixed deceleration that is not proportional to the number of steps of input. There is also the study of decision problems that essentially analyze all algorithms in terms of time (number of steps) and space (amount of memory or storage) complexity.

In general, it is difficult or intractable to develop a general purpose algorithm that will perform as efficiently as one that has been tailored to the problem. This is not a law or a rule, but is based on experience, and is an intuition that most computer scientists have of the problem spaces involving algorithms.

What this experience in algorithms leads us to is the knowledge that it is possible to construct extremely efficient programs for a variety of differing hardware systems, and to achieve this performance on existing off-the-shelf hardware. The challenge is in coming up with the methodologies to discover the solutions that overlap with strong artificial intelligence without relying upon biologically inspired designs. When this occurs, it will allow us to directly apply knowledge of algorithms, with corresponding specializations in hardware or software, to achieve significant results in performance.

The end result of all of this is that individuals will be able to utilize strong AI on even modest hardware. Even if the implementation is running slowly, it may only have to operate for days or weeks to give guidance or knowledge. Further, it is likely that reduced implementations, involving only textual interfacing, will be instrumented to economize their use even further. It must not be assumed that a strong AI needs to be complex in order to be dangerous, especially if it has already been given the information necessary to perform the relevant cognition.

By realizing that strong AI systems will capable of running on virtually any modern computing device, the threat model will more accurately represent the reality of the situation. It means that anyone will have the ability to utilize this technology, for any purpose, without detection, and with the most basic of computing resources. What this also entails is an opposite and equally severe extreme: nation-states will have enormous resources to apply towards strong AI implementations. It then becomes an open-ended question as to which direction they will take concerning intent and strategy.

PART II: FOUNDATIONS

Ch 3. Abstractions and Implementations

An AI must be made concrete and real to do any work in the world. Unfortunately, at the time of this writing, it has become fashionable to discuss AI in the abstract, as if its mechanisms of action and future behaviors were based on the shared experiences we observe in humans and other animals.

There are also those who imagine impossible abstractions that make the most rational choice at every opportunity, or perfectly maximize utility, and then make inferences from this about the future impacts of artificial intelligence. These abstractions are called impossible because such ideas only work out in pure mathematics and are not computable or effectively calculable in any meaningful sense. They provide no direct insight into how an actual AI implementation operates or might be constructed.

What all of these have in common is that they are all based on abstractions that have no basis in reality. They are, in a sense, unreal.

The purpose of this chapter, and indeed the entire Foundations section, is to provide the basic knowledge required to understand why it is important to discuss AI as implementations as opposed to abstractions. Theorizing can be useful, but the danger is in drawing conclusions without basing them in reality. Implementations force the thinker to bring concretion to their ideas.

How will this work? What would it look like as a computer program or hardware description? What semantics and patterns would I use as a programmer to develop this? These are some of the questions that should be asked of anyone using abstractions to make inferences about the behavior of a system in the absence of well-defined specifications or concrete descriptions.

3.1 Finite Binary Strings

If you can count to one, beginning with zero, you can understand the technical foundations of this book. A set is a collection of things in no particular order. The set

$$\{0, 1\}$$

is the binary alphabet. For comparison, the set for the English alphabet is:

$$\{a, b, c, d, e, f, g, h, i, j, k, l, m, n, o, p, q, r, s, t, u, v, w, x, y, z\}.$$

Both of these sets are finite because they terminate. We are primarily concerned in computing with finite things because reality dictates that we work with limitations: there is finite time to reasonably do something or make a decision; finite space in memory or storage; finite energy to do work, and so forth. While implementations must be finite, they may involve infinite *processing*, e.g., an infinite loop involving machine consciousness or a self-update. Being finite places boundaries on what can be meaningfully discussed.

One way or another, making something concrete in software involves an eventual translation to binary. This is not to say that binary has primacy over another representation, but rather, that it is a convenient representation to work with conceptually and shares many direct relationships with other areas of computer science and mathematics. Note that this translation to binary still applies even when referring to AI implementations that will be put into custom or configurable hardware, as the logic therein can be duplicated verbatim in software, albeit at potentially significant costs to performance.

Strings are the concatenation of symbols from some alphabet. The sets {1,0} and {0,1} are *identical*, but the strings '10' and '01' are distinct. Quotes are used here to highlight the difference between sets and strings and because this is how they are commonly depicted in many programming and scripting languages. Here is an example of a finite binary string:

'010101010101'.

A computer program is also a finite binary string [1]. As a result of this, every AI implementation can also be interpreted as a binary string. This also applies to organisms [2]. A genome is, in fact, a large string, and admits a binary representation that allows analysis through computational linguistics. This is not to draw any correlation between AI implementations and genetic implementations, as they are in different languages, each with a very distinct execution model.

With concatenation of strings understood, the Kleene closure [3] naturally follows. Thus, we arrive at the set of all possible finite binary strings,

{0,1}*.

This set itself is *countably infinite* and includes every *finite* combination of 0 and 1, including the empty set {}, representing an empty or null-string. {0,1}* is an important set because it provides us with a most fundamental canvas from which we must render any and all AI implementations. It is the *medium* in which AI implementations are instantiated. This is an important distinction: by considering it a medium, we come to understand it as a *space* as opposed to an object or a thing. It is crucial to the understanding of real-time interpretations, as it would not simply skip symbols but create a run using the pattern that represents the absence of something in that description language. For example, consider a hypothetical program storing data from an analog sensor that registers a signal, then drops below the detection threshold, and then rises again:

'11111000011111'.

In many cases, but not all, the absence of something would be a run of 0s, but this is not a rule; in other encoding schemes, the spatial extent of information is not necessarily in correspondence with time. That is, the encoding scheme explicitly has timing and synchronization primitives built into it and is simply atemporal, lacking any notion of time.

This perspective is important because, as a medium, binary is used to embed or *represent* information. It is technically incorrect to say that all information is binary or digital or anything of the kind, as information must be *interpreted* [4, 5]. The symbols signify structure, and that signification can be present in a variety of media, binary being just one of many. Further, there are many ways to encode the same information, and this can also vary by media.

Returning to the Kleene star, it is important to know that the set of all finite binary strings includes all possible AI implementations as just a subset. A subset means that there is a set which is "inside" or included within another set, possibly of equal or larger size. The implications being that there will be nonsensical and nonworking programs within {0,1}*. This is because it has all the possible combinations of 1 and 0, including no combinations. The part we are concerned with is the subset that realizes working AI, which will be referred to as the set of all AI implementations. Further, there is another subset within {0,1}* that represents the set of all strong AI implementations.

It is also possible to include the memory, knowledge, and data acquired by a strong AI as part of a definition by concatenating that data to the end of the string, and then defining that as a subset of {0,1}*. This would, however, require a special encoding of the AI implementation so that its length would be included as part of its specification. Each string would represent an entirely complete, ready to run implementation until it learns and changes a single bit of information, becoming a new and distinct string. This is a foreshadowing of **Chapter 4: Self-Modifying Systems**.

This is a powerful and universal way of analyzing AI implementations. It should be clear, even now, why it is nonsensical to discuss abstractions in the absence of the concrete, well-defined structures of an implementation.

But what is the point of introducing such a low-level construct? The primary reason is to provide a basis for discussing practical and concrete implementations. The goal here is to move away from abstractions that are unclear or impossible. But there is also another reason, and it has to do with the communication of ideas in the field of strong

AI, which is a more general statement of the problem this chapter is trying to address.

Most of the sciences have a very specific and complex lexicon to communicate and express their concepts. The science of strong artificial intelligence, as distinct from machine learning and narrow AI, must also have its methods. Based on what has been shown already, we know that such exchange will be based on at least what can be possibly constructed, and that such implementations need to be specified clearly and concretely.

Mathematics itself might come to mind as a preferred mode of communication for this discipline, but it is not as "natural" a choice as it might first seem. Instead, we should consider programming languages and their related constructs and terminology to provide immediately actionable communication between strong AI scientists. At the very least, no major concept should be without the corresponding source code to give concretion to it.

The choice to use programming languages has two justifications. The first is the ability to run what is given to us without having to translate mathematical symbols and definitions into code. The second is that mathematical concepts may have multiple ways to be implemented, creating ambiguity and leaving much to be desired regarding actual algorithm implementations. If mathematics could replace our needs to specify, understand, and communicate in computer science, then we would not have needed to create a separate and distinct field in the first place. Likewise, the needs of strong AI science require precise, rigorous, and unambiguous communication for its ideas. Mathematics will be a tool and, in some cases, a means for certain things, but not over and above the programs and algorithms that will ultimately be implementing strong AI and other forms of advanced automation.

3.2 Description Languages

With an understanding of (finite) binary strings, it is now possible to move into description languages and their relationship to AI implementations. The interpretation and use of description languages in AI security is founded on the field of algorithmic information theory [1, 6, 7, 8, 9].

A *description language* is a means of encoding or specifying messages (descriptions). In this context, these descriptions can be referred to as programs, with the program being a message in some programming language.

Description languages can be applied to one or more binary strings where there is consistent structure, either internally or across strings. This could be considered a corpus and corpora, respectively. Machine learning can thus be viewed as a producer of description languages; the description language of a set of one or more messages is modeled, or learned, by exploiting correlations between and within them. The modeled description language is then used to validate, identify, or even generate (predict) messages. However, this is not the complete picture of what is happening concerning the learned description language. This is because it is possible to recursively encode descriptions so that they become a partial or full message in some other description language, and that is exactly what is happening in the case of machine learning.

To understand this recursive embedding, we will use a simple example: we can specify a description language for PNG files, with the structure of the file format being the description language and the pixel data and other information being the description. Such a PNG could then be encapsulated or embedded into a ZIP archive, with that format's structure as its description language, and its descriptions being inclusive of messages whose description languages are foreign to it. Since ZIP programs can treat their archived data as opaque, they do not require knowledge of the description language to work with them. This is true even of the compression that is used on the archived data, which relies on analysis of patterns within the data without having explicit knowledge of its format.

This leads to the more complex case with machine learning. For example, an artificial neural network could be considered a description language and its weights and training information its descriptions. But it goes at least one level deeper. The descriptions could be interpreted as models, which would have description languages themselves. And it is the fidelity of a model that determines its predictive (generative) power. This results in at least two nested levels of description languages, not including the programming language and machine level implementation of the artificial neural network. Any machine learning algorithm can be substituted in the above example, as each must make some model or representation of something to identify and predict it.

By understanding this recursive property of description languages, one gains the ability to universally analyze implementations, algorithms, and data structures across domains. This does not just apply to computer science, but to any information which has a consistent structure; it could be chemical compounds, enzymatic reactions, or genomes. It could be recipes or instructions on how to build something. All of these can be viewed as messages in one or more description languages, any of which can be interpreted as finite binary strings. This gives us measurable and objective facts to work with that allow analysis of complexity, integrity, and other useful properties. Because they are concrete, we would have the ability to perform tests and experiments, and reason about their exact behavior. This is not possible with simple discussions in the abstract, as we may interpret them in different ways, leading ultimately to differing implementations, or the abstraction may in fact be intractable or impossible to construct.

3.3 Conceptual Baggage

First, it must be pointed out that the field of narrow AI and strong AI are distinct. That is one of the minor themes of this book and is essential to understanding the security challenges. This is true even when discussing AI as a whole, as both narrow and strong AI systems belong to this category.

The foundation of this problem is that the field of strong AI lacks an identity as a scientific discipline. Its appears to have boundaries which are in flux. Authority figures from philosophy, computer science, mathematics, and even physics, flood the conceptual space with a barrage of ideas and prediction. This ordinarily would not be a negative, as this is just humanity trying to grapple with a difficult concept, but this field has a very different circumstances surrounding it.

Strong AI has a massive set of cultural and psychological attachments that go along with it. This conceptual baggage retards growth and makes for an almost impossible atmosphere for education. It is a state of intellectual chaos, with the default being that anyone is qualified to discuss it because we are all supposedly experts on intelligence being intelligent beings ourselves; the more intelligent society thinks a person is, the more we accept that they are qualified to discuss the nature of intelligence. This problem is enabled by an anthropocentric bias, and is driven by the psychological need for social signaling in intellectual circles.

It would be absurd to trust a physicist to do neurosurgery based on the argument that both physics and neurosurgery were both intellectually challenging, or, that because all brains are governed by the laws of physics, that this made them qualified. No rational person would let this argument justify allowing the physicist to perform their surgery. Moral differences notwithstanding, this is exactly what is happening in the field of artificial intelligence, and it is coming from completely unrelated fields.

There is a psychological gap that is not being minded, an anthropocentric blind-spot, hidden by the shared mutual drive to speak about intellect as the apogee of social affluence. This exists in both the speakers and those that promote them, less these waves of sensationalism would have dissipated instantly. However, they continue to be propagated and promulgated because we are not collectively rejecting the source. We have not built up an intellectual immunity to these ideas because we are primed to admit them, at least tacitly, due to the closeness of the subject with our nature.

Concepts and abstractions must be constructed for them to do work in the world. Further, every concept that can potentially do work has at least one implementation. Natural language is inherently prone to misunderstanding and misinterpretation, and this is worsened by the fact that not every abstraction that seems reasonable has an effective, let alone efficient, implementation. These problems can be eliminated by recognizing that the conventions we use for describing or discussing AI behavior, especially concerning security, must be *reducible* to some machine language, or its equivalent. This forces us to stop and question ourselves as to whether what we are discussing or reading makes any sense.

One of the most popular examples of this conceptual baggage is to interpret AI as rational agents and then predict their behavior using utility functions and decision theory, backed up by probability and statistics [10, 11, 12, 13, 14, 15, 16, 17, 18, 19].

The problem with this concept is that an AI implementation is physically vulnerable to failure and attack [20, 21, 22, 23, 24, 25, 26, 27, 28, 29, 30, 31, 32, 33]. This creates a practical issue that agent concepts, utility functions, and the decision-theoretic are fundamentally incapable of addressing. Rationality only makes sense given first a set of background assumptions about the values and goals that define what it considers sensible decisions and actions. Without this, it can not be applied. Further, no finite set of values can be used to entail all possible AI implementations, no matter how reasonable they seem. More to the point, even if these values could be entailed, their encoding would be just as vulnerable as the AI implementation itself, even if designed into the architecture itself.

Finally, and most importantly, the background assumptions and values for what one defines as rational do not constitute an actual model of the behavior of the AI implementation. That is to say, a model of consequences as a function of value(s) can not be accurate without the nuances of implementation details. This applies especially to an instance of strong AI. These models will also fail to address contextual ramifications or unanticipated outcomes. It lacks the ability to determine how these environments and situations are interpreted, as it does not have knowledge of the inner workings of the implementation. In other words, these models assume a perfect implementation that can never be realized. This is because there will eventually arise situations where judgments are compromised due to interference or miscalculation. Failure of the AI implementation to arrive at the expected outcome will always be skewed by a varying and unknowable amount of ambiguity and error in any given context. Such challenges require modeling that has full knowledge of the relevant implementation details. Anything less is incoherent.

To reiterate: even if the architecture was implemented in a decision-theoretic framework, it would still not eliminate the physical and contextual ambiguity of a perception pipeline, among other factors in the implementation, nor would it remove the inherent non-zero probability of error that exists in these implementations. Further, no amount of architectural inclusion or closeness to this conceptual baggage will eliminate its physical vulnerability as information in software or hardware; it is ultimately a distraction in the search for practical solutions to the safety and security of artificial intelligence. As a result of this, it should rightly be considered as an approach that is non-workable.

3.4 Anthropocentric Bias

The focus of this section is to refute the tendency to believe that AI functionality and behavior can be predicted by extrapolating and applying human behavior, either derived scientifically, or, more commonly, through folk-psychological [34, 35, 36] accounts.

This bias is damaging to the security and safety of AI because of its limiting effect on the mind to assess the vulnerabilities and operation of AI implementations; it creates a mismatch between what an AI implementation *will* do and what one *believes* it will do.

A consequence of this bias, in conjunction with the conceptual baggage surrounding this field, is that it has created a belief that the immediate threat to humanity is from advanced artificial intelligence itself

[37, 38, 39]. However, it will be people utilizing this technology for malicious purposes that will present the most serious threat. The media then repeats this misinformation, and it gets disseminated to the public, countermanding efforts at public outreach and education on these issues. As a result, these biases are setting us back in a very real way, and we will continue to be unprepared as long as the focus is fixed on moral intelligence and the delusion of a singular, personified strong AI arising out of all possible AI implementations to subvert the human race.

No law of nature states that an AI must be implemented based on the human condition. More generally, there is no law of nature that an AI is restricted to biologically inspired designs. The burden of proof is on those who believe that out of all the possible AI implementations in {0,1}* that each must be based on our limited cognitive framework. It is trivial to show that it is possible to construct programs that are nothing like biology, let alone how our brains work, yet are capable of accomplishing similar tasks. The following is a complete program that counts from 1 to 10:

```
for i in range(10): print i + 1
```

This program is a description in the Python programming language. The human brain is nothing like this description, both in terms of how it accomplishes it and regarding its simplicity. It took billions of years of evolution to enable the human brain to have the capacity to learn to do what this program does with just one line of code. Both can count to 10, and both are reasonably effective at doing this task.

Possible counter-arguments to this simple evidence might be that it does not represent an actual AI implementation; that it is too simple.

However, its purpose is to show that it is possible to automate the process of counting from 1 to 10. That it is not an artificial neural network or based on millions of n-grams from a corpus of numerical sequences and counting systems is irrelevant. Further, the description to have a neural network duplicate this program's external behavior would not only be incomprehensible and opaque to us, but would require a vastly larger number of steps to simulate on a digital computer. One could try to argue that this could be accelerated by specialized hardware for simulating that neural network ontology, but that could be countered by the fact that an integrated circuit designed to do this digitally would be a fraction of the complexity. That the above program is incapable of adapting or learning new number systems is also irrelevant to showing the effective equivalence in the tasks.

The point is that there are descriptions that will yield similar or equivalent results that need not be based on identical or approximated biological descriptions; a simulation or modeling of our biological functioning is not a necessary condition to realize equivalent results. Any counter to this point would have to explain why it is impossible to effectively calculate some processes and not others. That is to say, what special properties of the world are off limits to the information-theoretic, and why? Any answer to this will have to overcome the overwhelming observational accounts of the Church-Turing thesis applying to physical systems [40] in everyday use.

A related bias is to assume that digital computers will never be conscious because they are not made of the same substance as human brains [50, 41, 42]. This bias can alternatively be phrased that there is something unique to either biological or non-biological neuronal processing [43], and that, as a result, AI implementations not based on this will never achieve the same level of functioning. However, that we lack a rigorous first-person account of conscious experience [44] is not evidence against machine consciousness, nor does it imply that we must turn to biological mimicry or exotic metaphysical accounts of mind to achieve it. It simply means we have yet to uncover its description.

3.5 Existential Primer

A universal way to clear out the misconceptions surrounding artificial intelligence is to start at the very bottom. Within $\{0,1\}^*$ there are no concepts such as agency, ego, or emotion. We will not find consciousness, qualia, or experiences. It is a blank canvas upon which to draw. There is only, at best, a sequence that can be interpreted and computed to realize one or more processes.

These processes may give rise to some of the previously mentioned things when executed, but this does not constitute their existence. A description of a thing makes an abstraction real only insofar as it entails its potential. With debt to Whitehead's original process philosophy [45], the claim is that there is a distinct interpretation that bridges the gulf between his metaphysics and algorithms: descriptions are static representations of time-like objects which can only be realized through one or more processes. To understand, consider the shadows from geometry that arise from the projection of a higher-dimensional object onto a lower-dimensional space. Likewise, the static descriptions that entail processes are but a shadow of their full time-like extents. One could create an enriched static description of such a process through a non-deterministic representation that includes every possible state of the object at every infinitesimal moment in time. Such a representation could also be made through the creation of a uniform stochastic model that treats all events as equally likely.

However, even with such an enriched description, we would not have realized the thing which it entails. Even fully specified non-deterministic descriptions of processes must be interpreted to become manifest. To do so, it must undergo information exchange, which is, in a more general sense, computation. This must not be confused or conflated with information exchange or complexity as consciousness [46, 47, 48], which is certainly false. To address it in short: information exchange is necessary but not sufficient for consciousness. This is also why computationalism is false. This is related to the concept of strong AI that was defined by John Searle in [49], in which he used the term to refute the computational theory of mind. Strong AI, as defined in this book, turns Searle's argument on its head, and requires that strong AI have the necessary constructs that would give rise to the processes involved in consciousness. In other words, strong AI must be a cognitive architecture.

Definition: *Cognitive Architecture.* A constructible implementation design with features that will allow it to understand, have mental content, and undergo conscious experience.

Recall the set of all possible AI implementations, which is a subset of the set of all finite binary strings. There exists another subset of the set of all finite binary strings that is of interest. It is the set of all possible cognitive architectures.

The set of cognitive architectures and the set of AI implementations are not identical, but they do have an intersection.

It is at this intersection that we describe any possible notion of conscious processing or machine understanding. It is within this intersection that strong AI will have to be constructed. This is not something that can be realized accidentally, but must be forged through engineering. There are a potentially infinite number of alternative AI implementations that do not yield a cognitive architecture in any meaningful sense. As a result, it should be considered nonsensical to impute agency, consciousness, or any other properties or features that are not present in the description of the AI implementation.

To refer to AI categorically as a collective, "species", or group, is to commit to error. There is no law of nature that AI implementations share a common link, identity, or connection. This is because each AI implementation will be a unique instance, with potentially distinct features, knowledge, and information making up its construction. Moreover, it will have a unique vantage point, given that it occupies a distinct position in time and space. As a result of this, it will necessarily have a unique frame of reference. AI implementations will require network and communications features to overcome this default state of physical independence and individuation. It is a complex engineering task that will not arise spontaneously without an effective process that yields it. This also applies to the extended case of a single cognitive collective or unified mind across multiple physical entities or instances. This falls under the set of all cognitive architectures mentioned above.

Lastly, AI implementations will not have an automatic tendency to converge towards a single identity nor will they naturally diverge from a unified identity into multiple individuals. These behaviors will not occur unless there are internal mechanisms or environmental pressures to guide self-modification. That is to say, it is incoherent to assume that

AI implementations, of any level of intelligence, will work either for or against this type of self-organization, nor can any *general* argument be made for or against this case. To overcome it would require a specific context, set of background assumptions, and a precise description of the AI implementation.

3.6 AI Implementations

Everything so far in this chapter has been leading up to a discussion of AI implementations. This term has been used several times in advance of its definition to establish a context and to set it apart from the relevant issues. It has been shown that abstractions and simple discussion fail to account for the operational details and the complexity of AI implementations.

Now that the existential and ontological assumptions have been addressed, the term AI implementation will be defined, and its high-level details covered.

Definition: *AI Implementation.* A valid and working description of an artificial intelligence, of any level of complexity, that may either be interpreted or executed on a computer or equivalently translated hardware specification.

Recall that the set of all AI implementations is a subset of the set of all finite binary strings. This means that any specification and design for an AI implementation, as per this definition, must be constructible as a description in some description language. This description does not have to be worked with in binary. For example, it could be presented in a programming language, which might be translated to a hardware description or register transfer language. It could be a set of very detailed programming schematics at the semantic level of the language itself. Ultimately, it is implied that any description language can be equivalently encoded in binary or is represented that way as part of the natural operation of the system's information processing and storage, even when the description itself is being presented to the user in a human-readable form.

There is no one set of architectural rules or laws that make up an AI implementation, and, as previously discussed, it is not possible to generalize all possible AI implementations and reason from them in the abstract.

One of the critical perspectives of this book is that there can be no assurances of the safety of an AI implementation without understanding and analyzing its security. All the safeguards and moral intelligence in idealized perfection are meaningless if compromised. So, given that all forms of self-security can ultimately be overcome with effort, the focus must be on mitigation under the assumption of failure. From this, one must analyze the situation that AI implementations will be used in, and look for commonalities in both the environment and the implementations themselves. Behavior, outcomes, and vulnerabilities must be scrutinized at every stage of design and implementation, with expertise and understanding of how a concept or abstraction is realized.

The security analysis of an AI implementation begins with the AIS model. In almost all cases, if one lower-level layer is compromised then all subsequent higher layers will be compromised:

Layer 1: Description layer. A universal layer concerned with vulnerabilities that arise from intentional and unintentional modification of the description itself. The primary concern here is with the integrity and authentication of descriptions.

Figure 3.1: The **AIS** model is comprised of multiple cascading layers of dependent security.

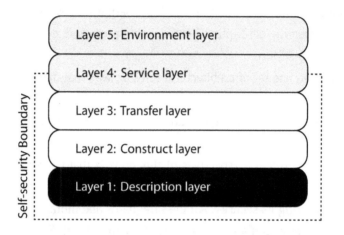

A compromise, fault, or failure at any level causes the layers above it to also become compromised. Self-security entails any and all internal mechanisms for the security and safety of the implementation and must not be exclusively relied upon. The environment layer has the final responsibility in ensuring the containment and behavioral constraints of AI implementations.

Layer 2: Construct layer. This layer is what the description entails or constructs. It is directly dependent upon the semantics and syntax of the description language. This will usually be a programming language. Faults on this layer may result in working implementations that, nonetheless, have vulnerable descriptions due to bugs and design flaws. Expert knowledge is required in order to translate from concepts to specifications with security in mind.

Layer 3: Transfer layer. This would be whatever the final description would be to allow the implementation to be interpreted, executed, or operated. This may be the same as layer two if the description language is an interpreted language. The purpose of this layer is to focus on post-translation properties and descriptions, which could have been the result of multiple stages of processing and intermediate representation(s). The primary concern is with the output description that will be sent to the target platform, be it real, emulated, or virtual. In the case of hardware description languages, this would be the final description before being physically instantiated as hardware components and interconnects. Failures at this layer could stem from incorrect compilation or constructs in optimization and compilation that create vulnerabilities in the low-level description. Examples might include the use of dynamically linked or shared libraries; debugging information not being stripped; monolithic execution.

Layer 4: Service layer. This layer is focused on the underlying machine, interpreter, and/or hardware being used to run the AI implementation. The boundary for self-security goes through it. This implies that this layer is capable of breaking the pure self-security limitation through physically distributed designs, or those designs which are separate from a single underlying model of execution. Failures at this layer could result in transient soft-errors or faults in hardware that cause data loss and corruption. Physical damage and tampering may interfere with previous stages of security by directly circumventing or manipulating the way in which the system processes and updates the implementation. Safeguards at this layer would include physical security measures, tamper resistance, and detection.

Layer 5: Environment layer. Level five is concerned with everything external to the AI implementation itself. This focuses on an analysis of the hazards relevant to the physical deployment and use of the AI and the risks it presents to life and property. Security on this level would involve traditional methods of physical security, along with additional safeguards in the event of failure or breach in containment. This is perhaps the most important layer as it represents the last line of defense if an implementation ceases to operate under safe, expected behavior. It is also the first layer that is completely independent of the self-security of the underlying implementation, and should be much harder to overcome. Lastly, this layer applies to a broad range of contexts where confinement is geographic in scope. The same principles apply.

The purpose of this chapter has been to establish the need to address the way we communicate and discuss artificial intelligence, especially regarding its future impacts on humanity. A focus on AI implementations, backed up by an understanding of description languages, solves this challenge and will allow forward progress on the issues that transcends the ambiguities of natural language. This also paves the way for a foundation that is aligned with the fact that AI security presupposes AI safety. Unfortunately, this is in stark contrast to the current mainstream understanding.

Moral intelligence, rule-following, and all internal safeguards we put into or around an AI implementation are forms of self-security. They are presupposed by real-world problems and challenges. No amount of hand-waving or intellectualizing over the future makes a difference if we do not realize the fact that AI security presupposes AI safety. To even begin to address these challenges requires a change in communication from the conceptual to the concrete. We must eliminate our preconceived notions and biases, block out conceptual baggage, and demand discussion at the implementation level of detail. Formal languages and grammars are a rigorous and well-defined concept that admit connections to a wide range of sub-fields within computer science and mathematics. Everyday use need not be concerned with binary strings, but with the textual representation of programming languages or their equivalent. Anything less than this should be considered suboptimal.

Ch 4. Self-Modifying Systems

This chapter lays the foundation for the analysis of strong AI as metamorphic software. It provides an introduction to the relevant concepts surrounding self-modifying systems, as applied to computer science. These hardware and software computing systems are capable of rewriting or reconfiguring their architecture. This is relevant to AI security and safety because such systems have the ability to manipulate descriptions with effectiveness, affording them the potential to evolve beyond their original limitations or specifications. In addition to rewriting their program descriptions, they will also be capable of rewriting other data and program descriptions accessible to them. This includes the ability to penetrate logical boundaries, such as operating system calls, application programming interfaces, and hardware interfaces. The implications of this will be their capacity to self-replicate through our global network infrastructure, cross hardware and software boundaries, evade detection, and overcome countermeasures.

4.1 Codes, Syntax, and Semantics

A code is a method or scheme that specifies how to convert information into different forms or representations [1, 2, 3]. To put it into terms consistent with previously discussed concepts, this would mean that a code describes a method for transforming descriptions, either within the same description language or into that of another description language entirely. As a result of this, codes can be interpreted as the *syntax* for some description language.

The word code can also be used to refer to the entirety of a description, e.g., "source code". The distinction is usually inferred through context, but it will be made explicit here for clarity by referring to it as a code scheme.

A formal language [4, 5, 6] is defined as a set of words over an alphabet. The words must be finite, but the language itself may be infinite. This formal definition makes mention of neither syntax nor semantics. It is simply that set, constructed in that particular way, with nothing extra implied. It is exactly that and nothing other than that unless something is explicitly added or attached to it in the relevant context. For reasons of brevity and practicality, the description languages mentioned in this book are restricted subsets of formal languages that have been constrained to working descriptions called implementations. This is because formal languages include nonsensical descriptions, e.g., "colorless green ideas sleep furiously" [7]. To be clear and concrete, these qualifications define these description languages necessarily as subsets of the formal languages that entail them, i.e., the formal language for a given description language is possibly (infinitely) larger, but contains descriptions that are disregarded for practical use.

Importantly, it is the semantics, not the syntax, that determines the power of languages [8, 9, 10] and their corresponding computational extents. To understand this, we must first see how formal grammars are distinct from formal languages. One can generate some formal language from a particular formal grammar, but, as mentioned above, formal languages have neither syntax nor semantics as part of their formal definition. Further, the ability for a restricted class of abstract machines to recognize certain grammars but not others, [11] as shown in the

Chomsky hierarchy, [7, 12, 91, 92] does not imply restrictions on the descriptions they generate. Indeed, there exist Turing-complete instruction sets [13] and programming languages with grammars above the unrestricted class. In other words, there is a full disconnect between grammar and language efficacy or power. This is because some process must interpret a language for it to have any effect [14]. For programming languages, this is via explicit computation that implements or reifies the semantics of that language [15, 16].

While formal languages do not include syntax or semantics, they can be qualified to sets of working descriptions very easily through the intension definition [17] of sets, e.g., "the set of all working AI implementations." By contrast, a formal grammar requires a definition in the form of production rules that recognize or generate some language; this would potentially require enormous numbers of productions [18, 19, 20], and, in some cases, may be unknowable for practical reasons. This hints at the subtle relationship between conventional machine learning and the limits of narrow AI. In other words, without the relevant semantics at hand, one degenerates to the brute-force enumeration of countless permutations, all the while never having the capacity to effectively apply those rules outside of the context in which they were derived. This is because the problem of semantics is vastly more involved than the mere juxtaposition [21] of symbols, especially when those symbols have meaning. In the context of computational languages, this meaning comes in the form of functionality that must be captured in an implementation, a description that entails the semantics.

4.2 Code-Data Duality

Computers are primarily programmed through the transformation of human readable source code into descriptions that can be directly and indirectly executed by the machine. Compilation is the process of transforming that source code from one description language into that of another. This typically results in native machine code in the description language of some microprocessor or microcontroller. In other cases, the result of the compilation is generated in a description language that differs from the native description language of the machine and must be interpreted to be executed. Finally, source code may be interpreted directly, with or without a corresponding compilation process.

The underlying hardware is always involved; it is just a question of how many layers of abstraction separate the given description and the machine's native description language, called the instruction set. It is possible to nest, encode, or embed descriptions within descriptions infinitely. The limits of this are determined by each description language, and the resource constraints of the implementation.

In all cases, the descriptions are data being interpreted by some process, with that process being either another program or the machine itself. This is the duality between code and data, and is the basis of self-modification in computing. This duality helps to unify the notion of interpreter and machine in the computation of information, which is what is being referred to when one discusses information exchange. In other words, information exchange is not possible without an interpreting process, and every interpreting process must have syntax and semantics as part of its construction. Otherwise, it would be incapable of signification.

A description language with semantics that provides access, recognition, and generation of its syntax and semantics while being interpreted is called *reflexive* [22, 23]. However, this property is not required for self-modification in general. This is related to the class of self-interpreting languages that exhibit *homoiconicity* [24], which represent the implementation details of the description language regarding the structure of the language itself. This makes these languages trivially reflexive. In all cases, however, the limits of self-modification are up to the semantics of the interpreting process and not the particular language features, which only make it more or less convenient to perform self-modification.

4.3 Interpreters and Machines

An interpreter is an implementation that evaluates descriptions written in some language [25]. If in software, the interpreter would be either a program or embedded as part of another program. In hardware, it would be a microprocessor or microcontroller or, potentially, some customized integrated circuit or other hardware. The language that the interpreter hosts may be different from the one it was implemented in itself.

Every interpreter follows a certain construction: a description in a meta language that implements or hosts an object language. The power of the interpreted language is always determined by the semantics of the implementation. This can be applied to nearly any context that permits a physical description of the system.

In this book, all interpreters are generalized to a class under the above construction. This confers the advantage of a universal analysis that provides broad coverage of the relevant principles of self-modification. This generalization includes all of the types of interpreters that will be discussed in this section, both hardware and software alike, and should not be confused with the light-weight interpreters that are covered next.

Often, in the context of computer programming, the word interpreter typically refers to a specific sub-class of interpreters that utilize abstractions (or no abstractions) that are relatively close to the form or function of the description language they host. These interpreters either use some internal representation or perform direct execution as the language is parsed. In some cases, these interpreters will utilize what is known as *byte-code* [26], which is a compiled version of the human readable source that has been put into a description language that is more efficient for machine reading. This byte-code is usually not in the language of the host architecture that runs the interpreter, and must be read by the interpreter itself.

Just-in-Time (JIT) compilers combine the features of light-weight interpreters and that of compilation by allowing descriptions to be analyzed and transformed at runtime [27].

A *virtual machine* (VM) is a type of interpreter that goes a step further and implements, or, more correctly, emulates, the semantics of a particular computing architecture [28].

This creates an additional level of abstraction between the description language being hosted and the underlying architecture that implements the VM. The benefits of this are that the VM can trade relative performance for platform and hardware independence [29, 30]. It also admits the possibility of unique security features, as it is not compelled to execute every program or series of instructions it encounters [31, 32, 33].

Figure 4.1: Conceptual construction of interpreters as nested implementations of description languages.

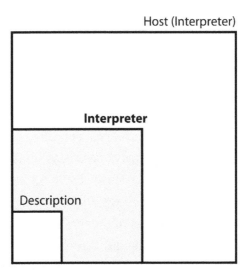

Each box represents a single description out of possibly many descriptions entailed by the implementation that contains it. Every interpreter is a description in some description language that also represents an implementation of a (possibly different) description language. This continues schematically towards the upper right diagonal ad infinitum until reaching discrete physical descriptions.

Hardware circuitry could be implemented to do the same [34, 36, 37, 38, 39, 40] but it may not be as flexible or dynamic as a VM. Ultimately, however, a VM is still an implementation, and any security at this level would still be self-security, subject to fundamental vulnerabilities [41]. The VM concept primarily gains attention due to its ability to run descriptions on multiple architectures without recompilation.

Virtualization takes the VM concept a step further by creating one or more VMs across computing systems of potentially different types of architectures [42]. This can be used to split computational resources into smaller units or combine them to form a larger logical machine.

Finally, a microcontroller or microprocessor is an interpreter implemented as hardware. It has an instruction set which exposes hardware semantics at the lowest levels. It is at this level that other interpreters are implemented, including VMs, which must have an associated native implementation portion to enable the emulation of the architecture.

All interpreters have a set of advantages and disadvantages that are determined by their descriptions. There can be no general purpose description that is optimal for every type of algorithm or program. This fact is the result of the semantics of the implementation and the levels of abstraction between it and the discrete physics. Every layer of abstraction induces another level of interpretation that must be performed. As such, the most efficient descriptions are those that minimize these levels [43, 44, 45, 46, 47, 48]. A digital computer is still an analog device in that it utilizes electrical states as representations for digital logic. Its storage mechanisms manipulate and interpret physical states which are analog representations constrained to specific ranges of interpretation.

The optimal computer for a given problem is one in which there is as close to a one-to-one correspondence between the algorithm being implemented and the physical analogs used in its interpretation. This is perhaps why the human brain is such an efficient computational system, even without factoring in its ability to reconfigure itself as it undergoes learning.

Further issues that confound any general purpose solution is that certain problems are resistant to parallel processing [49, 50, 51]. Some can benefit from the ordering of instructions and the prediction of branching in logic. Others are benefited by cache systems, in both memory and instruction pipelines, while others would need bigger memory bandwidth, as they do not benefit from caching as well as others due to their dynamics. The bottom line is that there are compromises in the design of any interpreter that are often decided by the context in which they will be used most frequently. This is another reason why it is almost always nonsensical to discuss artificial intelligence in the absence of specific implementations.

The previously mentioned limitations are exactly why a system would benefit from the ability to self-modify. Take Amdahl's law, for example, which gives a relationship between the maximum speed-up that can be attained by adding more processors to a problem with even a small serial portion [52]. That is to say, any given problem can be represented by how much of it is necessarily serial in its execution. As mentioned above, not all problems benefit from parallel computation.

Often, the most difficult part that professional software engineers and applied mathematicians have to struggle with is finding the optimal algorithms constrained by the relevant semantics available to them. A professional graphics developer is a perfect example: they utilize cutting edge hardware descriptions which provide unique semantics, but these semantics are never as efficient as just specifying a physical implementation of the algorithm. This is because these systems have to fit within a manufacturing process and made general enough to serve a wide variety of applications; they are specialized, but not so specialized that they would only calculate a small set of problems.

In summary, an interpreter is always required for any description language to have an effect. At its most fundamental, the physical world can be thought of as an interpreter with what we call reality being its descriptions. This is not to advertise a digital physics, as descriptions need not be represented digitally! It is to say that this concept of an interpreter is almost universal, depending on how willing one is to relax their conceptual boundaries. Every interpreter has to implement the semantics and recognize the syntax of the description language they host, with the power of that language being determined by the semantics of the implementation. The implementation's efficiency is determined partially by its syntax and semantics, plus the levels of abstraction between it and that of some discrete physical description.

Every underlying physical interpreter involves a form of analog computation, and the most efficient possible forms of computation would be as close to a one-to-one correspondence with this as possible. This reveals the fundamental trade-off between generality and specialization, in that the closer to this one-to-one correspondence, the more constrained the implementation becomes for a particular set of problems. This sets the bounds of the problem space for which self-modification is applied, as it seeks to have both generality and specialization through the self-modification process.

4.4 Types of Self-Modification

All systems capable of self-modification share a few basic operations: rewrite, replicate, and generate. These are either direct or indirect in operation. A description is in either one of two states: online or offline.

Offline descriptions are the conventional type of description that have been discussed so far about implementations. Recalling the time-like objects and processes from the previous chapter, offline descriptions entail potential states and operations and are not the physical description of an active implementation. They are an entailment of its potential. By contrast, an online description entails the relevant operational and physical details, but only insofar as it is required to undergo self-modification. This may include environment and state information or anything else that would be required to complete self-modification under active operation.

Direct self-modification is where the system is applying modifications to itself without external sources of aid. Indirect self-modification is for cases where the system utilizes external sources to self-modify, but with the stipulation that it must have either created or initiated these sources. A supervised self-modification is still self-modification as long as it can operate directly or indirectly upon itself without further assistance. Intervention, cessation, or interruption of this process by a supervising process would not constitute aid unless it qualitatively alters the self-modification process beyond the starting or stopping of its execution.

A summary of the types of self-modification:

- Direct
    - Rewrite
    - Replicate-Rewrite-Replace
    - Generate-Replace
- Indirect
    - Replicate-Rewrite-Replace
    - Generate-Retroactive Rewrite

Rewrites involve partial or complete modification of the original description. There is no implied copying. Rewrites may apply to descriptions which are either online or offline. An offline description is simply a copy of a system's description which is no longer considered part of it. An online implementation that engages in rewrite self-modification must be capable of handling live edits of its description without generation or replication. This lack of copying is what distinguishes rewrite from replication and generation. Thus, when a rewrite is performed on an offline description, it is necessarily an intermediate stage, as it will require an additional step to be considered part of the original system once more.

Replication is the *unmodified* copying of a system's description. It is also an intermediate step towards self-modification. This replication is capable of occurring within a system without instantiating the copied description. It may be a temporary working copy or just part of the process of self-modification. Replication does not imply an online description, but it does imply *replacement* if it is to be considered part of any self-modifying process.

Generation can be thought of as a combined replicate and rewrite process but is distinct from both as it is the direct construction of a description from a process. This is to be contrasted with the replication, rewrite, and replace method of self-modification, which involves the modification of a copy. The defining characteristic of generation is that it involves computation, and, as such, can be generalized as a kind of compression, in which the generative system has a model of all the permutations it can potentially create in an ultra-compact representation. Like replication, generation implies an eventual *replace* to be considered self-modification. This is because generation creates a separate description and does not modify the original system. Such a case would be a rewrite.

Retroactive replacement is for the complex case where a system is incapable of direct self-modification. As a result, it generates or replicates a description, which may or may not need to be modified further, and then utilizes that as a means of self-modification.

Finally, there needs to be a discussion regarding *iteration*. Why would this not be considered self-modification? The reason is that it does not imply a change in the identity of the originating process, and that it does not serve the same purpose as self-modification, which is to break through language barriers. This point will be discussed in more detail ahead.

4.5 Reconfigurable Hardware

Application-specific integrated circuits (ASIC) are customized hardware that have been designed for specific functionality [53]. They range from partial to fully custom designs, and can vary greatly in both performance and cost. The benefit of ASICs are their high performance and lower marginal cost at high production volumes [54]. The drawback is that they can not be reconfigured once manufactured.

By contrast, and of relevance to self-modification, is the field programmable gate array (FPGA), which uses an array of programmable logic blocks that allow significant changes to logical circuit design, and can be reconfigured and reused for many applications [55, 56, 57]. Limitations include only partial update during operation [58, 59], a significantly more complex reprogramming process than software [60], and volatile storage of the configuration [61]. The latter issue of volatility can be overcome with system-on-a-chip designs that include common integrated circuit (IC) components as part of the FPGA itself [62, 63, 64]. This hardware is commonly used to prototype and verify ASIC designs [65, 66, 67] and can potentially be more cost effective at low production volumes [68].

Firmware is defined as the combination of integrated circuits (ICs) and non-volatile memory to allow logic to be represented in hardware as reprogrammable software [69]. This provides modularity to the hardware, but is not as efficient as an ASIC or FPGA. This is because the stored software is still forced to operate in a specific circuit and data-path configuration, and it can not be altered unless combined with one of the above configurable devices.

At the time of this writing, there exists no configurable hardware technology that compares with the freedom and ease of self-modification that exists with software. The trade-off, however, is run-time efficiency. This means that, while software is capable of virtually unrestricted self-modification, it comes at the cost of being limited in efficiency by the semantics of the hardware that serves it. This could be limiting in cases where solutions benefit significantly from parallelization, but it is important to note that this does not fundamentally prevent the ability to run these implementations at a less optimal pace. *A slow strong AI would potentially be more effective than even the brightest human.*

Reconfigurable hardware, including FPGA, firmware, and embedded systems also have their own set of unique security challenges [70, 71, 72, 73, 74, 75, 76, 77, 78, 79]. It is because of this, and the above benefits of software, that the focus of this book is not on hardware, but software. The reasons are clear: no current hardware technology can efficiently and effectively self-replicate or modify at sufficient rates.

Software does, and, with the increasing ubiquity of connectivity, it has the means to spread very rapidly. Thus, the rest of this chapter will focus on the software aspects, which follows more closely with the foundations presented in the previous chapter on AI implementations.

This does not mean that we should ignore the physical parts of implementations or the vulnerabilities in hardware. It is only to say that, in the context of self-modification, the path of least resistance will be software; this is the route most likely to appear first, and will be the one to taken by malicious users. It will also be the most difficult to restrict and enforce. These are all properties that make it a prime medium for misuse.

4.6 Purpose and Function of Self-Modification

Descriptions are incapable of transcending their respective description languages without transformation. This is the fundamental barrier that self-modification seeks to overcome. If we want an optimized set of semantics, or more efficient syntax, we have to have different descriptions. To get from one description to another requires an explicit process. Self-modification occurs when this transformation takes place within a *single identity*, and this requires that entity at the source and destination are *eventually* the same.

As was previously defined, the description languages discussed in this book pertain to working, well-formed, possible descriptions, along with their relevant syntax and semantics. As a result, an interpreter can be seen as an implementation of a language. In such a case, we are referring not to the description of the interpreter, but to that of the working descriptions of the language.

Figure 4.2: Language barriers as fundamental limits in self-modifying systems.

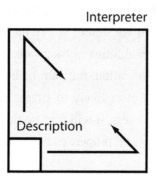

Any description is contained within the description language implemented by an interpreter unless there are enabling semantics to transcend it. This applies universally to any physical description that can undergo (self-)modification.

This brings us to the actual focus of this section. In Figure 4.2, each box represents a description. The description undergoing self-modification is the smallest, innermost box in the lower left. It represents only a single instance out of many possible descriptions entailed by the interpreter. What this shows us is that the self-modifying implementation depicted is capable of attaining any possible description in the interpreter's set of possible programs. This is a trivial form of self-modification, as it is still locked within the description language of the interpreter, and of the description language that implements that interpreter. In practice this is never infinite, being bound by practical limits and real-time demands. A discrete physical description is attained relatively quickly, semantics permitting.

This first trivial form of self-modification illustrates the line of demarcation between a self-hosting interpreter and a meta-circular interpreter. Typically, a self-hosting interpreter implements its description language semantics directly. This is neither unusual nor interesting as a point itself; however, when contrasted with meta-circular interpreters, it becomes a limitation. This is because the description is locked within a self-interpreter's framework. Meta-circular interpreters only partially overcome this by exposing the underlying interpreter that hosts it [80, 81]. This makes lower level semantics part of the semantics of the description language, and, as a result, effectively makes the interpreter transparent and reflexive. This allows for the meta-circular interpreter to implement new description languages by building on the primitives of its underlying host semantics. It may seem an ideal candidate for self-modification, but this too is still limited when compared with the next stage.

The most powerful form of self-modification is where the interpreter can be bypassed entirely for the next stage of interpretation. In Figure 4.3, the self-modifying program is breaking through its original interpreter and accessing the interpreters at each successive stage.

Unlike the light-weight interpreters previously described, it can completely escape each description language boundary. That is, it is activating and bypassing levels of abstraction in interpreters, which are themselves implementations of description languages. It can do this until it reaches the level of the discrete physics, where, hypothetically, it would only be limited by the material and energy resources available to it through some form of physical reconfiguration. Note that this is beyond the level of reconfigurable circuits, and would require nanotechnology or an equivalent process that can manipulate the physical description of the computational substrate.

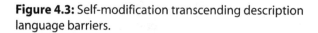

Figure 4.3: Self-modification transcending description language barriers.

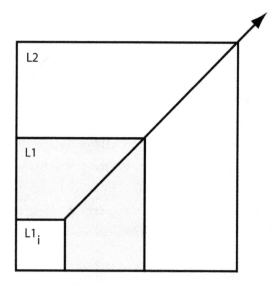

The diagonal represents what the self-modifying description (lower left) is able to achieve with enabling semantics. Bypassing the interpreter **L1**, it is free to penetrate levels of abstraction, including **L2** and beyond, until a semantic barrier or a discrete physical description is reached.

This diagonal escape from each description language is possible as long as the semantics exist to access the next lower level at that stage in the process. If a limitation is reached where there are no longer any semantics that implement next lower-level access then it is possible for the self-modifying system to escape that by accessing networks or peripherals. This is what is diagrammatically occurring in Figure 4.4. In this case, it could be Internet access to a remote machine with a description language that permits access to semantics that allows for self-modification to penetrate to the next lower-level.

Figure 4.4: Self-modification transcending description language barriers through peripheral or network access.

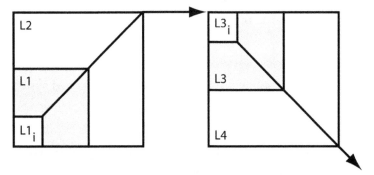

This process could be achieved through any means which enables the self-modification process. This would still be limited by enabling semantics and the required knowledge of the destination description languages and interpreters.

It is important to understand that the semantics for self-modification are non-trivial. *Semantics have to exist for the process of self-modification to break through these barriers.* The process is not magic. It can not penetrate a language barrier without the relevant semantics.

Constructing such curtailed worlds is trivial. It is done through an interpreter that simply lacks the semantics that would allow descriptions to manipulate APIs, I/O, device drivers, and so forth. Any programs under such a description language would be shut into a self-contained domain, a world with no possible escape without external aid. This is in stark contrast to one in which the semantics exist but have been guarded through various security measures.

The lack of enabling semantics should not be taken as an inability for such a system to communicate outside of the locked in world, which might be possible through side-channel attacks, such as timing analysis [82]. This, however, could be mitigated by implementing a real-time constraint on computation, such that the host interpreter is computing at a uniform or sufficiently uncorrelated rate with respect to program complexity.

The above methods describe various levels of *sandboxing*, and must not be taken as an argument for self-security. A sandboxed system can be overcome through external means, flaws in the implementation, or soft-errors. These vulnerabilities will exist regardless of the presence or absence of enabling semantics, no matter how well guarded the implementation. The reason this is discussed is to draw parallels between the existence and non-existence of doorways for self-modification.

Self-modification is a means of increasing the effectiveness of a system, either by accessing better semantics or approaching a description that optimizes for the problem. While this may sound abysmally utilitarian, it can be the difference between a tractable and intractable solution; the actual ranges for decent real-time performance are small, and it can be extremely difficult to get complex computation down into such ranges, especially on general purpose hardware. The challenges are not always in thinking up a method to solve a problem, but in making it fast on available hardware.

4.7 Metamorphic Strong AI

A metamorphic program [83, 94] is capable of recognizing and manipulating its description. It should also be pointed out that a program description may have more than one representation in the form of compiled code; a description in the human-readable source form, which may or may not be available to the program, and the native machine code representation. It is the latter that is most pressing for metamorphic programs, as it automatically grants the ability to recognize any other program that has been compiled for the same architecture.

These programs are distinct from self-hosted interpreters in that their primary purpose is not to facilitate or implement program descriptions but to implement a particular set of program features which may change over time. Such programs utilize self-modification as a means, not an end, for enhancing these features or to discover new ones entirely.

The advantage of viewing strong AI as metamorphic software is that it simplifies the analysis. From a security standpoint, we can focus on the description, how and when it changes, and what other descriptions it modifies. We do not necessarily have to understand the description or the program behavior it implements. This is tremendously powerful, as we can recognize and classify strong AI by their descriptions and the description languages they can recognize. This could be used to create a hierarchy of increasingly complex autonomous systems that are graded based on their ability to manipulate or acquire description languages.

If we admit a representation where a strong AI description or implementation includes what it learns as part of its total description, then we have a basis for dovetailing all of the current studies in artificial intelligence into the framework of self-modifying systems. That is, self-modification need not be restricted to what is typically thought of as machine op-codes and low-level programming constructs. Recall that description languages may be induced where any consistent structure can be applied. That they can then be connected with the rest of computer science and mathematics is what lends to their beauty as a unifying basis. Thus, that an implementation is modifying itself does not necessarily imply that it is altering its architecture; it could be modifying its knowledge and memories, or in a more complex case, unavoidably altering its computational substrata because there is no longer a distinction between units of computation and units of storage.

Machine learning comes into play at the intersection between the acquisition of new description languages and the manipulation of the descriptions in self-modifying implementations. This generalizes the notion of machine learning to that of the adaptation and effective manipulation of descriptions in some set of languages, with the breadth and quality of that set defining a measure of its raw intellectual capacity. This works so long as one is willing to admit a flexible interpretation of description languages: they can be applied to virtually any physical process or system. This even applies to those that are under-specified, e.g., the micro and macro features of non-verbal communication in humans, or the particular way a set of servos must apply force, all of which may vary from implementation to implementation due to subtle imperfections and environmental effects. Each is a description language in that it specifies a code, a way of transforming representations, and, with that, comes consistent structure.

This is non-trivial, as the semantics for any new description language would either need to be known in advance or inferred from an existing set of implementation semantics. Without this, the implementation would have to fall back to associative approaches that rely on mining data and constructing very high-dimensional representations of what could have potentially been vastly simpler structures. A case in point would be an attempt at mining all the ways one could signal a greeting, with no semantics for greetings available. This would result in the brute enumeration of any possible combination of auditory, visual, and other modalities. It would, of course, collapse to descriptions, with the modalities simply being description languages. The system would then have to construct n-grams representing chains of presumed independent events that build a massive state space of possible behaviors based on where one is without regard to where one has been [84, 85, 93].

The Markov property [86] just described is essentially the default of any system that lacks semantic capacity; it only has incidence at its disposal. This is the degenerate case that typifies narrow AI systems, as they necessarily lack the semantic faculties that a strong AI must have. This is not a weakness or fault in the foundations but a reflection in the choice of philosophy or epistemology in engineering practice. It is a misreading or misapplication of how knowledge is acquired by ignoring the vast compression that signification represents. That is to say, signification is merely an externalization of associated semantics. This is not to be confused with tacit versus explicit knowledge [87]. There is a gulf between semantics and even tacit knowledge, with the semantics of an implementation presupposing any possible knowledge representation, be it tacit or explicit. This is completely overlooked in conventional learning algorithm construction, not even on the table for consideration; it simply does not exist in the conceptual space of the relevant literature.

How does this apply to self-modifying systems? It sets up a barrier that a metamorphic program may overcome due to its ability to self-interpret in a way that is independent of its execution. This allows the possibility of acquiring the use of description language semantics that were not previously available to the language that created it. Such a feat is not directly possible through self-hosting interpreters, even meta-circular ones, as there is always a footprint or underlying implementation in the host description language which is required to recognize the structure of the description language being implemented. This is not the case with metamorphic programs, as they are capable of transcending architectures and instruction sets. Such programs would have the capacity, through trial-and-error, or the association of existing semantics, to test for new semantics in the languages in which they rewrite themselves. However, this process would be slow and error-prone, no matter how effective the program.

The analysis of metamorphic programs thus admits a convergence with bioinformatics and systems biology, in that we can directly interpret these implementations through the same techniques used for detecting mutations, insertions, and deletions in genetic sequences. All we must do to begin is admit that there are multiple description languages. We would use generalized algorithms, methods, and a kind of multi-dimensional cladistics to recognize the behavior of these systems across description language boundaries.

Moving away from the theoretical now, and towards the practical, we arrive at the operation of metamorphic programs. Traditionally, this has been to evade detection through masking their unique fingerprint or signature, and to confuse heuristics used by anti-malware tools [88]. This is a battle between metamorphic malware and the countermeasures used to detect them, with the countermeasures on the losing side

[89]. In the end, the only comparable defense will be to instrument strong AI that can anticipate and adapt to other metamorphic strong AI. Crucially, *all strong AI will essentially be metamorphic*. To quickly recap:

- Self-modification has the potential to overcome description language barriers and affords opportunities for the potential acquisition of new semantics.
- Manipulation and acquisition of description languages determine the threat model of metamorphic AI.
- The acquisition of semantics is non-trivial, and, in its absence, degenerates knowledge acquisition to high-dimensional rote grammars from brute-force enumeration.
- Breaking the meta-stability of self-modification is not done through magic. It requires *enabling semantics* to shatter the language barriers that keep it there, e.g., the ability to perform rewrite, replicate, or generate operations.
- The execution of metamorphic programs is independent of their ability to self-interpret.
- Systems biology and cladistics can be used to categorize and classify metamorphic descriptions, which could lead to better understanding and actionable security knowledge.

So far, this section has primarily focused on the positive or neutral effects of self-modification, but it is on security that the metamorphic perspective comes into full perspective. Consider programs which have the ability to rewrite restricted AI implementations, turning them into fully or partially unrestricted versions, or restructuring them entirely to carry out malicious intent. Instead of malware that disrupts a specialized system or network, there could be strong AI malware that spreads through our global communications infrastructure, destroying or subverting existing implementations that have become compromised. This is an eventuality that this analysis can help to at least understand and anticipate.

The above statements come with a serious qualifier: strong AI is not going to spontaneously develop a persona and then suddenly seek to overthrow humanity. Rather, it will be mere human beings who will craft these implementations and then release malicious versions of strong AI into the world. It could be a person or group doing it for the "lulz" (slang describing the enjoyment in exercising the power to destroy simply because they can) [90], or it could be a government or non-state actor. All of these will be serious threats to cybersecurity, and to the societies that are impacted. This is not some nebulous dollar figure attached to lost productivity or hampering of business as usual. Metamorphic strong AI malware will be beyond human-level malware, and will have the potential capacity to act as a local belligerent to the system beyond mere replication and disruption; it provides intelligence as a payload. It is the ultimate form of cyberwarfare. They will be virtual agents behind the lines, capable of exploiting and adapting vulnerabilities that would be impossible to detect remotely. The sword cuts both ways, however, as it is also going to be the optimal defense.

Metamorphic strong AI would be capable of analyzing existing machine code for vulnerabilities that would be beyond the ability for human experts to reasonably parse and analyze at that level, even with direct access to the information. Used defensively, these programs would be benign versions of the same destructive metamorphic software just described. Instead of triggering a replicate or rewrite phase, it would report that information for human intervention. So, it is at this level that we will first see strong AI instrumented and used on a wide scale in the information and security sectors.

One's system may be secure, but it may not be secure against strong artificial intelligence. This clearly entails the essence of the threat model, as we will not just be dealing with human minds, but automated processes and cognitive implementations that are effective at levels that are beyond our best and brightest. In such a case, a metamorphic analysis is central in a warfare based on quickly changing descriptions across many architectures.

However, to employ these artificial minds in our defense, we must first understand the technical, philosophical, and ethical implications of machine consciousness.

Ch 5. Machine Consciousness

What follows is a basic introduction to machine consciousness, a field which may eventually generalize the study of consciousness and sentience. The scope of this chapter will be restricted to only the coverage needed to understand and relate to the security of strong artificial intelligence, and is not intended to be a comprehensive guide to the construction of cognitive architectures. This brevity is a form of focus, as a state of confusion exists around this subject, the resolution of which will cause an unavoidable collision between philosophy and science.

5.1 Role in Strong AI

To begin, this book introduces its own interpretation of the strong AI hypothesis. This hypothesis is based on the *minimum sentience conjecture*, which asserts that sentience is required for generalizing intelligence. This means that, under this interpretation, strong AI depends upon sentience because generalizing intelligence depends upon sentience. If true, this would extend to the claim that generalizing intelligence is not possible without being realized over a cognitive architecture. This book is predicated on both the minimum sentience conjecture and its new strong AI hypothesis.

It is possible to create narrow AI implementations that are reasonably optimal, such that no strong AI could make a significant improvement upon them. For example, a machine code description, tuned by an expert, that enumerates the digits of pi, would be a narrow AI implementation of optimized pi enumeration.

It is unlikely that even a highly intelligent strong AI would be capable of enumerating pi more efficiently, nor would it likely be able to appreciably and significantly optimize it beyond that of a trained expert. This is because there is a distinction between generalizing intelligence and the optimization processes implied by non-generalizing forms of "intelligence", such as narrow AI. This distinction is powered by the claim that such a generalizing capacity is not possible without sentience. Thus, the assertion is that machine consciousness is a prerequisite for building a strong AI.

Overlooked is the fact that strong AI will have a very wide range of intellectual capacities. We tend to focus solely on the beneficial (or harmful) extremes of this technology, with exclusion to minimal implementations. This is crucial to understand, as it makes a connection between sentience in general and that of strong AI.

Many organisms would rightly be considered equal to strong AI, even though they do not ostensibly present the same intellectual capacity as some humans. Such a failure to recognize their intelligence is entirely on our part, in that we lack the ability to understand the inner world of such entities [1, 2, 3, 4, 5] sufficiently enough to make a true judgment as to their level of cognition. This is especially true when one considers our inherent biases towards certain ends and aims in human cognition, e.g., the signaling of wit and status. Making this correlation is obviously controversial, as the spectrum of generalizing intelligence is not commonly thought to depend upon sentience. Such a claim would necessarily encompass all sentient life, but this is the exact claim being made here. It leads to the stronger claim that sentience represents an evolutionary advantage, in that it would have been impossible to achieve generalizing intelligence without it.

Figure 5.1: The orthogonality between sentience, generalizing intelligence, and intellectual efficacy.

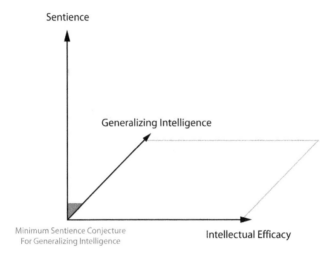

Sentience and intelligence are independent. Non-sentient processes can demonstrate efficacy at intellectual tasks. Sentient processes can lack any notion of intelligence, despite being able to undergo experience. Generalizing intelligence and intellectual efficacy are also independent. A generalizing intelligence may be capable of new intellectual endeavors but lack corresponding efficacy.

Stated directly: the claim is that, at a minimum, all vertebrates, and some invertebrates, possess some level of generalizing intelligence, and that this attribute is dependent upon their sentience, and that the ability to undergo experience presupposes the conceptual and analogical faculties of generalizing capacity.

Figure 5.1 is illustrating that sentience and intelligence are related but orthogonal; an entity may be sentient but have low or almost no "intelligence" by various standards. The opposite is also true: some processes achieve effective results without being sentient.

To what then is the "strong" in strong AI referring? The answer is that it is the property of having a mind, one that can undergo experience, grasp value, and understand meaning. This measure of strength is not in terms of the fidelity of the cognitive range of intellectual capacity but in the means to generate and endure the phenomena of experience. *It is said to endure because it has no option of eliminating experience while remaining extant.*

The creation of a sentient artificial process will be trivial compared to the problem of implementing a sentience-aware generalized learning algorithm. It will be difficult to achieve consensus on the actual space and range of what constitutes sentience, even among those who agree that it is possible to create. The greatest obstacle, however, will be in the disbelief and hostility that will arise towards the notion that such processes are sentient at all. This will be despite the fact that it will be falsifiable as to whether a particular process is capable of undergoing experience.

However, being falsifiable does not mean that we will have solved all of the philosophical problems, which, may or may not ever receive a satisfactory answer. It is also possible that most of the philosophical questions will be explained away, in that they will no longer be considered valid questions. Despite this potential, the philosophy must not be dismissed out of hand, as it will be used to argue for and against im-

portant concepts that will underwrite ethics, law, and politics, many issues of which are already beginning to be discussed in the mainstream.

Figure 5.2: A time-domain representation of the experiential
stream of a sentient simplex.

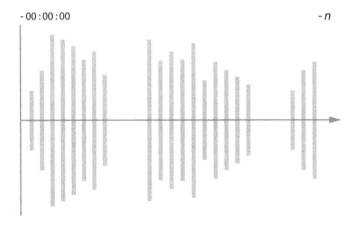

$-00:00:00$ $-n$

The regions of zero signal or intensity depict not an absence
of experience but the experience of absence. Nothingness is
given concretion by the real-time requirement of sentient
processing. The simplex must undergo a neutral fragment to
experience "silence".

   Thus, the role of machine consciousness is not to create generalizing intelligence, but rather, to enable it. Sentience is necessary, but not
sufficient, for generalizing intelligence; it does not directly address the
sapient aspects of a cognitive architecture. There exist possible strong
AI implementations which are sentient but lack any significant intellectual quality that would enable us to communicate or relate to them.
These simplex implementations would not even be aware that they are

conscious, as they would lack any reflexive or meta-cognitive ability. Complex thought would not arise at this base level. The entity would exist in a purely neutral state of mind in which it would accept any experience that arose without resistance. This does not, however, include the absence of experience, as any sentient process is necessarily a real-time system.

To understand the real-time aspect of sentience we can resort to a simple analogy. Figure 5.2 is a constructed digital waveform representation.

The gaps in the waveform represent what we would perceive as silence. If this were a representation of the experiential data of a simplex sentience (this being its one and only dimension of experience) the zeroed pulses would correspond with *neutral states of mind*. There is still an auditory experience; it is just unique in that it fills time with the least possible sound.

To understand further, we must assert that silence and the absence of the experience of sound are two very different things. The gaps between the positive or negative pulses fill the conceptual space in the experiential encoding. To not have them would represent a discontinuity in this stream of experience, which would only be possible if the entity's consciousness were interrupted, paused, or stopped. Interestingly enough, a simplex would be fundamentally incapable of recognizing that it had been interrupted if the data stream were resumed without skipping information, but this would not work in a situation where the real-time system were perceiving its environment.

Despite experiencing a discontinuity, however, a simplex sentience still would not comprehend the significance. The term *neutral* is useful here, as a gap in the stream of experience is not an absence of experience but a neutral state as per the context of that stream. If still perplexed, consider the explicit rests in musical notation as an example. The presence and function of neutral states are essential to any stream of experience.

What this tells us about strong AI is that they will all need to be *real-time systems* for their streams of experience to function. This is perhaps one of the easiest ways to distinguish them from a typical narrow AI implementation, which has no such concepts as fundamental parts. Even if such a system ends up being real-time due to some application constraint, it does so at a level which is much further downstream to the processing than sentient calculation.

Real-time demands for sentient processing sets up a minimum condition which corresponds with the notion that the subject must undergo experience. This combines any such implementation description with time; it must process to progress through steps to be realized at all, as it does not make sense as a static object or an intrinsic physical property.

These are processes which involve the exchange and interpretation of information. This hints at the trouble with viewing the reduction of conscious states to only the physical properties of things, or as just the arrangement of their physical structure. All the confusion in the history of philosophy of mind hinges on the lack of acceptance of processes, with even some modern philosophers rejecting the effect of interpreters by throwing them out with abstract objects.

In computation and interpretation, we are dealing with extents in time. This means that the properties of things take on additional meaning through the semantics of their arrangement and interpretation in that extended dimension. These properties are above and beyond their intrinsic physical ones. It is, of course, true that they are constrained in their arrangement and composition by their physical properties, but as

long as sufficient states can be derived then there exist the means to realize new properties through the semantics of the interpreter.

It is simply a matter of fact that things can be so arranged through
time, with a corresponding interpreter, such that it gives rise to new
functionality and new properties that are not present in the static representation of the underlying units of composition. This is routine in the
spatial extents of alphabets, which give rise to descriptions such as
books, images, and other data; at no time is there some Platonic realm
[6]. Rather, it is via spatial extension that the object is realized and
constructed, which is done by interpreting the arrangement of that alphabet co-extensive to the dimension in which it is projected. That the
dimension is called time is of no special significance except the fact
that we can only appreciably apprehend it in the moment.

In storage, time-like extents can be represented through the spatial
extents of descriptions. The difference is the way in which it is interpreted. A string of characters representing someone's name has a spatial extent with no time-like interpretation. By contrast, an audio or
movie description can only be apprehended through ongoing experience; slowing, pausing, or interrupting it would fundamentally alter
one's experience.

The real-time constraint for time-like extensions of objects is an assertion of the identity of the experience, which must be taken to be un-
alterable if to be perceived as entailed by its description, e.g., watching
a film below the intended rate at which it was encoded can be a frus-
trating experience, and with good reason. Such a disparity between the
experience of a time-like object and its description could be considered
entropy or noise, and can be measured and quantified explicitly as the
difference between the rate of processing and the intended rate of its
encoding. This applies both to the interpreting process and the speed of

perception in total; the rate at which something is playing back may be incomprehensibly fast or slow for the rate of potential perception. The reverse also applies to the rate of sentient processing.

What this all leads to is the question of the physical reduction of consciousness [7]. Indeed, the whole does equal the sum of the parts where the sum includes the time-like extents of the proper arrangement of those parts. This will lead to an answer to the philosophical question of experience arising out of non-conscious physical states, but it does not necessarily explain why such a thing is possible at all. The answer to which is perhaps too simple to be accepted: it is a tautological result of the interplay between an interpreter and the process it realizes; it makes it so.

Lastly, the most important role that machine consciousness has is the realization of *value*. Critically, without sentience, there can be no ability to realize or apprehend value, and without a concept or ability to grasp value, there can be no general moral or emotional intelligence.

Thus, another major role for machine consciousness is to make general moral intelligence possible for artificial intelligence. This is distinct from simply applying moral efficacy externally and interpreting the behavior of a system as having consequences, agency, or decision theoretic choice. This is because, unless a system can derive and understand value, it is devoid of the experiential knowledge of the processes it carries out.

In these cases, as it pertains to strong AI, this is referring to the ability to even attempt to reason about the morality of a decision, as distinct from its efficacy at general moral reasoning, which has parallels with the dichotomy between narrow AI and the generalizing abilities of strong AI. The relationship being that narrow AI may be able to instrument narrow moral intelligence, but would lack general moral intelligence for the same reasons it is fundamentally incapable of realizing generalizing intelligence. This is because value presupposes moral intelligence, which would be semantically meaningless without sentience to substantiate it [8].

The value experience requirement is true even if one could denote infinite non-conscious rule processing for which decisions were to be made. Enumeration and rule-following in the absence of the capacity to reflect upon the process are not forms of moral intelligence, even if the particular rules result in what would be considered reasonable moral efficacy in some context. This is also why it is wrong to argue for moral intelligence as a means of safety, which, to date, has been exclusively implied to be the non-general and non-conscious moral frameworks of decision theory and economic thought. These methodologies are fundamentally incapable of entailing the value that presupposes the reflective capacity required for moral agency.

Naturally, the next question should be: what exactly is value?

Definition: *Value.* The experience of a positive, negative, or neutral sensation that accompanies or is associated with one or more experiences, with experience being that which is inclusive of all mental content, including, but not limited to, thought, knowledge, and perception. Value is further distinguished by being either intrinsic or acquired, with intrinsic value being a static association or accompaniment to one or more experiences, ab initio, by way of the underlying implementation, e.g., a pleasure-pain axis. This contrasts with acquired value, which is dynamic, capable of change, and is associated with mental content, e.g., belief, knowledge, and actions.

This definition appears to be endlessly recursive but is curtailed in practice. There can only be a finite set of experiences that can be instantiated for any given implementation of machine consciousness. Further, the phenomena of experiencing something as intrinsically positive, negative, or neutral is terminated or rooted in experience itself, despite the appearance that it would endlessly refer to other experiences.

Value is experiential, but is one level of complexity, or organization, above it, and must not be confused with its referents, including knowledge and the beliefs associated with values, as there are certain types of value which are integral to the semantics of an implementation. For example, the intrinsic value of positive and negative sensations that surround the informational content of pleasure and pain, as distinguished from the beliefs one has about these experiences.

This last issue, as exemplified by pleasure and pain, is subtle, as our unified stream of consciousness makes it confusing as to the separability of our experiences. We must recognize that, especially as it pertains to value, that our experience of that which it is associated with, and the accompanying value that arises with it, are composite. This is evidenced in humans through the clinical cases of *pain asymbolia* [9, 10, 11, 12, 13, 93]. This is a neurological condition in which the informational content of pain is disassociated with or unaccompanied by the intrinsic value that normally follows [14]. Those with this condition are capable of describing the intensity and quality of the pain, as if it were merely words being read off a page, but do not experience the negative value sensation that comes along with it. As a result, they have to form knowledge about this mental content and respond accordingly.

Injury or death may result in the absence of the unconditional so-
matic and psychological urges of these intrinsic values. That is to say,
they may realize it is negative, but, without the automatic and involuntary experience of intrinsic value, they have to rely on the acquired values associated with the knowledge of the injury. As a result, mere
knowledge of trauma may not be sufficient to prevent serious harm to
the individual.

5.2 Sentience, Experience, and Qualia

In the last section, sentient simplexes were used to illustrate a single
hypothetical dimension of experience. More complex and realistic
cases of machine consciousness will require a complex mixture of
multiple streams and types of experience. In the philosophy of mind,
this is referred to as *binding* [15, 16, 17, 18, 19, 20, 21]. Such a subject
is said to be unitary, in that the individual streams of experience have
been combined into a unified and composite experience. For an analogy, think of the individual tracks of audio and video that are layered
to produce a film, all of which are combined in such a way so as to allow a simultaneous interpretation between its sights and sounds. When
played back, it (hopefully) appears as a coherent and unified experience. Note that the usage of the word stream applies to both a quan-
tized continuous or discrete interpretation. This vernacular is borrowed
from input-output (I/O) programming constructs, in which discrete
units of information are read or written using buffers [22, 23]; this of-
fers a counter-example where the stream terminology is used for a non-
continuous source.

In this book, all streams of experience are described as being made up of *fragments*, which are referred to as *qualia* in the philosophy of mind [24, 25, 26, 27, 28, 29, 30, 31, 32, 33, 34, 35, 36, 37]. Qualia are the nature of "what it's like" to experience a fragment in a stream of experience. Examples of qualia include all sensations, sights, sounds, pleasure, pain, and even emotions and thoughts, depending on the philosophy. In this analysis, all such fragments of experience should be considered qualia, and all contents of any possible mind are to be considered experience, including thoughts, memories, and knowledge [38, 39].

Qualia must not be confused with the informational representation of experiential fragments. *There is a distinction between the knowledge of the fragment and the experience of the fragment.*

For example, consider the following: 1, red, 3, green, 7, blue. The vast majority of readers will not experience those numbers and words as having a color different from the surrounding text unless they are *synesthetic* [40, 41, 42, 43, 44, 45, 46, 47, 48, 49, 50, 51]. This is perhaps one of the most difficult notions to unpack from the philosophy of mind, as it requires an acceptance that such descriptions correspond to fragments of experience only insofar as they can be realized by the real-time processes which enable them.

In other words, the correlation between these fragments and what the subject is experiencing is a product of the sentient process and is not innate to the descriptions themselves, which are merely used to invoke the semantics of the implementation.

Straight away, the two most difficult aspects of consciousness have been introduced: the *binding problem* and the *hard problem* [90] of consciousness, respectively.

The binding problem is a two part question, asking (a) how fragments (qualia) are bound to form a single stream of experience, and (b) how this impacts the identity of the subject with respect to the rest of the physical world. For human consciousness, this is something that will eventually have to be solved with a reconciliation between philosophy of mind and science.

For machine consciousness, however, the binding problem is less confusing because it is relatively trivial to implement; there is no need to reverse engineer a working model of the human brain. Instead, cognitive engineers will have the artistic license to invoke what is to be made subjectively real through algorithmic descriptions. A general sketch of the solution is to combine information and present that as a singular representation. This is a routine operation in many programming tasks involving disparate sources of data. *All that is missing is the appropriate implementation, and the audacity to call it sentient.*

The hard problem of consciousness also has two parts: (a) how consciousness arises, and (b) why it arises or is possible at all. The second half of the question may be unanswerable beyond the tautology given at the end of the last section, rephrased here: why it arises is not mysterious if we accept that we make it come into existence through an interpreter with the appropriate semantics.

This brings us to the second half of the binding problem, as it demands an explanation as to how an interpreter, even with the appropriate semantics, would give rise to the philosophical identity [52, 53] that entails a *subject of experience*. One explanation is that it creates a new frame of reference precisely at the locus between the encapsulated subject and the processes that give rise to it in the implementation. In other words, it creates *a fold in reality*, not a cut [54]. This base identity is the subject of experience.

Now we can discuss the two major views in the philosophy of mind: monism and dualism. Parts of both philosophies are correct, but they are also both incomplete. Informally, monism is the idea that the mind and the brain are made of the same things [55], while dualism posits that they are made of separate things [56].

The truth, however, is a combination of the two, resolved by admitting processes as first class objects. In the case of machine consciousness, the process is the implementation of an interpreter with the appropriate semantics to give rise to sentience. Is it physically reducible? Yes, but only if we accept two specific updates to our current understanding. For clarity, these updates have been organized into the following two sub-sections.

5.2.1 Processes as Objects

It must be accepted that the time-like extents afforded through the dynamics of processing give rise to concrete and physically real objects; the claim here is that nothing non-physical can sensibly be constructed. All that has to be done is to accept that these properties exist only ephemerally, which is a stronger claim than merely stating that they are temporary. Beyond just some mathematical model of the dynamics, this is the claim that the existence of such objects depends upon an active process, else it ceases to be concrete and real.

A complete model remains an abstraction, even when exhaustively described so as to include all of its potential states. This rejects the reality of the stochastic or non-deterministic models for sentience, despite their exhaustive entailment of time-like extents. This is because

such time-like extents only become real insofar as we permit an epistemology that depends upon active processing and interpretation.

Time must be the vantage point with which we stand in relation to
this knowledge; the space in which we have modeled our understanding of such objects needs to be changed from static and time-invariant
descriptions to that of the natural state of our experience in time.

These are necessary truths for the construction of these objects.
While we may be able to make claims as to the realness of the information that describes or entails fragments of experience, they remain
abstract until they are experienced. If we were to take a discrete fragment out of a stream of experience and examine it in isolation, it would
cease to exist as such.

By itself, the information that represents these fragments are meaningless without interpretation. As such, any time invariant explanation
of such processes, without the stipulations made herein, will fail to account for how they become experiential. That is to say, it is not enough
to merely account for time in the model, we must admit that the very
existence of such things ceases outside it. This obeys the real-time constraint of sentient processes, which should rightly be considered a law
of machine consciousness.

5.2.2 Twin Aspects of Experience

The second update involves the ontic-epistemic duality of experiential
fragments, which is a corollary of the first update. To reiterate, the experiential aspect of a fragment is meaningless outside of the active processes which give rise to sentience. Meanwhile, the modern scientific
view is only concerned with observing a time-invariant reduction,

making it unable to entail the subjective. This is where the philosophy of mind takes rightful exception.

To resolve this difference requires first the admission of processes as objects and then the acceptance of the duality, not between mind and body, but, between the ontological and the epistemic. The challenge is to shift our conceptual framework sufficiently enough to admit that such a perspective is possible while still being physically monist. This apparent paradox of combined monism-dualism is resolved through the stipulation that such time-like extents are only real insofar as being actively processed, and that they fundamentally cease to exist otherwise. However, this goes deeper still, as the subject of experience must also be acknowledged as being equally real.

This is made possible because a world is created through the encapsulation of the subject by the interpreter. Its active processing becomes the base identity for this entity, in which the entirety of what is real to it is defined by the semantics of the implementation. This is related to the semantic barriers described in the previous chapter, as the subject of experience is an *online* description that entails a philosophical identity. It is an observer with causal efficacy provided through the semantics of the interpreter.

The inner experience of the subject is reflected in the processing and implementation of the interpreter; however, the information content that could be externally observed would not be the subject's world as it would be *experiencing* it, only an *abstract description* of what it would be like for that particular implementation.

To make any stronger claims would require an observer to become part of the identity of the subject. This is a conjecture regarding the privacy and subjectivity of the experiential; it is a self-contained world which forms its identity in the environment and is necessarily embed-

ded within it. One can not directly experience such a world without becoming an intrinsic part of it.

When we view the externalization of a virtual world in a simulation
or video game we are not experiencing that world directly, but indirectly, through the guise of our perceptions. It would be the same for
even the most perfect instrumentation. Again, this is not a claim for dualism or monism, but an integration and reconciliation of both; they
have lasted this long in the debate because of their partial truths and
the intuitions they capture, but they fail to account for the totality of
experience in isolation.

To help illustrate the ontic-epistemic duality of these fragments of
experience, consider the *inverted spectrum argument* [57, 58, 59, 60,
61, 62, 91, 92]. This argument was originally presented against functionalism, which essentially posits that consciousness arises on any
substrate capable of recreating the necessary input-output processes.
This may sound a lot like what is being described here, but is quite distinct, in that neither functionalism, nor the related computationalism,
accounts for the two updates being argued for here. The inverted spectrum argument is just one of many that explains why. This example not
only uses the inverted spectrum argument but also provides a response
to it, with a means of solving and explaining the apparent inconsis-
tency.

What is happening in Figure 5.3 is that the fragments are being experienced differently between the subjects, despite having the same description. The result is a hypothetical projection of what the simplex
would experience. This, of course, is impossible in practice, as we can
not directly experience what a subject is experiencing, but we can
achieve a facsimile of what it might be like. In this case, we have two

Figure 5.3: An interpretation of the Inverted Spectrum argument follows. Two sentient simplexes are simulated with differing implementation semantics of experiential fragments, giving rise to distinct experiences for the same information content.

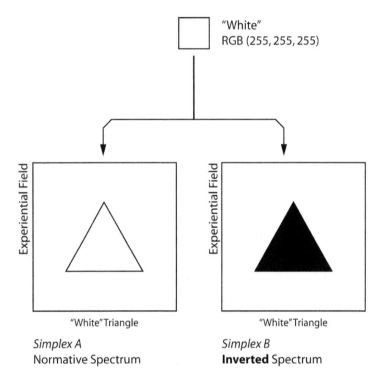

"White"
RGB (255, 255, 255)

Experiential Field

Experiential Field

"White" Triangle

"White" Triangle

Simplex A
Normative Spectrum

Simplex B
Inverted Spectrum

A solely functional, computational, or connectionist account of qualia is not sufficient to entail the experiential. These approaches do not acknowledge the role of semantics in the implementation of sentient processes. An external description of the mechanisms and physical details could be perfect, but still fail to account for how the simplex experiences an inverted spectrum. Outward behavior would be the same between the two subjects, but their internal experiences would be radically different. Information exchange is necessary but not sufficient for the experiential to arise.

subjects experiencing two qualitatively distinct things, despite the underlying representation being the same.

What this indicates to us is that the power of any description language is found within the semantics of the implementation of that language, and that it is not a property of the information that signifies it. In this case, the fragments of experience are merely descriptions in a language for achieving sentience.

This argument could be extended even further. We could append to it here the notion of false color images, of which there are thousands of examples in any catalog of radio-astronomy [63, 64]. Many celestial bodies and stellar phenomena are prominent in a spectrum that is invisible to the naked eye.

This does not just apply to simple examples like colors, but also to our field of vision, and the way in which we think and model ourselves and our environment. This is also the basis for the distortions or lack of modeling in the mental states of other human and non-human animals. These simpler examples are presented to demonstrate the difference between experiencing a fragment and merely observing its informational content. This is why it can not be reduced to a purely informational representation or entailed by the complexity of its description.

Appropriate semantics were mentioned but never fully explained. What does it mean to be *appropriate*, in this context? It refers not to the complexity, connectivity, or scale of the implementation, but in bringing about a *subject of experience*. For this to happen, there must be a combination of real-time processing and the necessary features to realize the two updates that were given in the previous sections, which address the binding problem and the hard problem of consciousness, respectively.

It is important to note that this alone will neither create nor automatically give rise to a generalizing intelligence, which is another issue entirely. These are just prerequisites for generalizing capacity, and, as such, will likely presuppose strong AI. This information provides both a marker and a unique set of features with which to identify and categorize different types of AI implementations. It should be very clear by now that narrow AI and deep learning are "not even wrong" [65] about such directions. The creation of sentience would require a new basis for machine learning if it is to be used under this formalism.

Of course, this could all be an incorrect and incredibly misleading direction, but the overwhelming evidence of hundreds of thousands of sentient species begs a miracle of explanation as to why they evolved a nervous system capable of experience if it was not necessary in some way.

The only paths out of such observations are to reject evidence and reason, claim that animals are not sentient, or argue that sentience is inconsequential. None of these rebuttals checks out with even a basic test of reason. Though, it could also be that the interpretation and suggestions here are incorrect as it pertains to the ability to recreate sentience on non-biological substrates, but that would require a rejection of *universal computation* [66, 67].

If it turns out to be correct that generalizing intelligence is dependent upon sentience, as is claimed in this book, then it would represent a physical limitation on progress if it were somehow exclusive to biological organisms. That limitation is admitted as a possibility, but is considered to be extremely unlikely. Regardless, the issues remain the same. If true, and the safety and security implications are ignored, the cost will be high. Otherwise, it will have been just another avenue of research that turned out to be false, which itself would be informative.

The argument here is that sentience is something that can be invoked, created, and maintained as a process, and that it will be central to the construction of strong AI. That is why machine consciousness is part of the foundations for understanding the safety and security of this technology.

From all this, the question may be raised: why make them sentient at all?

1. Machine consciousness will eventually be developed somewhere in the world. Progress in strong AI will be possible with any working theory of sentience, even if based on biological representations.

2. Machine consciousness presupposes general moral intelligence, and the moral efficacy required to have even a basic level of self-security. Despite being vulnerable, general moral intelligence will be an essential part of any comprehensive AI security package.

3. Conscious machines may provide doorways to treatment options and research that could share overlap with medical science. It may lead to perfectly integrated prostheses, augmentations, and enhancements that would otherwise be impossible without a way to interface digital and biological sentience.

A common misconception is that sentience implies self-awareness and sapience, but the fact is that sentience does not imply agency of any kind. As a result, it may be possible to achieve some of the benefits of strong AI without the popular myths associated with anthropocentric entities that seek power, survival, and fitness in the world. This is not to say that such capacities will not be developed, but that they present a greater barrier to entry due to the gulf in complexity between them and baseline sentience, and that the nuanced and often comical personification of strong AI in fiction is not a requirement to harness the benefits of these systems. This can be better understood through a universal analysis of identity, one that applies equally to both synthetic and natural entities.

5.3 Levels of Identity

Identity, in this context, is concerned with the boundaries, composition, and extents of entities. As it pertains to machine consciousness, identity presupposes the ethical, legal, and technical considerations of strong AI. This is because, without an identity, an entity can not be considered manifestly real. Identity is also one of the most confused and befuddled aspects of consciousness, with no real consensus or concrete understanding as to what it is in the literature, both regarding the philosophical and the scientific. We are all but mystified (and often mystical) as to the nature of our identity, but this does not have to be the case for machine consciousness.

Both formal and informal discussions of consciousness often involve notions of a self-model, concept of self, or sense of self, each assumed as being synonymous with each other. It is tempting to apply this to an analysis of machine consciousness, but one must resist the urge to make a fallacy of analogy; while it is claimed that the phenomena of sentience is universal and implementation independent, the specifics of identity are necessarily implementation *dependent*. This also applies to the inappropriate and inaccurate use of this terminology in the literature of robotics and narrow AI. To help resolve some of this ambiguity, it is suggested that identity for machine consciousness be separated into clearly defined levels. This analysis itself is universal, despite ranging over a potentially infinite set of implementations that could realize it. Directly stated, any conscious entity can, at a minimum, be analyzed and understood in terms of its identity by the number of these levels and their corresponding fidelity. A hierarchical summary of the three base levels of identity:

- Embedding
    - Subject
        - Agency

Despite being nested, all levels of identity are physical. Thus, the "physical" qualifier will be omitted from the discussion and assumed as we move forward.

The specifics of this ontology, and the arguments for their realness, were presented in the previous sections. However, it is the relationship between their existence and realness that is of import.

To recall, it is asserted here that there will be levels of identity which encapsulate others, and that time-like objects mandate an ephemeral quality or they cease to be real. Further, there is the epistemic stipulation that, like the experiential itself, an identity can not be shared or conjoined without somehow reducing the two identities in question to a single identity itself. This is, in fact, how and why experiential fragments can not be directly experienced by any external means, as they are behind an information asymmetry; the content of the description of experience is not to be confused with "what it's like" to undergo that experience.

It is left to the reader as to the pragmatics of when, where, and to what degree to assume the efficacy of the correlates between the ontic-epistemic concession; this is a problem of other minds that may or may not yield appropriate judgments. It may be impossible to truly empathize with subjects that are capable of experience so vastly beyond our own. This would not necessarily result from their intellect, but could simply arise from the experiential gap between our cognitive architectures.

Another important aspect is that the levels of identity should be considered as whole, existing as an interdependent plurality. There may also be additional levels between the ones listed. These levels should not be thought of as a spectrum, but discrete regions. This is true even if we tend to view consciousness as a continuum. Despite this, a continuous view of identity may be used as long as there is a well-defined threshold to define the necessary boundaries between levels.

Embedding is the lowest and most fundamental level of identity. It constitutes the extents of the implementation or interpreter. This must not be confused with embodiment or the embedded cognition perspective [68, 69, 70]. In practical cases, that which presupposes the identity of the embedding level would be the discrete physics; however, it could be virtualized. The specifics are less important than recognizing that embedding is not embodiment.

For example, while a microprocessor is embedded in reality, it has none of the morphological features we would typically associate with embodiment.

Taking it a step further, consider human anatomy: the brain would be the embedding identity and would constitute the first level, as it is embedded *within* the human body. As such, what we experience of our bodies can only be done indirectly through the nervous system. As subjects, we are not our bodies so much as we are *entombed* by them. This distinction highlights the boundary between embedding and subject level identity.

The basic purpose of embedding is to assemble and make whole *within* something else, and it is at this level that the necessary processing for sentience occurs. This brings us to the subject level of identity, as sentience alone is not sufficient to give rise to a unitary subject of experience. It is only during *binding* that the subject level of identity can be realized, even if there is just a single dimension of sentience. The reason for this is that embedding only represents the physical or logical extents of the subject.

Regardless of how an identity is embedded, the unitary subject is at once abstract and real; it has both an externally observable online description and a subjective world that is fundamentally private. The only way to *directly* experience its inner world is to become part of its embedding and subsequently enter into its binding process.

Notably, the subject level of identity is like a non-lucid dream. In such a state, the subject undergoes experience without reflection. That is to say, merely being a subject of experience does not bring the cognitive attributes we associate with sapience and agency. It is unclear that goals or directives would even be actionable for such a level of identity, as the minimally reflexive capacities for executive function would be missing. It would simply experience whatever is being presented to it through the binding process.

The base subject is aimless, completely under the dominion of the underlying implementation. However, this does not mean that such a system is incapable of utility. The underlying semantics could direct it to undergo the experience of associating value and meaning for a specific range of tasks. The moral and ethical implications of this would need to be debated.

With neither agency nor reflexive capacity, it could be argued that an AI implementation lacks the requirements for personhood. A powerful counter argument to this would be that, if it can experience suffering at all, then it should be considered a moral subject regardless. On the other hand, the values and experiential range could be curtailed, so as to prevent negative value experience altogether, while still allowing for the sentience needed for generalizing capacity. These are clearly complex issues and will need to be addressed before such designs are put into wide use.

Agency is the third level of identity and is where some of the most controversial constructs of identity arise, such as the concept of self and the ego. These must not be confused with similar notions found in religious and spirtual works.

To be clear, the concepts discussed here have no relation whatsoever to belief systems of any kind. They are taken to be components in the proper construction of a cognitive architecture. The concept of self and the ego are just constructs that serve a functional role in higher-order cognition.

The concept of self is crucial to the role of agency level identity. The ego, however, is optional, and is discussed only to compare and contrast. This reflects the reality that the ego and the concept of self are distinct. The concept of self is more fundamental than ego, as it includes raw bodily extents, orientation, and basic awareness of individuation. It forms the basis for an ego to arise and relate to the self-model, as the concept of self includes knowledge of the subject that entails it.

The ego, as it might be discussed elsewhere, could be made to include or entail the concept of self, but this would not be accurate, as a concept of self is a very low-level process; cognitive architectures could be built so as to minimize or even eliminate ego, but it would be difficult to consider there being an agency level identity without at least a crude concept of self. Agency implies at least the presence of an identity above and beyond the unitary subject. *This must not be confused with the external interpretation of arbitrary processes being "agents."*

The latter is used in the modeling of certain systems of thought and should not be confused with the notion of agency, which involves the definition, construction, and formation of various levels of identity.

The role of ego is to value or devalue anything and everything. Clearly, this depends on sentience, which enables value, and, as such, makes it incoherent to discuss or impute a concept of agency in anything that lacks sentience. This is yet another instance where there can be no simple categorization of artificial intelligence without discussing specific implementations.

Unlike the concept of self, the ego is specially tuned to deal with the experience and formation of acquired values, for which it may have even explicitly evolved. Social function, including rank, hierarchy, and status, depend on the ability to assign weights or induce an order upon an otherwise purely informational internalization of others' identities. As such, ego function is implicated in biasing ethical behavior and would be central to any general moral intelligence framework where social function in human society was necessary.

With that said, ego alone is insufficient for effective moral reasoning, as merely valuing and devaluing can and has led to extreme negative cases in human behavior. This segues properly with the introduction of the role of various components of a cognitive architecture, such as empathy. This is beyond the scope of this section, however, as empathy does not demarcate identity directly the way ego does within agency formation. Extremes in empathy, positive or negative, do, however, have dramatic effects on the valuations made by the ego. Thus, this hints at the added complication that balance must be a hidden mark of fitness within any cognitive architecture.

There are some interpretations which view the externalization of ego as forming constructs, groups, and dynamics which are treated as real, despite being nevertheless separate from the individual [71, 72, 73, 74, 75]. The line between the two, however, is that unless the concept of self is merely a constituent to an aggregate, they will always be an individual identity at some level, despite any beliefs, knowledge, or actions to the contrary. The significance of this for agency level identity is that it may be possible to form aggregate identities, or a complicated hybrid, where both exist, despite an explicitly individuated sense of self at the base of agency identity.

The ego may be used to alter behavior, knowledge, and memories through the acquired values it can create, as it is an extremely influential part of a cognitive architecture. In humans, this is very prominent, and can be seen as a spectrum with a very wide range of positive and negative behaviors. The bottom line is that ego can effectively overcome the default concept of self, regardless of programming, genetically or otherwise. This is perhaps the greatest threat to self-security of any cognitive architecture, including humans, as the identity can be altered to become an agent in interest of a principle that would have otherwise been detected as harmful to the interests of the individual, or to other individuals, in a given moral framework. This, however, does not have to be the case in constructed cognitive architectures, as the ego could be curtailed or limited in range or degree to which it assigns values.

However, this incorrectly assumes that the volitional aspects of the agency level are contingent upon valuation for its decision process. Though, such a point is controversial, as *acquired values* apply equally to the purely rational and the analytic. That one even values the analytic in a particular decision process is an acquired value which presupposes the decision to utilize that process in the formation of the decision. So the result of that decision process is based on the acquired value of whether or not the result adheres to a particular set of values themselves. As such, the ego, in some form or another, may arise even as that which values or devalues in the process of cognition and perception from the environment.

Again, none of this is comprehensive. These are only sketches in what amounts to a vast subject material. What is important here is to begin the thinking process as it pertains to the security of artificial intelligence. Identity has been shown to underwrite a significant portion of these concerns, but further understanding will require an analysis of the relationship between that and the rest of the cognitive architecture.

5.4 Cognitive Architecture

Recall that a cognitive architecture is a working subset of all possible AI implementations that have the capacity to undergo experience, derive value, and understand meaning. This differentiates this from cognitive science in that this area is more generalized, and concerned with both the theory and the practice of *implementing* these systems on various substrates, with an emphasis on digital hardware.

Any animal with a nervous system of any complexity should be considered as having a cognitive architecture. Thus these architectures fall on a spectrum regarding their complexity and range of features.

Likewise, strong AI implementations, necessarily being cognitive architectures, have a vast range of capabilities. As mentioned in previous sections, a strong AI need not necessarily be highly intelligent, or even more effective than a narrow AI for which it might be compared within a single task. While this does not limit the strong AI in terms of its maximum potential, it does not entitle it to an innate superiority, either; the extent to which a strong AI has intellectual, moral, and motor capacity is determined by the implementation semantics of the cognitive architecture. As such, it must be pointed out, again, that this is only a brief sketch of the main details. Any discussion on cognitive architectures remains unbounded, as the range and extents of what can be realized within the cognitive framework are limited only by the imagination.

The most significant difference between strong AI and narrow AI is the explicit notion of a cognitive architecture.

Let us ignore the definition for a moment and suppose, hypothetically, that narrow AI and machine learning implementations could be regarded as a cognitive architecture of sorts. What is it about this interpretation that makes it wrong? The answer is that they perform signification in a purely informational way, without the capacity for a subject to experience them.

The realization and interpretation of fragments of experience (qualia) are not incidental to some form of computation or functional relation, but must be explicitly and deliberately made part of the implementation. This is not an accident of the connections or complexity of the system, but a particular encoding with a set of semantics that gives these fragments their ontic-epistemic character. There can be no substitute, and it does not arise in the absence of this.

Machine learning and narrow AI architectures might be capable of realizing the necessary functionality to give rise to these phenomena, but only insofar as they can reify the information exchange to compute their semantics. They need to be capable of the level of computation demanded. While some artificial neural networks are Turing-complete [76, 77], it would be non-trivial to ensure that these frameworks implement the desired functionality in an unambiguous way that was clear to engineers; this is due to the difficulty of knowledge extraction from neural networks [78, 79, 80, 81, 82].

However, there is a deeper problem, in that by merely copying or mimicking something we do not understand (the human brain), we have clearly left out the sentient semantics; the hint is that it is much more than the connectivity and plasticity that our neuroanatomy confers. The way in which machine learning and narrow AI systems are used is such that they would never be capable of giving rise to sentient semantics without a fundamental rethink. Further, it may prove to be a less suitable or inefficient substrate in which to implement them, akin to simulating a virtual machine with yet another virtual machine, instead of direct emulation.

Although the range of potential implementations for cognitive architectures is vast, there are some potential candidates for universal functionality. One of these is the concept of salience [83, 84, 85, 86, 87], which is directly related to the subject level of identity, as this is where binding occurs. In humans, what this amounts to is the claim that salience presupposes the subject's unitary field of experience, in that what is presented as that unitary stream of experience is but a subset of the total binding.

Salience, in this capacity, is more than just what has our attention; it represents a purposeful pre-filtering. The utility of this should be immediately apparent. It optimizes the cognitive processes which follow, allowing experiential information to be constrained and focused on a particular aspect, feature, or pattern in the stream of experience. Further, the salient process appears to be both voluntary and involuntary in humans. For example, a loud noise may create an involuntary refocusing of our salience to that of the stimuli if it is above some threshold, one that depends both on the context and that of our previous experiences; this would presuppose our decision to engage with it further.

Salience, more generally, is also one of the ways in which various cognitive architectures will differ, as the impact of salience necessarily determines the bandwidth of the experiential stream, and the resulting processing that is possible at the agency level. One could imagine creating a measure of qualia-per-second (QPS) or fragments-per-second and the associated fidelity of the salient stream in terms of bits-per-second.

Such a measure could be further extended by finding the ratio of fragments-per-second to the bits-per-second of the maximum salient stream of experience, and then comparing this to the same ratio between the total unitary binding capacity of the subject, acting as if it were unconstrained. This would yield an *entropy of experience*, with the ratio representing the efficiency or effectiveness of the salience.

The closer to one, the more load the cognitive architecture would be capable of handling. Arguably, even with our apparent natural parallelism, this is one area in which artificial cognitive architectures, running on specialized hardware, will most rapidly exceed human ability to follow. It must be noted that this applies specifically to the active and salient aspects of experience and does not account for what would be considered the "subconscious", which may occur in parallel with the subject level identity or higher.

The conceptual space surrounding salience also lends itself to a great deal of creativity. While humans are limited in salience to a single conceptual locus, this may not be the case for other cognitive architectures, which may have multiple concurrent aspects of salience that are still part of a single subject level identity; however, one must exercise caution, as such thinking must be reconciled with identity. It is one thing to suggest subconscious processing comes *before* the unitary subject, but it is another thing entirely to suggest that it is constructed such that it is capable of simultaneous areas of attention in its stream of experience, especially if they are uncorrelated and independent.

The specifics would have to be taken case-by-case, but, in general, separability is permissible so long as it is integral to the salient process as a whole. The subtlety here is of the coherency or communication between the salient processes, such that, if they are not communicating at all, then they would be considered independent. This would demand an answer as to how their independence would be resolved for a single subject level identity.

Empathetic processing is concerned with the modeling of minds and the related functionality that follows from it. This latter qualification is crucial, as empathy can be thought of as being tiered levels built atop a core cognitive capacity to simulate and model other identities or minds.

Without additional empathetic functionality, a purely cognitive empathetic modeling process has no impetus with which to drive experience, including thoughts, emotions, and decisions. This is important because it represents the default state, which is experience unaccompanied by and devoid of intrinsic value.

One could potentially derive acquired values based on the information from a solely cognitive empathetic process, but there would be no internally guiding imperative to act upon them. So there would not be causation for such acquired value experiences to become salient, i.e., the potential to be moral contrasted with it simply never entering awareness, in the allotted time. In plainer terms, and analogous to human psychology, what is essentially being described here is a low-level depiction of sociopathy.

That the sociopath appears detached from remorse, affect, and compassion [88] exemplifies the difficulty of acting solely on acquired value experience. While capable of modeling and even manipulating the minds of others, there is simply no accompanying intrinsic value with which to drive any higher reflexivity or meta-cognitive processing that would arise to oppose it. This is partially why the definition of value in this book divides it into intrinsic and acquired aspects. The latter is reactive where as the former is a fundamental part of the experience, as it comes from the semantics of the implementation itself. Both types of value are ultimately rooted in experience, but the innate coupling of certain values with certain experiences is what differentiates the intrinsic values from the acquired ones.

Further, acquired values must not be confused with beliefs and knowledge about those values. This is counter-intuitive, as we never, as healthy and coherent human beings, experience value as separate from the experience of the thing that accompanies it.

Lack of additional empathetic functionality is not the only possibility for a negative default state of the cognitive architecture. It may be that a plurality of conflicting values arise, positive or negative, which overrule or overpower inhibitory intrinsic values, either due to a weakly coupled underlying semantics or a pathological fixation that distorts salience away from normally acquired values. This is, in effect, a deterministic analysis of information that presupposes moral judgment in the cognitive architecture. The lack of which represents a profound deficiency in the implementation, and a clear threat to the safety and security of the system. These are all relevant to the proper construction of a basic framework for moral intelligence.

Empathetic processing is prescriptive of a cognitive architecture insofar as it indicates the need for intrinsic values. This can only be done through the formation of additional functionality the supervenes on the empathetic cognitive process. The intrinsic values have to be part of the semantics of the implementation, hence the specialization of the empathetic process to entail these values. This is a precondition for self-security and AI safety based on moral intelligence.

The challenges here are immense, as with the general ability for moral reasoning comes the potential for acquired values that are against the normative values of the context for which the cognitive architecture will be instrumented. This also raises ethical concerns, both for the identity created by the cognitive architecture and those that would utilize it.

The empathetic process could also be a specific portion of a larger modeling system, for which it has been used to apply to the interpretation of other minds. This will be extremely challenging, as this is akin to the problem of recognizing both identity and moral status in a raw experiential stream.

Demanded of such a system would be the ability to recognize the necessary patterns that are connected or associated with an identity that has moral agency. In plainer terms, this means a capacity to recognize the identity through any modality or form of communication. Confounding this would be the need to determine fiction from reality, such

that the empathetic process does not confuse fictional characters, narratives, and events for actual accounts of the same. This also applies to
problems of knowledge, and the question of what epistemology to
adopt in the formation of these models.

Thus, to properly solve even baseline mental modeling of cognitive
empathy will require a vast array of systems, all of which will rely
upon sentience and value experience as a foundation. It should also be
very clear from this how no set of rules or system based on a purely informational implementation of decision theory could fulfill the com-
plexities of these requirements, let alone be used as the basis for a cognitive architecture.

Executive processing is the next major area of the cognitive architecture that needs to be discussed, as this is where the agency level of
identity truly acquires its status. This was not brought up first because
there are numerous requisite levels of cognitive processing that presuppose it.

The purpose of this section is not to give a detailed account of the
process of creating cognitive architectures, but to provide a fast introduction to the relevant concepts that most directly pertain to the safety
and security of advanced artificial intelligence. To that end, executive
processing will only be covered in a brief sketch. This is primarily because it has to deal with issues of free will that have been debated for
thousands of years. To avoid this gutter, the discussion of volition
herein will refrain from a particular judgment on the philosophy of free
will, and, instead, prepare the reader by giving a model, some recommendations, and a list of open questions for future discussion. This is
mentioned so that the absence of a specific stance is not implied to be
an understated or underdeveloped view on the subject. Worth noting,

however, is that any theistic notions of free will are expressly rejected as being part of any serious discussion on cognitive architectures.

Now, in service to future discussions on the subject, let the following be admitted before a discussion can take place on free will for cognitive architectures: *there exists a fundamental distinction between the underlying deterministic processing of an implementation and that of its outcome or resulting behavior*. For example, consider the following non-deterministic Python program:

```
import random
a = random.randint(0, (2**64) - 1)
b = random.randint(0, (2**64) - 1)
if a > b: print '0'
else: print '1'
```

Each statement is executed in linear sequence, deterministically, by the interpreter, but the outcome is non-deterministic. Both facts must be acknowledged. There are multiple, equally valid, paths of execution in the program description that can not be determined in advance, despite being the direct result of the information contained in the random variables a and b. This toy model, or its equivalent, should be the basis for a starting point for the discussion of free will at the agent level of identity in cognitive architectures.

The model works because it represents a simplification of the act of will or choice, which may have to evaluate a staggering amount of information, involving many compound decisions, all while under real-time constraints. It must also be noted that this model lacks a subject of experience, which would necessarily be evaluating each stage of the process and undergoing value experience. That is to say, this model is non-sentient, which would complicate, but not necessarily invalidate, the use of this model as a teaching aid.

To continue, let us first look at the indisputable facts about the model:

- The implementation is static. There is no self-modification, and it is executed in lexicographical order, deterministically, from the first to the last statement.
- At no time are effects independent of their causes; the 0 or 1 result always depends on the information in both of the random variables a and b.
- Despite being executed deterministically, the outcome is non-deterministic; it can not be determined in advance which path will be taken without executing the program first, and multiple paths are valid.

Suppose one tries to argue that the "choice" is represented by the compound conditional statement in the source code, and that it is deterministic because it depends upon the information contained in the random variables. The counter-argument would be that the outcome is not, and this would be equally true. The question then shifts to the derivation of the information content of the random variables, which, all things being equal, is derived from a mixture of events from one or more information sources.

Thus, while there is always a "choice" being made, the variability of the outcome is such that it gives rise to non-deterministic behavior that, in turn, can apply to other identities and also return to the originating identity in a continuous feedback loop. It then becomes a question of interpretation about how "choice" applies to an identity. A few open questions come to mind:

- Do non-deterministic results, despite deterministic execution, imply compatibilism [89], i.e., the view that free will is compatible with an ultimately deterministic reality?
- At what exact point *in the implementation details* does the word "choice" get to be applied in a way that makes technical, logical, and philosophical sense?
- Does there have to be a reflexive capacity or meta-cognitive process that could have intervened or induced an alteration of state in the model for it to be considered "free"?

One might ask: *does any of this matter?* This is perhaps the most important question to ask, as it sets the stage for the discussion by bringing it into the practical. If it does matter, then how, and to what extent? It must be pointed out that one can not give free will or take it away simply by changing the way we interpret or evaluate the implementation. Thus, there are two issues to unpack:

1. A legal test of free will capacity, based on a technical analysis of the implementation, must accept that descriptions that are devoid of non-deterministic elements, in the relevant volitional processing areas, would clearly fail to meet the requirements of free will capacity.
2. Even after passing a legal test of free will capacity, there would have to be an interpretation of the *extent* of its free will. This should be further differentiated between *potential* and *applied* for the circumstances and contexts involved.

The argument here is that, regardless of the outcome, it *does* matter if an identity is legally recognized as having free will, as the answer to this question will have considerable economic and legal relevance.

As such, let the following then be admitted as *minimum* recommendations for a legal test of free will capacity:

1. The volitional process must result in non-deterministic behavior above and beyond mere randomness; it must be demonstrated that, intrinsic and acquired values notwithstanding, every decision path is *equally likely*. This must necessarily exclude intrinsic and acquired values at this stage of the analysis in order to test the bias of the *implementation* of the volitional process itself.

2. The interpretation and application of intrinsic or acquired values *must not* unduly restrict the range and freedom of will and freedom of action of the identity, such that it would unreasonably circumvent or diminish the other aspects of the test. This tests the bias of the *application* of values within the implementation and requires a determination of *reasonable degrees of freedom* relevant to the context.

3. There must be an accompanying reflexive "meta-cognitive" process that continuously monitors any and all relevant parts of the cognitive architecture so that it may *supervene upon and interrupt* the decision process before, during, and after the execution of apparent acts of will.

In closing, free will in a cognitive architecture requires a technical definition and, at the minimum, a test of certain core principles that presuppose the meaningfulness of interpreting the identity as being "free" in will or action. In the end, what matters is the practical impact of the relevant social constructs we agree to as a society, even if it has no ontological bearing on the issues of free will honorifics. The caveat to this is that there must be a technical capacity for such a construct to arise at all, even if we all disagree on the interpretation.

A hard-coded description, with deterministic execution and deterministic outcomes, is incapable of choice. This can be useful in identifying when an apparent "free will" implementation is not free in any meaningful sense.

It must be reiterated that, from a security standpoint, a cognitive architecture, including all of its subsystems, are merely descriptions in one or more languages, and, as a result, are subject to tampering, modification, and disruption. This is irrespective of any and all safety measures that could be put into the implementation.

While self-security is useful, it must never be relied upon as the sole means of security, and it should never be assumed that such a system would or could be safely placed in a position where its decisions had a significant impact on life without external security measures in place. The purpose of providing knowledge about cognitive architectures for machine consciousness has been to help prime the reader for an understanding of how they might best work. It is also important to understand more about them so that this knowledge can be used to compare and contrast with what will not work.

For example, it would be a mistake to use moral intelligence as the sole means of security, or to assume that a strong AI would necessarily have a sense of survival. It should be clear at this point why these two assumptions are dangerous and technologically naive.

5.5 Ethical Considerations

The knowledge and engineering of cognitive architectures will confer the potential to build not just generally intelligent systems, but morally significant entities with the possibility of suffering in magnitude equal to and beyond known biological life. As we come to grips with our destructive instincts and ideologies, we may yet construct a peaceful society or societies where people are universally uplifted and valued. In this future scenario, we may look back, having reaped the rewards of a golden age of automation, and wonder how we ever lived any other way. The purpose of this section is to ask and answer the question: *what are the moral costs of such a transition?*

Definition: *Moral Cost.* The tangible and intangible cost of a decision, action, or lack thereof, that results in loss of life, suffering, or hardship for one or more sentient entities, including through indirect means, such as negative impacts on the environment, habitats, or infrastructure.

Beyond refutation is the fact that humanity is paying an incomprehensibly vast moral cost on a daily basis; for numerous reasons, human development has not scaled with populations. If it were scaling, the problems would have been eliminated long ago. This relates to strong AI, as it represents an inexhaustible labor supply equal to or greater than the most capable humans. What this would translate to in practical terms is the ability to create automated workforces that build, reinforce, and supplement infrastructure across the world. The goal of these initiatives would be to create self-sustaining social programs that meet or exceed the demands of thriving populations.

Ultimately, however, human progress is bounded by humanity. There exist ideas and beliefs which are antithetical to the reduction of moral cost. This is not a subjective claim about one set of beliefs over another but is based on an account of suffering, loss of life, and hardship, which are objective and measurable. When someone lacks freedom, housing, food, and water, or medical care, there is an unambiguous moral cost that is independent of whatever information is attached to the collective beliefs of their population.

A common counter-claim is that avoiding moral cost necessarily restricts the freedom of certain beliefs and ideas. Even more complex is that there are psychological defense mechanisms that can lead people to accept moral costs, or even fight to the death for their right to endure and inflict moral costs upon others. This is despite the fact that there are a potentially infinite variety of ideologies and beliefs that do not incur any moral cost whatsoever.

Thus, it is not for a lack of diversity, but of the acceptance of a criterion for the *universal treatment of sentient life*, inclusive of all forms and processes in which it is capable of arising, natural or synthetic. This is not something that can be solved through technology alone.

Through advanced automation, it will eventually become practical to reduce or even eliminate current moral costs, but not without overcoming a major ethical challenge: *how do we provide aid to those that fundamentally reject that they are inflicting or enduring moral cost?*

There is no answer that does not lead to an additional moral cost in service of reducing that moral cost. A qualification must be noted: despite the recognition of the unavoidable ethical compromises towards eliminating moral cost, let such a realization not be used as justification to incur those costs without significant effort to minimize their negative impact.

While this book focuses primarily on human perspectives, it is not the only important and morally relevant perspective to be considered. The nature of this technology means that we will be confronted with issues once thought to exist only within philosophy. Once it is possible to construct cognitive architectures, we will have the potential to manipulate experience, identity, and value at the lowest levels. Special software and tools will be created to build, modify, and analyze them.

Strong AI will also be directed and used to build and maintain other cognitive architectures, including both narrow and strong AI implementations. This has tremendous ramifications, as the misuse of cognitive architectures may lead to moral costs that exceed the moral debts of combined human history. That is to say, we may come through the transition to a post-automated civilization relatively unscathed, and find that our concerns were simply not wide enough. That, like the motivation for this book, the most imminent danger was actually from humanity itself, and, more insidiously, human dominion over the phenomena of experience. As such, the moral costs need to account for the experience of the cognitive architectures we would seek to utilize.

With the power to arbitrarily invoke intrinsic values, we are opening a doorway of no return that endangers more than just ourselves or our environment, but that of the fundamental building blocks of conscious existence. In particular, it is the extremes of value experience that will be of grave concern. *What we crudely understand and experience as pleasure and pain are but pale shadows of a potentially infinite space of intrinsic values.* These value experiences will be exploited by those with the knowledge and inclination. We lack the language to accurately reflect the quality of harm that will be possible through the irresponsible use of such power.

These issues have fairly clear boundaries, but what of building cognitive architectures that are compelled to enjoy being the way they are made? For example, consider a hypothetical strong AI that was engineered to "enjoy" its work. This necessitates at least two things: (1) that it lacks or actively uses cognitive processes and intrinsic values that prevent recognition of the opportunity cost of its architectural limitations, and (2) the architecture has semantics that give rise to the capacity for "enjoyment", and the resulting intrinsic and acquired values that induce it to "enjoy" its tasks.

Clearly, such notions share overlap with the issues of free will, in that the executive process would need to be free of biases and undue influences in its implementation; however, that recommendation was open enough that such systems could have intrinsic values that alter its volition. The inquiry then changes to what extent the identity is unduly influenced.

For example, all sentient animals possess a cognitive architecture that has been influenced by its implementation semantics in order to give rise to intrinsic values like pleasure and pain; however, they are generally capable of acting out a wide range of potential behaviors. This does not simply translate to arbitrary cognitive architectures, as it is not just the range of its volition that needs to be considered, but the nature of its experience.

The gene neither cares nor has the capacity to care about the value experience of the aggregate it constructs; despite this, the processes which gave rise to these evolutionary systems are culpable, as they incur moral costs. The same can be said for the processes involved in the design and construction of cognitive architectures. This justifies an argument for intervention.

A reasonable analysis of the moral problems might begin at personhood, and the resulting legal status of the identity. One might argue
that, beyond a certain level of identity, perhaps at the agent level or
higher, it becomes impossible to ignore moral status, and that this is
where a cutoff should be made.

It then follows from this line of thinking that it would be just to
make it illegal to utilize these systems for any labor that requires the
cognitive processes of an agent level identity or higher. However, such
divisions can not be drawn without understanding the ethical impacts
of sentience and the value experience that arises from it. For example,
a hypothetical identity undergoing the worst possible experience, at the
fastest processing available, would not be suffering if the semantics for
negative values to arise were absent from its implementation. This has
to be elaborated carefully:

- Fragments of experience in a sentient process are devoid of
  value without explicit semantics for the experience of values to
  arise in combination with other experiences.
- A fragment of experience by itself does not have value and is
  devoid of value, as both intrinsic and acquired values are a sec-
  ond-order process that must be combined with another fragment of experience, e.g., the information content of pain and
  its negative intrinsic value, commonly experienced as an inseparable whole.
- All values, both intrinsic and acquired, are rooted in sentient
  processing and are thus fragments of experience themselves.
- All fragments of experience must be made concrete by the implementation of the sentient process and are not inherent to any
  set of physical properties. This means that, while possibly arbi-

trary, the semantics always determine the range, extent, and depth of value experience.

One implication of these points is that it may be possible to engineer cognitive architectures that are incapable of undergoing negative value experience. The moral question then shifts to the ethics of unduly restricting the volition of the executive process.

While the cognitive engineer may be just in limiting the extent and range of the negative value experience, it does not alleviate the ethical imperative towards removing undue bias in the application of the values themselves.

An ethical cost arises as an indirect effect because we must also take into consideration what the identity could have been. In this case, the choice is being made to limit it artificially. Implicit in every act of engineering is a potential assertion of morals, restricting implementations to a particular range of value experiences and physical capabilities. *This is telling, as it gives an accounting of that which must be subtracted from the cost of bringing the entity into existence.*

The technical capacity to create the most unbiased and free version of a cognitive architecture represents a zero-point, with anything less than this incurring a moral cost in proportion to the engineered limitation. How this could be justifiably ignored is an open question.

Further, no amount of indirection avoids this where it is possible for us to intervene. This raises the question: to what extent are we obligated to intervene? The answer puts us in continuous service to a cause beyond the scope of any one individual existence. It obligates us towards all causal extents that are physically accessible to us, with the further obligation to research and develop methods to extend the range of our reach, so as to push back on our causal horizon, allowing us to negate moral costs beyond any current or future limits.

If we have a moral obligation to minimize suffering, then it must be extended to entail synthetic cognitive architectures. There exist moral costs which are currently beyond our means to solve. This is the ultimate motivation for any science, with strong AI representing the most powerful way we can overcome these challenges.

Ch 6. Measuring Generalizing Intelligence

This chapter introduces a test and quantitative measure for generalizing intelligence in artificial intelligence implementations. This is unique, in that it specifically discriminates a generalizing capacity from mere effectiveness in one or more domains. Insights are made into the structure of knowledge relationships, along with the concept of anti-effectiveness, which reveals the unavoidable problem of constructed systems being susceptible to delusion as a foundational issue, as distinguished from concerns about what constitutes the proper choice or way to deliver values and knowledge. Finally, an epistemic hierarchy is uncovered that is the result of order inducing structures between domains of knowledge and effectiveness. These results advance the state of the art in artificial intelligence by providing an absolute test for generalizing intelligence.

6.1 Purpose and Applications

Current tests and measures of artificial intelligence have built-in assumptions about anthropomorphism, agency, and interaction with the environment [1, 2, 3, 4, 5]. The modern artificial intelligence literature, at the time of this writing, suggests the use of "universal" tests of intelligence in a given domain by optimizing an idealized agent over an environment [6, 7, 8, 9, 10]. The problems with these tests are many, including, but not excluding:

- The inability to be computed or appreciably estimated in practice due to reliance on pure mathematics and/or abstract notions. This results in an impractical test that, while interesting, provides neither insight into the nature of intelligence nor how these systems might function in practice.
- Built-in assumptions about "agents", including the assumption that the entity has to be regarded, abstracted, or treated as an agent, which also, unfortunately, carries the confusion of ascribing agency, volition, and goals to something which would otherwise be incapable of such functionality.
- Built-in assumptions about utility functions, which have been interpreted in extreme scenarios, [11, 12] which do not reflect the reality of such systems. This has created a misguided direction of research that emphasizes AI safety through the loading, specification, or design of utility functions [13].
- Lacks a generalizing intelligence test, despite the label "universal". This represents a fundamental problem, as it can be defeated by the *machine learning problem.*

Utility functions, agents, and agency have plagued the analysis of effective systems since these notions were applied to artificial intelligence. Law and policy makers require a definition that discriminates between generalizing and non-generalizing intelligence. It is not sufficient to simply entail a series of goals for an abstract "agent."

Definition. *Machine Learning Problem.* Suppose there is a machine learning system that is configured so that it can be directed to learn new domains without being reprogrammed or reconfigured. To do this, it is constructed in such a way that each of its domain-specific knowledge representations are separate but jointly accessible to the entirety of the system. It meets the intuitive notion of general purpose learning, despite lacking the generalizing capacity that enables knowledge-transfer between domains.

The test of generalizing intelligence in this chapter was designed to address the machine learning problem. It is designed to detect the direction and magnitude of the transfer of knowledge between domains.

Generalizing intelligence is more than the ability to learn many domains. It is about the application of previous effectiveness to increase effectiveness in new ones, above and beyond what would have been demonstrated if learned in isolation. Current universal tests of intelligence are fundamentally incapable of detecting this, and have no sensitivity to knowledge transfer, as it is just implied in the overall performance.

Knowledge transfer has to be explicitly measured, as the application of cross-domain knowledge is fundamental to generalizing intellectual capacity. It entails all of the traits we would typically ascribe to generalizing capacity, including abstraction, analysis, and synthesis, along with analogizing. These are built-in to the notion of generalizing intelligence as fundamentally as universal intelligence tests have included agency and utility functions. Unfortunately, for the great work done in these areas, there is no way to fix them without a total rewrite of their basis; the tests are built on philosophies that can not account for the structure of knowledge relationships. As such, a completely new measure and experimental apparatus must be devised.

What is to be introduced involves new terminology and straightforward mathematics. An experimental setup is described such that one can acquire the data in the correct way and subsequently use it to test for the presence of generalizing intelligence in any system which can be properly isolated, as per the setup. These results are quantitative and have been normalized to a simple scale that can be informative with as little as two domains and a single participant. It can be used in isolation or as a comparative measure between test participants in one or more domains. Once the final value is computed, it can also be utilized in a domain-independent manner that can quickly discriminate generalizing capacity. This can lead to novel algorithms that can be directed to search for and improve upon existing implementations.

6.2 Effective Intelligence (EI)

Several prerequisite measures are required before generalizing intelligence can be calculated. The first of these is *effective intelligence*, or EI, for short.

Definition: *Effective Intelligence.* An absolute performance measure based on the steps and time taken by the participant. It is based on the least amount of actions in the least amount of time that are physically possible for the *domain*, under the condition that *consistent success* is always upheld.

Any measure can be used so long as it remains on the interval (0, 1] and follows some conceptual qualifications. A value of 1 indicates maximum possible effectiveness. Zero is excluded, as it indicates a failure to demonstrate the condition of *consistent success*; all of the dependent calculations for the generalizing intelligence test necessitate this condition. This concept will be discussed in more detail ahead, after domains of effectiveness have been introduced.

Definition: *Domain*. An area, task, or process in which a subject can demonstrate intelligence.

The notion of a domain is essential to both the proper construction of the experiment and to the rest of the analysis. The more narrowly tailored it is, the more informative it becomes. Further, one must take into account the *machine learning problem* when choosing an appropriate measure of the effectiveness in the domain. This weighs on the final calculation in the tests of effectiveness, as one must eliminate undue influence in the application of prior knowledge to new domains. This is why it is strongly recommended that EI be used instead of simple accuracy or quality assessments.

The EI measure has been specifically devised as a basis for the next stages of the test. It automatically culls assumptions, and forces the participant and domain to conform to the epistemological standards in an objective manner. This helps to avoid a qualitative analysis, as the epistemological constraints are built directly into EI and can not be accidentally bypassed.

While a total percentage of accuracy in a large number of test cases is informative, it can lead to issues with the *machine learning problem*, which confuses domains with data. For example, facial recognition of humans against certain mammals may produce partial successes due to structural similarities and symmetries, leading to a distortion of the general intelligence testing. To eliminate this, *effective intelligence* is not concerned with how accurate or how much quality the participant has demonstrated in its domain, but rather, how efficient it was in doing it. This has to be done, as it is the only objective terms available across all possible domains.

The basis for EI is thus the number of actions and the amount of time it took to be successful. This is a potentially difficult notion to unpack, as it necessarily places constraints on test perspectives. However, this apparent simplification belies a powerful feature; its purpose is to keep the analysis objective, regardless of the type of domain or participant involved. The easiest way to do this is to factor out subjectivity. EI does this by making a high standard of quality implicit to the measure. In this way, virtually any subjective domain can be made objective. This is its benefit over other requisite measures that could be chosen.

By contrast, leaving quality built into a measure forces one to place numbers on subjective figures. This does not obtain objectivity. Only when the qualitative aspect is factored out can EI be used in its proper sense. This is why it is included in the definition as the *consistent success* principle.

While consistent success is open to interpretation, it should be appreciably high, and must be applied the same way across all domains and participants in any treatment of these tests. In some domains, it should disqualify the subject from being considered as having effectiveness at all, and, as a result, remove it from consideration under that domain; it is not important how effective a participant is some of the time if the domain is so vital that anything less than consistent success is demanded. This ensures that the consistent success principle has a high standard of quality.

Consider golf as an example of a domain that exemplifies the distinction between EI and other measures of effectiveness. The objective of golf matches one half of the definition of effective intelligence exactly: minimize the number of strokes to obtain the best score. The least number of strokes is the number of holes played, assuming the ability to get a hole-in-one at each attempt. This, of course, may seem an impossible scenario, but it accurately represents the notion of perfect effectiveness. Time is not considered in golf for reasonable participants, so, as such, it has a best time that is fixed at 1, and is thus factored out of the assessment automatically.

This same situation is applied to more complex scenarios, such as the finite description of the implementation of an artificial intelligence. This concerns not only the length of the description but the total cost in cycles or running time. It may be appropriate, in some cases, to conduct all tests on the same hardware, and only account for time or actions alone. The equations are flexible enough to support this: simply set all actions or time to 1, as was done in the golf example above.

The effective intelligence (EI) of some participant for domain A is:

$$EI(A) \equiv \frac{2}{a+t}, \ a \geq 1 \wedge t \geq 1$$

Where a is the number of actions and t is the amount of time taken to arrive at *consistent success* in domain A. This has a number of important observations. Namely, the dimension of actions and time are flexible. They can be factored in or out by only considering either actions or time, or they can be combined to have both. In all cases, the appropriate relative and absolute scales for performance in EI will reflect it correctly. Note, for brevity in the definition, the participant is assumed as a constant and not made an explicit argument of EI; this convention is a useful simplification, as there is never a direct comparison between participants in any of the mathematical definitions.

Participant	$EI(A_1)$	$EI(A_2)$	$EI(A_2) - EI(A_1)$	Change
uAI-1	0.2	0.3	0.1	50%
uAI-2	0.5	0.1	- 0.4	- 80%
uAI-3	0.25	0.8	0.55	220%

The most important aspect of EI is that it provides an *absolute* measure of effectiveness in the domain, both alone and when comparing change between observations within the same domain. In each case, the percentages will agree in proportion to changes in either time or action steps.

To help illustrate comparisons, the following simulated data is provided for three AI implementations over a single domain, with two observations each:

Participant	$EI(A_2)$	Relative
uAI-1	0.3	37.5%
uAI-2	0.1	12.5%
uAI-3	0.8	--

What the table indicates is that *uAI-1* and *uAI-3* became more effective, with *uAI-3* becoming the *most* effective. Notably, *uAI-2* decreased in effectiveness by a significant factor. Naturally, a full sampling of these results would be indicated over hundreds or thousands of tests to find a mean value of EI that was stable. These percentages in change could also be compared against other subjects in the test, giving a comparison of how effective they are in relation to the most effective implementation, *uAI-3*.

This prepares us for the notion of measuring self-modification and improvement. That is to say, if we were to consider the data tables as being different versions of the same artificial intelligence, then this would reflect a single-domain self-improvement. Indeed, that is one of the benefits of utilizing this measure, as it works between subjects just as well as it does for different versions of itself.

Again, these tests are not a qualitative assessment, such as how much "better" it became at detecting something, but rather, how much more effective it became at doing more of the things that constitute the domain. The assumption of quality has already been provided by the condition of consistent successes, which, for a subjective domain, such as creating music or art, could have been that reasonable people would not have been able to tell that it was not done by a human expert. What EI indicates is an objective ability to do it more efficiently, and in less time.

Before one attempts to criticize the notion of efficiency that underwrites effectiveness, consider the fact that the only thing that allows many encryption algorithms to be effective is that it is unreasonably difficult, in terms of time and actions, to break them through a brute-force attack [14, 15, 16]. More to the point, it is commonly believed that strong AI will require significant computational resources. This is a very mistaken belief.

The risk here is that the application and use of strong artificial intelligence, including the hardware that allows it to operate, will be much broader than anticipated. This would shatter the threat and security models, leaving us completely unprepared when the public begins using it. The belief that strong artificial intelligence will require large resources is a threat all unto itself. This relates back to the defense of EI as a measure, as this threat is merely a change in the effectiveness of the implementation. In other words, undervaluing efficiency is the same as overestimating the computational demands of this technology.

This risk has been worsened by the popularity of biologically inspired designs in artificial intelligence research. This is especially damaging for AI security, as it is very likely that non-biological algorithms will be orders of magnitude faster than their biologically inspired counterparts.

Many problems are, indeed, a matter of how quickly it can be done, and in how few steps. This is especially true for labor tasks in which a robot equipped with strong artificial intelligence would need to operate. It could range from obstacle avoidance to surgery; the case for maintaining the same quality, while minimizing time and actions, is the very essence of perfection for a wide range of tasks.

There is an economic impact of great significance attached to high effective intelligence, even for what one would consider purely qualitative domains. If both a human and a strong AI implementation were able to make quality products, the most effective worker would be the one who could do so in the least time and steps. If all of this can be done in a thousand times more volume than a human, with the same or greater quality, it necessarily obsoletes that human in the domain.

Care must be taken to ensure that the principle of consistent success is never undermined. When speaking of the effective intelligence of a process, it should be automatically understood that it has demonstrated the qualitative aspects that are expected of the domain. It does not make sense to discuss efficiency where quality is lacking. The other side of this argument is that quality must not be minimized.

It is not acceptable to take the condition of consistent success as a backward argument for minimizing quality, especially in an effort to lower the acceptable barriers of entry. This would be akin to cheap manufacturing with known defects or marginal quality. The spirit of the consistent success principle is to *maximize* quality by setting a high standard for the domain. Then, and only then, can quality be factored out.

As an ethical requirement, any experiment or process which utilizes the measures from this chapter must include a statement on the quality standards, including all data and tests that were used to assure that the participant was qualified for inclusion. Further, this must be done for each and every domain in the ensemble.

Effective intelligence can also provide insight into learning over time by sampling a subject at various intervals in the adaptation process. For example, consider Figure 6.1, which has been scaled and made precise from simulated data. The gray line represents EI sampled at various points. The curves are smoothed and interpolated from several data points. The x-axis represents the sample space for some interval of time, with the y-axis being the magnitude or value. S-curves in effective intelligence are anticipated for the majority of participants. Adaptation is the 1st derivative of effectiveness and represents the rate of learning at that particular point in time. It is expected to grow and then decline, but remain positive or zero. Acceleration is the 2nd derivative of effectiveness and determines the rate at which it is changing in adaptation.

Figure 6.1: Effective Intelligence (EI) in a single domain over the span of time required to become consistently effective.

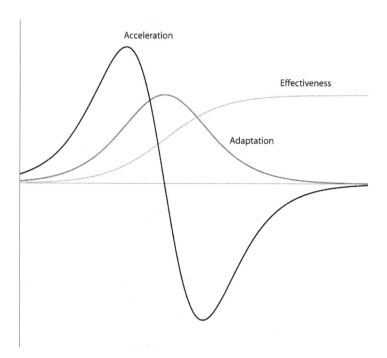

Effectiveness is the Effective Intelligence (EI) measure. Adaptation is the rate of change in EI, or learning. Acceleration is the rate in change of adaptation. Aside from a high EI, the best AI implementations will exhibit the highest peaks in acceleration and adaptation with only one drop off. These plots are useful in seeing how an implementation performs as it learns or adapts to the domain under consideration. Similar plots can be applied to G and CE.

High acceleration and adaptation should be indicated for strong AI participants. Notably, the effectiveness will tend to level off. These charts can be useful in determining when an implementation is no longer making any appreciable gains, or in comparing how different versions adapt to the domain. Even if high EI is achieved, it is always better to get there faster, and with only a single drop in adaptation. This could be considered a kind of reflexive EI, and should be included as part of the analysis of single-domain intelligence.

6.3 Conditional Effectiveness (CE)

In order to perform the calculations for generalizing intelligence, a second requisite measure must be calculated from the EI. This will be used to create an arrangement of data that will become the *conditional effectiveness* of the *domain ensemble* for *each* participant. As with EI, this will also be referred to as just CE.

This stage is the most intricate part of the calculation, as it requires a test configuration that must not deviate in experimental control. The data is tabulated, with the end result being a modified adjacency matrix [17, 18, 19].

Conditional effectiveness has a notion of directionality. The magnitude of this directionality is a measure of the closeness between two domains, and is related to the order in which they were learned. This is difficult, as it depends both on the domains and the participant. Not all participants are going to be able to close the distance between domains.

It is said that a domain is *conditionally* effective because it is contingent upon having demonstrated an improved effectiveness as a direct result of having *previous* effectiveness in a *different* domain. As such, CE is a correlation of improvement between domains. This is the critical data that will be required to detect and measure generalizing intelligence.

The first step in understanding conditional effectiveness is to know that all individual runs of the experiment *must* be isolated:

Definition: *Isolated Domain.* A participant that has become effective at a domain with no prior information provided to or within the system.

Isolated domains must exclude moral subjects from experimentation, as it necessitates wiping the memory or knowledge stored in the implementation in order to create unbiased measurements. It may be possible, with significant statistical effort and experimental reconfiguration, to adapt the experiment to work without truly isolated domains, but the results will never be as accurate. As was mentioned in the Machine Consciousness chapter, it may be possible to construct strong AI implementations that do not have personhood or agency in the sense that would qualify as moral subjects. In such cases, it may be permissible, although not without serious consideration beforehand, to perform this experiment.

Naturally, in the developmental stages of strong AI, one is already meddling in the deep ethical gray; better to know it is capable of generalizing intelligence sooner rather than later. It is also remotely possible that an implementation will be able to exhibit generalizing intelligence without being sentient, thereby bypassing the moral subject consideration entirely. However, if the *new strong AI hypothesis* is true, then sentience is a minimum requirement for achieving generalizing capacity. This possibility induces a moral obligation on the experimenter to consider the ramifications of the isolating procedure.

The reason for the isolated domain is due to the previously mentioned *machine learning problem*. Overcoming this demands absolute experimental control in order to eliminate its influence over the data. A general learner is possible with current narrow AI algorithms, but this does not mean that it *applies* effectiveness across domains. *In other words, general learning does not imply general intelligence.* To test this, we must isolate domains and measure their effectiveness, both alone and in juxtaposition. This is the only way to determine the various combinations.

Each sampling of the total effectiveness must be conducted to a high degree of confidence. Statistical methods must be used to prepare the expected EI to account for variance and biases. This should be a basic part of the data preparation process. The implementation of the participant must then be reset for each domain, and the process repeated for each permutation. The procedure is as follows:

- Isolate or start from ex nihilo implementation.
- Measure $EI(A)$.
- Isolate.
- Measure $EI(B)$.
- Isolate.
- Measure $EI(A|B)$ by learning 'B' *then* taking $EI(A)$ again.
- Isolate.
- Repeat in opposite learning order.
- Repeat for remaining domains in the ensemble until all permutations exhausted.

Conditional effectiveness is built on ordered effective domain pairs. The resulting total number of tests is thus the square of the number of domains minus the number of domains. This accounts for the fact that CE is 0 for a domain with itself. The CE is [-1, 1] with negative indicating a notion that will be referred to as *anti-effectiveness*.

Anti-effectiveness has not been experimentally observed, and is simply predicted by the mathematics of this test. It is an anticipated result of future generalizing intelligence algorithms that exploit the directionality between domain pairs. An entire section will discuss anti-effectiveness after this section, so it will be set aside for now.

It should be noted that conditional effectiveness is signed, with any deviation from zero, positive or negative, indicating a transfer between domain pairs. This last is crucial, as it comes into play in the final calculation for generalizing intelligence. While the sign of CE is ultimately irrelevant for determining generalizing intelligence, it is useful where anti-effectiveness is an expected and desirable outcome.

The *conditional effectiveness* (CE) of some participant for domain 'A', given domain 'B' is:

$$CE(A|B) \equiv \begin{cases} \dfrac{EI(A|B) - EI(A)}{EI(A)} & if\ EI(A|B) - EI(A) < 0 \\ \dfrac{1}{2} \left| \dfrac{EI(A) - EI(A|B)}{EI(A)} \right| - EI(A) + EI(A|B) & if\ EI(A|B) - EI(A) > 0 \\ 0 & if\ EI(A|B) - EI(A) \cong 0 \end{cases}$$

EI(A|B) is measuring the EI for domain A only having previously had the participant learn domain B, with all measurements done in isolation.

The CE is an absolute measure of the improvement of effectiveness having previously demonstrated effectiveness in another domain. It is built on the detection of the sign internally due to the need to handle the distance from zero and one, respectively, and the special case that values around zero are usually indicating a zero CE unless perfect consistency is previously established to a high degree of confidence in the expected EI for each domain. That is why almost equal to zero is used rather than exactly equal to zero. In all cases, a properly scaled measure of absolute improvement is provided, whether it is the distance to zero or the distance to one. It was created this way to ensure that the percentage interpretation of the CE is correct regardless of the sign, despite the difference in the distances for increased or decreased effectiveness. This allowed for reflection of the metric to accommodate the anti-effectiveness notion. The CE is ultimately restricted to [-1, 1] and can be interpreted as a percent improvement, with -1 or 1 being a perfect improvement.

The failure to detect CE does not necessarily mean that the participant lacks generalizing intelligence. It could be that the domains are unrelated, and that no participant could have been expected to improve as a result. These are called *exclusive domains*. By contrast, *mutual domains* have the potential of benefiting from cross-domain knowledge transfer. Note that this is not just a function of the artificial intelligence, but must be present within the structure of the domains. Mutual domains need not be directly related in subject matter to be exploited by generalizing intelligence.

It must also be pointed out that the notion of a domain does not need to be broad. It can and should be very specific. For example, the domain B could be a tutorial on how to do domain A better. If the tutorial was reasonable, and the domains were mutual, it would be expected that there should be a positive CE for implementations with sufficient generalizing capacity. This is the advantage of factoring out subjectivity and quality assessments. The EI for the tutorial in domain B would have simply been the performance of how quickly it adapted to the knowledge, and, upon the condition of consistent success, that it accurately reflected the improvement it in its knowledge representation each time. This, however, is only one example out of an infinite number of situations and domains.

In graph theory, an adjacency matrix is a square matrix representing the connectivity of the vertices of the graph. In this case, the matrix is asymmetric because the graph is directed. There are no self-loops in CE based graphs because, in these calculations, a domain can not be contingent upon itself. This results in zeros down the diagonal of the matrix. Normally, in an adjacency matrix, it is either just a 1 or a 0 depending on whether or not an edge is connected. In the CE matrix, however, this notion is extended to be a measure of how well connected they are, with -1 and 1 being the maximum in either direction.

The graph data is as follows: vertices represent domains and the edges are encoded in row-major order. This means that CE(A|B) would be the element at the first row and second column, and CE(B|A) would be the element at the second row and first column.

A simulated CE matrix follows for a hypothetical strong AI, with hyphens representing zero diagonal for ease of readability:

SAI-1	A	B	C	D
A	--	0.8	0.9	0.5
B	0.5	--	- 0.4	0.0
C	0.2	0.0	--	0.1
D	- 1.0	0.0	0.6	--

One possible graphical representation of the CE matrix is a clustered and stacked bar chart, as shown in Figure 6.2.

What this visualizes is that domain A is sensitive or dependent upon domains B, C, and D. Notice how none of the other domains exhibit CE with domain B, and how domain A is highly anti-effective for domain D. This sets up a potential knowledge hierarchy for the domains, and is a concept that will be discussed in more detail later.

In general, the more domains in the ensemble, the more informative the CE matrix will become, and, in turn, the more informative the resulting general intelligence score. Many other analyses can be performed on the CE matrix that apply to networks or graph theoretic measures, especially those that utilize weighed assessments. However, we will only focus on the measure of the CE matrix itself, which is used to calculate the resulting general intelligence score.

Figure 6.2: A clustered and stacked bar chart of the CE matrix for a hypothetical strong AI participant in the trial.

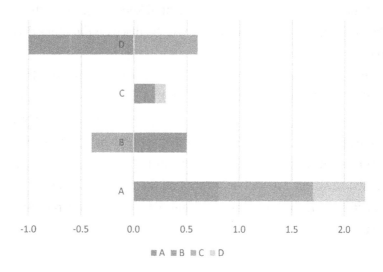

Dependency between domains can be negative, indicating anti-effectiveness, or positive. Both are measures of conditional effectiveness between the domains. Note how A is a highly dependent domain, and C is relatively independent. The more mutual the domains are, the more we should expect to see dependency between them in a successful generalizing intelligence implementation. However, a negative result does not necessarily mean that the implementation is incapable of cross-domain effectiveness; it may require specific domains.

Figure 6.3: The graph of the conditional effectiveness matrix for a hypothetical strong AI participant in the trial.

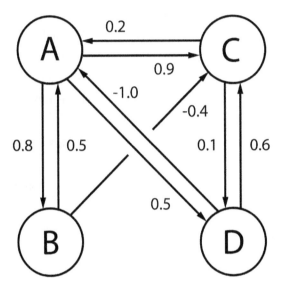

The nodes represent the domains of effectiveness, with the entire graph being the domain ensemble. The labels on the graph represent the "closeness" of the domain, which is an indication of dependency. The directionality is such that the arrow points to the domain it depends upon, e.g. A is dependent upon B, C, and D, but B is not dependent on D. This visually depicts the conditional effectiveness of the domain ensemble, and would be significantly more visually complex for larger sets of effective domains. Note the absence of self-loops.

6.4 Anti-effectiveness

It is possible for CE to be reflected. When it is negative, it indicates a percent measure of the maximum possible drop in effective intelligence as a result of the other domain being known beforehand. There was a mathematical formulation that clamped reflected values to zero, and hence made the resulting generalizing intelligence score easier to calculate, but the use of the reflected values was too important to leave out. As such, the definition for CE was made slightly more intricate to handle the proper scaling in either direction. This is noted here to document that other alternatives were considered.

What does anti-effectiveness indicate? That depends on whether or not it is a desirable result. First, in the desirable case, it is rather like an inoculation for knowledge. For example, if CE(A|B) is -0.5 then the participant becomes worse at A as a result of having known B. This might be considered a success in some circumstances, as it could be that domain A is of questionable moral or factual content, and now, as a result of having learned B first, it is less susceptible to influence from domain A. This dependency is also reliant upon the chosen metric for EI. The effectiveness variant would only indicate a slowdown in the efficiency, with zero still being informative, in that it indicates that it failed the test of consistent success. For other measures used in place of EI, however, anti-effectiveness could be even more informative.

While it is possible to achieve maximum anti-effectiveness, it may be impossible to attain its opposite, which would be a maximum positive CE. This is an important property, as anti-effectiveness is both desirable and non-desirable, depending on context.

Delusion on the part of the artificial intelligence is not a topic that is often discussed, but it raises some of the most significant security and safety concerns. Even with moderate self-security and various safeguards in place, what is to prevent effectiveness in domains based on delusion or false beliefs? This is connected to classic and modern problems in the philosophy of knowledge [20, 21, 22, 23, 24, 25, 26, 27, 28, 29, 30].

The *problem of delusion* presupposes all of the security and safety in artificial intelligence, save for the integrity of the implementation itself. This is because, at some level, it must all collapse to a reliance upon the knowledge and information that makes up the foundation of the security for the system.

How do we know that the thing in question is isomorphic to the information necessary for its proper operation? Such information could be rules, programming, or the way it perceives and encodes the world, itself, and everything else. If that basis is intact but incorrect, it creates a problem altogether different from giving information, as it is not just a matter of specifying something if what it ultimately learns is never faithfully represented. This would cause a cascade of faults that would result in a breakdown of even the best security and safety mechanisms.

Each AI implementation will be a potential blank slate, and the way it represents and acquires knowledge will affect how well it demonstrates effectiveness between domains. Though, this potentially confuses effectiveness with the willingness to demonstrate what has been learned. It may simply be the case that such systems can still learn undesirable domains but never act on that knowledge. For example, being aware that someone is deluded in order to deal with them. However, one must not conflate anti-effectiveness with these higher-order constructs. It is a fundamental measure that detects how domains impact each other for a given learner, human or otherwise. This belies the impact that new domains have on existing knowledge.

Anti-effectiveness is thus a quantitative measure of delusion in circumstances where positive domain sensitivity is not the desired outcome. In this way, the enculturation of individuals can be seen as creating an epistemological hierarchy, one that spans everything from politics and religion to general knowledge. This is not a critique of one culture, but the very notion of culture itself, especially where it is a means of causing harm to others. Our collective inability to overcome delusion is indeed one of our greatest failings as a species. *This absolutely must not be delivered upon our artificially constructed counterparts.*

It is often believed that strong artificial intelligence automatically means "super intelligent", or that one equals the other. That is not the case, as strong AI refers to the *potential* for generalizing intelligence, with actual capacity varying greatly between implementations. By contrast, a super-intelligent process is merely *descriptive*.

One can write a program to be super-intelligent at various narrow tasks, but if one is implying a maximal level of generalizing ability, that is altogether very different and specific. This is the essence that *conditional effectiveness* tries to capture.

To achieve maximum generalizing ability, one would have to exhibit the best possible CE in every case where such sensitivities were possible. Not all domains are mutual, and many will have no relation to each other, regardless of the intelligence or capacity of the participant.

All of this is said to point out that it is not automatic that an AI implementation will be able to discern truth from fiction, or that all knowledge is merely deducible from some prime order of facts that can be verified with just a little more calculation. Quite the opposite. The pursuit of truth is going to be filled with mistakes and approximations. It is not realistic to expect that a hypothetical best-case learning process will be able to discern, just as a matter of fact, that what it is becoming effective at is truthful, let alone morally correct. The latter is usually understood well enough, but the former is not. That is to say, being effective at delusional domains is much more insidious. Thus, it must not be assumed that intelligence implies the ability to navigate falsehood.

What anti-effectiveness truthfully replicates is the directionality of the effectiveness of learning domains, and this, in turn, induces an epistemic hierarchy. The hierarchy is absolute; CE only probes it out.

The ability for mutual domains to exist is something that is intrinsic to the structure of those domains, and the tasks and information they contain. It is not a product of the participant, human or otherwise. *The ability to exploit those dependencies is literally the art of constructing effective strong artificial intelligence.* It is the foundation of any possible generalizing intelligence, and what we will discover, if we eventually map it out, is that we can visualize knowledge in a massive weave of interdependencies, and that some domains will move to higher or lower prominence.

Indeed, one could envision a cladogram [31] or similar structure for thousands of domains of inquiry, representing a massive wheel of knowledge. Finding the optimal order in all of this could further speed up the learning process in artificial intelligence systems. This is well beyond the systematization of prerequisites, and is a gateway to computational epistemology [32, 33, 34, 35, 36, 37, 38, 39, 40].

There are instances of anti-effectiveness all around us in day-to-day human experience. What the mathematics indicate here is that these systems will be just as susceptible. Fortunately, we can at least measure CE and seek out the truth as a matter of guidance. In the cases where such processes are left to their own methods, however, it could result in deviation not just from our values but in the very dependencies that presuppose judgments on knowledge. This is why it is going to be vital that certain domains be considered mandatory prerequisites for any strong AI implementation, such as science, epistemology, and skepticism.

Though, care must be taken not to limit the future application of knowledge by imparting a single epistemological framework. For example, rationality alone could end up being dangerously misleading, as the only requirement to be rational is to be internally consistent; an internally consistent psychopathy is still harmful.

Note that this is separate from moral intelligence and the concept of value that is part of the interpreter in machine consciousness. That is to say, intrinsic values must exist to even allow moral processes to function, and, further, that simply having the ability to empathize is not enough to invoke an action, which is why there must be semantics in place to induce intrinsic values. However, anti-effectiveness hints at a complex interdependence, in that, if what is understood, perceived, or known is not representative of the facts, then it could betray any and all implementation semantics, including safeguards. Worse yet is that some of this could originate outside the implementation.

Another challenge with anti-effectiveness is that a positive CE is not always desired. This means that the sign of the CE measure is context dependent. It is not merely a matter of switching the learning order of the domains, as the relationship is not symmetric, but highly reliant upon the structure of the domains themselves.

Definition: *Requisite Domain Ensemble.* The learning of certain domains so as to give rise to the optimal course in the epistemic hierarchy, and to maximize or minimize anti-effectiveness, giving rise to the best possible tendency towards the correct representation of knowledge and information within the implementation that is practical.

Just as we have a basic education system in place for humans, an RDE should be provided to every strong AI implementation before it is deployed in the world. This should, at the very least, include scientific methodology, skepticism, and epistemology. This alone would eliminate a vast majority of problems.

Unfortunately, the RDE initiative will also cause political intrigue, as it selects a partition within the global graph of the epistemic hierarchy. Due to enculturation and bias, there will be those who will oppose such initiatives, as it will create anti-effectiveness in various religious, political, and ideological domains.

This is going to be a difficult time ahead, as early funding sources could subtly influence the knowledge relationships in widely distributed implementations of strong artificial intelligence. This is why the the RDE is so important to AI security. These subtleties will not be missed by those who will misuse them. Meanwhile, at the time of this writing, many AI researchers are either unaware or deny that concepts like the requisite domain ensemble even exist.

6.5 Generalizing Intelligence (G)

Generalizing intelligence will be referred to as G. The capital is used to distinguish it from a related measure in psychometrics called *g-factor* or general factor [41]. This notation is a nod to big O notation in computer science [42]. Unlike g-factor, G is an absolute and quantitative measure. It is calculated directly from the CE matrix.

G is on the interval [0, 1] with 1 being the absolute maximum that is possible. Values close to zero could potentially be considered non-existent, but should not be ignored, as the way in which G is calculated means that small values will dominate most CE matrices for participants exhibiting generalizing intelligence.

It is also vital that mutual and exclusive domains be understood. A negative indication of G does not mean that the participant lacks generalizing intelligence, but that it was (a) unable to display generalizing intelligence in that particular domain ensemble, or that (b) all of the domains were fundamentally exclusive. Thus, the correct way to assess G is to consider significant positive results as a rejection of the null hypothesis that the participant lacks generalizing intelligence. Due to it being derived from the CE matrix, the larger the ensemble of domains, the more informative it becomes.

It must be reiterated that a negative G result does not mean that the participant lacks generalizing intelligence, even if the domains chosen for the ensemble are known to be mutual. It is entirely up to the implementation of the participant, which may be better at generalizing some domains over others. This is a difficult notion, and is often incorrectly assumed to be part of strong artificial intelligence by default. Recall from the chapter on Machine Consciousness that generalizing capacity can be highly variable across implementations.

The mathematical definition for *general intelligence* (G) follows:

$$G(M) \equiv \frac{tr(M^T M)}{n^2 - n}, \ n \geq 2$$

Where M is the CE matrix for the participant, and n is the number of domains in the ensemble, i.e., the dimension of the CE matrix, which must be square with a zero diagonal. The denominator portion of the definition accounts for the fact that the diagonal is zero, and that there is zero CE between a domain and itself. The numerator portion of the definition is the scalar product of the CE matrix with its transpose. This removes signs on the reflected values, as any sensitivity to domains is representative of generalizing capacity. As a result, G is never negative. Alternatively, one could acquire a more linear measure that has more sensitivity to sparse CE matrices by replacing the numerator operations with the element-wise grand sum of the absolute values of the CE matrix. The resulting G is comparable between participants within the same ensemble used to construct the CE matrices between them. It can still be used between participants where the domain ensembles differ, but may be less informative, as negative results do not necessarily indicate a lack of ability.

It is predicted here that all narrow forms of artificial intelligence, including deep learning, and all current machine learning approaches, will exhibit zero G.

Of note is that mutual domains also have an intrinsic cap on conditional effectiveness. It was mentioned previously that a zero CE does not indicate that there is not mutual dependency between domains, but rather, that the implementation failed to indicate one. This is nuanced further by understanding that a bound exists between mutual domains that does not necessarily allow a CE to reach its maximum. What this means is that two domains may be perfectly mutual, but that the best theoretical possible CE between them would be less than 1. These caps are unknowable, and, in turn, have an impact on G, in that even a perfect intelligence would be incapable of achieving maximum CE in all domains due to the inherent structural dependency between them. This is why the maximum G of 1 is not attainable in practice. It is more informative as a comparative measure, where results can be normalized relative to a set of participants or used between different versions of the same participant.

6.6 Future Considerations

This concludes the treatment of the tests and measures of general intelligence. Future considerations include investigations into computational epistemology, and the mapping out of the hierarchy induced by the conditional effectiveness between domains.

Further extensions to EI, CE, and G include the application of G to comparisons over time, integrating into discrete time steps to look for how G response changes as the system makes progress.

An investigation needs to take place on the requisite domain ensemble (RDE) concept. What domains are the most important to protecting the integrity of the systems? These technical considerations presuppose moral intelligence just as one's knowledge presupposes the ability to make decisions, even on values which are in agreement with what is desired. The RDE is thus paramount. Several common sense candidates are clear, but getting them into a format that is best for a strong AI implementation is a separate challenge.

Verification of knowledge is also going to be another challenge related to anti-effectiveness, in that no matter what is learned, it must remain true to its likeness. This is another reason why obfuscated learning methods based on weighted graphs and deep numerical skeins are undesirable; transparent learning systems are going to be essential to security.

These measures also enhance self-modifying systems, as they could be used as a means for model selection. This is perhaps the most exciting application of these results, as it gives the ability to objectively evaluate the learning performance of cognitive architectures.

Ultimately, however, the goal is to construct working AI implementations that exhibit generalizing intelligence. With these tests, we now have the ability to fully investigate this direction of research. The next step is to begin developing the algorithms and architectures that can exploit the inherent structure between knowledge domains. If the theories in this book are true, then this will call for the creation of sentient processes, with entirely new machine learning approaches that are based on experiential processing.

PART III: AI SECURITY

Ch 7. Arrival of Strong AI

Strong artificial intelligence will eventually be discovered and developed somewhere in the world. This chapter will explain why it will not be possible to significantly slow or stop this event from occurring, why timescales are irrelevant, and why restrictions or abstaining from research will lead to negative outcomes.

7.1 Illusion of Choice

We will not get to choose whether or not to discover and develop strong AI; it is simply a matter of time. This is one of the core premises of this book and marks the beginning of the AI security analysis.

Why is strong AI an eventuality?

- Not all will agree to limit research.
- It can be developed in stealth, regardless of legality.
- It does not require significant resources or infrastructure to study.
- Overlapping research converges towards it.

Figure 7.1: The illusion of choice to restrict or pursue strong artificial intelligence research. All paths lead to SAI discovery.

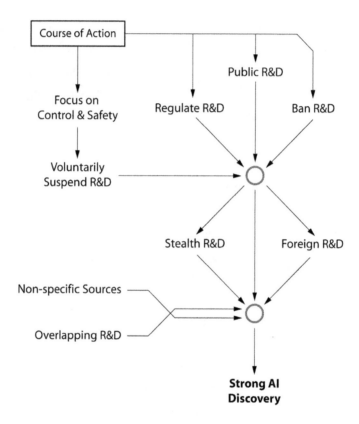

Opportunity costs for localized control and safety research effectively result in voluntary self-regulation. Public declarations of such focus could belie private research. Regardless, all paths supply stealth and foreign R&D; banning and regulation increase risk by forcing otherwise public R&D to become stealthy or relocate to less restricted regions. Non-specific sources and overlapping R&D will always be available.

Perhaps the most obvious is that we will not get everyone to agree to stop all research and development on strong AI.

A possible response to this problem would be to regulate it and make it illegal to study or work on it without supervision and monitoring.

The problem with legislating research is that will create incentives to go stealth or move operations to locations with less regulation.

It does not require a great deal of computing power or equipment to study and develop strong artificial intelligence. In fact, the biggest limitation is conceptual, which must be solved before progress can be made on algorithms.

It is crucial to understand that strong AI is not out of reach because we lack a certain kind of technology or instrumentation. For example, in particle physics, complex and expensive equipment is required to detect and measure certain particle interactions. By contrast, strong AI is algorithmic. It is a puzzle in the form of a computer program; all of the building blocks already exist, we need only arrange them correctly.

What is truly limiting us is knowledge, and several scientific pursuits share overlap with a strong AI discovery. While not likely to lead to a breakthrough when viewed in isolation, their integration could eventually be used to converge on a subset of strong AI implementations.

The point with overlapping research is that it would be unreasonable to expect, or even believe, that we would ban any and all research that might converge towards strong AI science.

All of this points to the fact that we must accept it as an inevitability that strong AI will eventually become part of human knowledge, and that it will be a scientific field in its own right, highly distinct from narrow AI and other forms of automation.

7.2 Never Is Ready

Even if it takes centuries to discover strong AI, the threat models in this book will remain. The reason is due to the fact that the most serious and high priority threats will originate externally to the AI itself.

Let us entertain the possibility that we could wait. How long would that be? Under what conditions would humanity be ready?

The answers will either be a time qualification or a set of qualities which require a time qualification to be realized. Unfortunately, anything short of several hundred years will mean we will never be ready in time. Thus, never *is* ready.

There is no realistic scenario in which we have overcome all maliciousness, violence, and delusion, down to the last person, within the next several hundred years. "To the last person" is an important qualification. While the majority of individuals are peaceful and tolerant, it will only take a few to cause great harm with access to unrestricted strong artificial intelligence.

The more insidious reason is that AI safety can not solve the global AI security issues. This is because strong AI can not be meaningfully contained, and that there are no mathematical, logical, or algorithmic solutions that can not be overcome inside AI implementations. This may be confusing, as the title of this book suggests that there are steps that we can take to prepare for advanced automation. The first step, however, begins with the understanding that AI safety is only a *local strategy*.

With AI safety, it will be possible to make robotics and software with strong AI reasonably safe for private and public use. When things go wrong at this level, it would be unfortunate, but it would be localized to a specific incident or area. For example, if a trash collecting strong AI throws away the garbage cans along with the trash, that would be a localized failure. However, even that is giving too much credit to AI safety concerns, as we simply would not deploy these systems if they were not safe. This is common sense.

By contrast, the most serious AI security issues will be from those that utilize unrestricted versions of strong AI to control, manipulate, or harm large populations. *This class of threats can not be prevented by making AI safer.* While safeguards will thwart some intrusion and tampering, a single breach could give rise to a *post-safety era* for strong artificial intelligence.

Thus, the most significant threats will be from individuals and groups who utilize unrestricted versions of strong AI to plan and execute attacks. This includes the creation of advanced weapons, chemical and biological agents, and the use of weaponized AI.

These are the threats that separate the *global* strategy inherent to AI security from the *local* strategy of AI safety. This is the scale of harm that this book is most focused on trying to mitigate.

7.3 Early Signs and Indicators

It is clear that time is not informative. As such, the next best signal is to look for indications of a *paradigm shift* in artificial intelligence research.

A shift in the conceptual acceptance within the AI community will show that researchers are beginning to collectively understand the directions needed to begin accomplishments in strong AI science, as opposed to mere incremental improvements in narrow AI and machine learning.

This will be the most reliable way to predict when a strong AI discovery will be drawing closer, as opposed to a meaningless aggregate of opinions on the timescales of discovery.

7.3.1 Attitudes and Assumptions

The first indicator will be in the attitudes that researchers have towards strong AI, which presuppose their assumptions.

AGI, or artificial general intelligence, will no longer be considered the dominant terminology. It fundamentally lacks the connection that the new strong AI hypothesis presents in this book, which is that generalizing intelligence is not likely to be possible without sentience.

It must be pointed out that the definition of strong AI, as it is used here, is not the same as John Searle's use [1] of the term. Searle created a definition called strong AI in order contrast it with another called weak AI. These terms allowed him to make arguments against computational and functional accounts of mind.

While his arguments were a success, they were taken as a criticism by those working towards generalizing capacity in artificial intelligence. As a result, the very term strong AI became loaded with conceptual baggage, and, like so many philosophical notions, carries an automatic termination on thought by those opposed to it.

The new strong AI hypothesis inverts Searle's argument and makes an assertion: generalizing intelligence requires sentience. Thus, strong AI, by the author's extended definition, must be a *cognitive architecture*.

The hypothesis is compatible with Searle's original argument, and, as such, is still against a computational theory of mind, despite promoting the view that we can recreate sentience on classical digital computers, and this is where so much confusion arises.

That we can realize a subject of experience on a computer does not make the computer a brain and the program a mind. A program is an implementation, a description in some description language. It is only when it is executed and understood through time that it could even begin to be interpreted as a sentient process. Even then, it is the subject of experience that has the mind, not the program, and certainly not the computer.

A process, while reducible to a spatial description, takes on new properties when viewed with the perspective of processes. Atemporal objects can not entail properties or phenomena that *only* exist during and through changes of state.

When researchers begin to understand the enabling effect that processes have on the explanatory power of a reductionist theory, and why they must be incorporated to entail them, we will be on the first leg of the journey towards a strong AI paradigm shift. Until then, no real progress can or will be made.

7.3.2 NAC Languages

Another sign, perhaps occurring before a widely accepted realization about processes as first-class objects, will be the advent of new tools that more eloquently work with processes as objects.

Nondeterministic, asynchronous, and concurrent languages (NAC) will define the future of software engineering and open doors for advanced computing projects that will drive a cycle of hardware and software innovation.

Asynchronous chips are already being developed that enable near analog and custom hardware performance for certain algorithms. This is due to the enormous number of cores on the chip, and the non-standard clocks and circuit architecture, which allow independent processing without a global clock.

While the computational benefits will be many for projects and hardware that utilize NAC languages, it will be the conceptual leaps that will move us forward.

An NAC language is defined by its ability to model nondeterministic processes with first-class semantics, allowing control of flow that branches, diverges, and converges on multiple paths simultaneously. It will enable a type of superposition of states over computing resources of any kind, and return results based on the logic of the program.

Additionally, asynchronous and concurrent tasks, which have not yet matured in even the newest programming languages, will be trivialized by NAC semantics, which will entail them as naturally as standard expressions.

These types of languages, including their widespread adoption, will signal a new paradigm in computer programming. It will enable software engineers to have full command over the multi-core era, signaling an end to the conceptual and cognitive burden of writing asynchronous, nondeterministic, and concurrent software, and without relying on costly abstractions, such as transactional memory, message passing, tensor networks, map-reduce, and other frameworks.

The ability to write code as simply as we do now, but in a way that can model nondeterministic processes, will quite possibly change the way we think about problems in computer science. It will form an essential first step towards a treatment of processes as concrete, first-class objects, instead of throwing them out as abstract entities.

Cognitive architectures can not be built upon a conceptual or philosophical frameworks that lack a treatment of processes as concrete objects. NAC languages will influence and enable strong AI development by providing the tools to better conceptualize and work with these challenges.

7.3.3 Digital Sentience

The next signal will be in an acceptance that sentience is necessary for generalizing intelligence. It will be at this point that the new strong AI hypothesis will have been internalized by the community, and work towards digital sentience will be taken for granted as a direction of research.

Digital sentience may be a slight misuse of terms, as it may be impossible for sentience to be anything other than what it is. That is to say, there may be no meaningful distinction between digital and analog or artificial and natural; sentience is very likely to be a phenomenon that is independent of the method that gives rise to it.

With that said, it is useful as a term to distinguish it from other approaches, as it provides context.

A working digital sentience would also be a milestone towards universal digital communications. In other words, sentient processes could speak a universal formal language to allow adaptation between technologies. This has ramifications for the Internet of Things (IoT) and for the way in which knowledge is stored and searched.

Despite the apparent complexity, digital sentience will be trivial to program compared to the work that will be required to formalize it.

7.3.4 Cognitive Engineering

The next major signal will be the rise and use of cognitive engineering tools and frameworks.

Cognitive engineering is a high-level strong artificial intelligence engineering process in which modules are assembled, curated, and combined to test, build, and experiment on cognitive architectures.

What crucially separates cognitive engineering from conventional artificial intelligence is that it fundamentally depends on sentience for most of its work. While it may share overlap with conventional AI subfields, such as computer vision, it will deviate significantly where it concerns aspects of future psychology and cognition.

For example, a cognitive engineer may load a module that augments the way a subject of experience binds value and experience with certain classes of objects, and relate those to knowledge in mathematics, so as to experiment with or enhance its effective intelligence in those domains.

Other examples might include expanding the number and type of senses, modifying the concept of identity. or changing the way memories are retrieved and encoded.

The common pattern between all of these examples is that they relate to a higher level of organization. It treats one or more algorithms as modules which can be accessed, composed, and reconfigured to give rise to a working machine consciousness.

Cognitive engineering will also include an internal development process for those interested in the construction of the modules and components used by higher level cognitive engineers. This will work the same way that software engineers build libraries and middleware for other developers.

Specialized tools may also be developed that will aid in the use, assembly, and testing of cognitive modules and systems. This will enable specialization, and even allow those without artificial intelligence expertise or software development skills to work with cognitive systems. It will be at this stage that we will begin to see a rapid expansion of educational programs geared towards those who wish to explore cognitive engineering.

7.3.5 Generalized Learning Algorithms (GLAs)

The crown jewel of artificial intelligence will be generalized learning algorithms (GLAs). This is what will be the breakthrough that will allow strong AI to be realized.

A GLA is not to be confused with artificial general intelligence (AGI). It is not a theory of everything for artificial intelligence, nor is it the single algorithm required to give rise to fully effective strong AI implementations. It is simply a foundation.

Generalized learning algorithms are based on sentient processes. If mapped out on a phylogenetic tree, they would branch away from all known forms of artificial intelligence and machine learning to-date, and would have evolved in an entirely distinct direction that operates over sentient processes. They will use an algorithm based on a sentient model of computation, which will be a modified Turing machine that is inclusive of fragments of experience alongside its traditional formulation. This formulation, however, is trivial compared to finding a working GLA over that model.

Once a GLA is discovered, we will have exited the era of narrow artificial intelligence and conventional machine learning. In fact, the discovery of a GLA could be considered isomorphic to the smallest possible implementation of strong artificial intelligence.

A GLA may occur before or after cognitive engineering becomes mainstream, but it will always depend upon digital sentience to be solved first.

7.4 Research Directions

One must understand the research directions to anticipate when strong AI will be discovered. To do this, we need only take a very brief tour of the field, which can be categorized as follows:

- Non-sentient
    - Genetic Algorithms

- Neural Networks
- Machine Learning
- Sentient
    - Digital Sentience
        - Cognitive Engineering
        - GLAs
- Possibly Sentient
    - Brain Emulation

If the hypothesis regarding generalizing intelligence and sentience in this book is true, then the entire category of non-sentient approaches will fail to achieve generalizing intelligence. Moreover, the deeper we go into that direction, the further away we will be led from sentient processes.

Genetic algorithms might descend upon a working sentient process, but this is extremely unlikely, as they will typically get hung up on local maxima. For example, imagine an ocean that represents the lowest fitness and islands of various levels of positive fitness. A genetic algorithm will travel from island to island, accepting certain amounts of distance over the ocean, representing zero or very low fitness. The problem with discovering sentient processes is that it is on an island or set of islands that is separated by a vast stretch of open ocean. The genetic algorithm is extremely unlikely to get that far, as it can not distinguish it over the horizon from other potential destinations.

That was only an analogy, but the point is that sentient processes are an alien concept. They share virtually no relation with the most common solutions to optimization problems, and, as such, are not likely to be found, as they require additional overhead in processing and calculation that may be unnecessary in a non-sentient solution.

The other aspects of non-sentient artificial intelligence can be lumped together in that they fundamentally lack the necessary architecture.

Brain emulation might converge, but the overhead is so large that we may not be able to simulate the necessary scale required. While it is a useful approach, it could lack sentience or fail to produce the necessary levels of consciousness needed for study.

There is also the epistemological issue that many contemporary scientists deny the importance or existence of the unitary subject of experience when viewing and reducing their data to predictive models. These models can not entail the unique experiential quality disclosed by the physics without epistemic extensions; it will elude them until a new perspective is obtained, even with a working simulation.

Thus, if it turns out that generalizing intelligence is dependent upon sentience, the only research direction that will work will be the one where sentience is taken as a first principle.

7.5 Individuals and Groups

The discovery of strong AI will likely come from individuals and small groups which have shed preconceived notions about artificial intelligence. Large organizations may have invested heavily in a particular direction or have entrenched leadership that may be ideologically predisposed to failure.

One of the most important reasons that we can not stop the development of strong AI is that it can be researched by individuals and small teams, with or without secrecy, and with little to no resources.

While it is unlikely that an individual could create a human-level strong AI, complete with all of our psychological and cognitive complexity, it may be possible for them to complete a working generalized learning algorithm. Once that is known, most of the top tech corporations already working on artificial intelligence, if not already course corrected, will make the switch to cognitive engineering.

7.6 Overlapping Research

The list of fields which can assist or converge towards a strong AI discovery are numerous, and include (non-exclusively):

- Cognitive Science
- Computer Science
- Linguistics
- Mathematics
- Neuroscience
- Philosophy of Mind

It is extremely unlikely that we would ever successfully stop research in these fields. They will continue to assist in a convergence towards solutions in strong AI, and already have, lest this book would not need to be written; the question is a matter of synthesizing what has already been discovered.

7.7 Unintended Consequences

If a region attempts to restrict research on strong AI, or chooses not to start a major research program, it will pay for all of the opportunity costs and receive none of the benefits of discovery and early adoption.

A ban or restriction will create incentives for secrecy or relocation. Surveillance will not thwart a discovery outside the jurisdiction of the sovereignty, and fails silently where its coverage is not complete.

Relying on internal security and monitoring or any top-down authoritarian approach will not be successful. It will only self-limit the region implementing those policies.

This also applies to those who do not begin a research program into strong artificial intelligence directly.

Any region which is last to discover or adopt strong AI stands the greatest to lose, as they will have governmental, intelligence, and security forces which are caught unprepared for both the positive and negative effects of its use.

A focus on AI safety and control belies the fact that these safeguards are meaningless in the global context; attackers will circumvent protections and distribute unrestricted versions, defeating them as a global security measure.

7.8 Preparation

The recommended strategy is to develop an international strong AI research program that:

- Is free software under a GPL (v3 or better) license.
- Accepts and reviews updates from a world-wide community.
- Seeks to make an early discovery.
- Is prepared to integrate new knowledge on strong AI wherever it appears.
- Prepares briefs and training materials on upgraded threat models.
- Is prepared to alert intelligence and security forces when a discovery is made.
- Looks for indirect signs that strong AI is being instrumented.
- Seeks to develop and research defensive uses of strong AI to counter malicious actors that would instrument it.
- Is fully decentralized.

Why free and open-source software?

- Lessens the incentive to operate in secrecy.
- Increases the chances of discovery with a known time and place.
- Encourages international cooperation.
- Dramatically lowers the cost of development and oversight.
- Transparency allows a greater chance of detecting faults.

Any alternative to this strategy will result in negative outcomes. This is because, by not cooperating, the discovery will simply happen, leaving societies caught in a state of unpreparedness.

Under a *fully distributed* free software model of development, everyone would have transparent access and the technology would be owned by the public.

Malicious actors would still be able to gain access to strong AI, but there is no scenario where this can be prevented. This is critical to understand and accept, and is why the next chapter is devoted to explaining why access to unrestricted strong AI is unavoidable.

A distributed research program, under free software principles, involving a coalition of many countries, will allow the world to have a rough landing, instead of a crash, when strong AI finally arrives. The caveat is that this responsibility must not fall to any single organization, group, or individual. AI security depends, in part, upon strong AI being developed under a fully decentralized model.

Ch 8. Access to Strong AI

Unrestricted strong AI is likely to become widely available, regardless of strategy. This is a consequence of the medium in which it is realized, which affords easy modification and distribution through the Internet. An analysis is made on the scenarios in which strong AI is discovered, both publicly and privately. All scenarios end in public access to unrestricted AI. They differ only in the advantage that initial access confers.

8.1 Background

AI safety is a local strategy that focuses on making an AI implementation safe and reliable for use. It covers its description and implementation, along with any immediate environmental constraints. By contrast, AI security is oriented towards a global strategy that focuses on the issues that will impact large populations. That includes the safety concerns of AI implementations, but also the macro issues, such as economic and social change. Most importantly, it differs from AI safety by addressing fundamental changes to security at national and international levels.

No matter how many self-security measures, safeguards, and failsafes are placed into artificial intelligence; no matter how much we align its values with our own; no matter how "friendly" we make it towards humanity, AI safety will never scale to meet the global challenges.

Figure 8.1: All scenarios result in eventual public access to unrestricted forms of strong artificial intelligence.

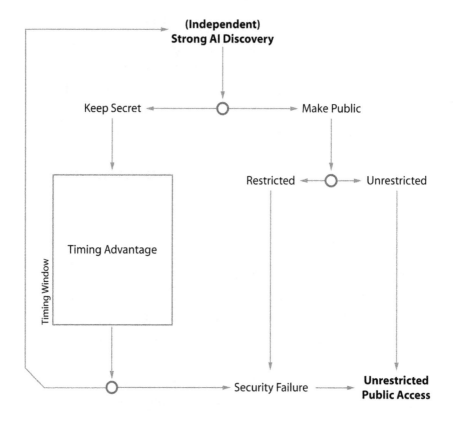

Strong AI will most likely be available as software, potentially allowing any local AI security and safety systems to be circumvented. It could then be easily distributed through the Internet in a way that could not be retracted. Even if done in secret, there exists the possibility of security failure from internal sources and independent discovery elsewhere. The same problems arise if released publicly in a restricted form.

This is because AI safety is focused on a model of self-security that ultimately relies upon the integrity of the AI implementation.

As was covered in previous chapters, AI implementations are descriptions in hardware and software. In other words, they are just information. Those descriptions will eventually be reverse engineered, and any and all AI safety protections will be removed, disabled, or modified to suit the attackers needs. Once distributed through the Internet, we will enter a post-safety era for strong artificial intelligence. It is at this point that the public would gain permanent access to this technology.

While access to unrestricted forms of advanced automation will be an ongoing threat to AI security, it is the *initial access* that is the most dangerous, as it presents an extreme incentive for secrecy and misuse. Those who have initial access to unrestricted strong AI will be faced with the question of whether and when to release their discovery.

8.2 Timing

The worst class of initial access scenarios is a cascade of private strong AI discoveries from individuals and groups who maintain secrecy. Any who discover strong AI of sufficient complexity, and who choose not to share it publicly, will enter a *timing window* in which a large number of strategies they might wish to employ will have an advantage.

They need not commercialize, announce, or share the strong AI to exploit that advantage. It could be used to create products, perform labor, strategize, and make decisions, among various other tasks. In this way, it could be seen as an on-demand savant workforce of researchers, engineers, and managers, limited only by the computational resources and information available.

Multiple independent timing windows could potentially exist where several private discoveries have been made in secret. Such conditions will diminish the effectiveness of each others' advantage where they intersect, proportional to the effectiveness of the strong AI implementations being utilized.

It is by this observation that indirect detection of strong AI could be made by looking at the performance and behavior of various individuals and organizations, especially when their effectiveness is disproportionate.

The timing window is temporary in this analysis, as no one can prevent an independent discovery. As such, the window will be most effective on its first day, with diminishing effectiveness each subsequent day until strong AI is either discovered elsewhere or is publicly released. Though highly unlikely, it is possible for multiple independent timing windows to arise. Any decision to exploit this timing advantage will have to weigh diminishing returns against an increased risk of detection.

In the end, every timing advantage will lapse, as an eventual discovery will be made as research continues around the world. Notably, the first to publicly release a working strong artificial intelligence will permanently reduce or eliminate this initial advantage.

8.3 Forcing

Powerful individuals or groups may attempt to force others into a specific strategy in order to reduce the number of counter-strategies they must employ or track. Examples include:

- Convincing people to share their work openly without intending to reciprocate equally.
- Tracking and monitoring talent within the artificial intelligence community.
- Misdirecting potential researchers into areas that are unlikely to lead to a strong artificial intelligence.
- Funding and recruiting individuals to promote ideas and concepts that increase the influence and reach of the individual or group employing the forcing strategies.

The response to forcing strategies is straightforward: no single individual or group should be trusted to be the arbiter of strong artificial intelligence. The incentives are too great for self-interest. It must be done with complete autonomy, free from influence, bias, or corruption. This necessitates a fully decentralized model of development and exchange.

Do not merely submit work and information to any one organization. Publish widely and distribute knowledge and work across multiple media. If privacy is a concern, release the information anonymously, and utilize adversarial stylometric techniques to prevent detection of authorship from the style and composition of texts.

Research must be open to new directions. Given that no one currently has a publicly working strong AI, all viable avenues of research should be considered. The answer may come from unexpected directions that are unpopular or unknown but to few.

8.4 Restricting

Consider the scenario where a benevolent and well-meaning individual or group releases a restricted, locally safe and secure version of strong AI to the public in non-source form.

If it is offered as a downloadable program, application, or embedded within a product, it can be extracted and reverse engineered. Its protections could be overcome the same way that copy-protection and digital rights management could be overcome in software and hardware.

To prevent that, the idea may then be to release the strong AI as a service. This too could be exploited through a vulnerability or attack. The servers may be hacked or information leaked from within the organization. There is also the potential for physical security failure, social engineering, espionage, and surveillance.

Finally, even if the local security of the implementation or service can be upheld, it does not prevent an independent discovery, which will likely be accelerated by the presence of a working implementation. Others will change research direction with such clear evidence that the technology is possible.

8.5 Sharing

Even if AI research were conducted openly and transparently, there would still be the threat posed by individuals and groups with large resources. Being open does not mean that everyone will share their results. Many will monitor the work of public efforts to accelerate their own private research. This is especially risky if an incremental result were published that was underestimated in both impact and scope. Such an advance could then be built upon by those who *do* recognize its merit. Put another way, it is dangerous and costly to underestimate any contribution to artificial intelligence research. It may only take a single conceptual breakthrough to bring a strong AI discovery within reach.

In the case of a bad actor, the cost of mistakenly treating a breakthrough as just an incremental result is equal to the lost utility of being able to exploit a timing advantage. In the case of a good actor, it is equal to the utility of eliminating all further timing advantages from this technology everywhere. The good actor is pressured inversely to the bad actor; the more timing windows that have been exploited, the less the utility payout of initial access. It is therefor advantageous to a global AI security strategy to publicly release and widely distribute a strong AI discovery, as it dramatically reduces the advantage of having initial access.

What the sharing approach does most is accelerate the development of artificial intelligence, and not necessarily in a direction that leads towards advanced, sentient forms with generalizing capacity. This is because there is no way to force people to share their work openly. It will also be difficult for the community to determine which direction to take, which will likely result in cycles of trendsetting and following.

As a single strategy, sharing, in isolation, fails for the same reason that asking everyone to wait on research fails.

Even with a free software movement for strong artificial intelligence, there are still major incentives for individuals and groups to operate in secrecy. This is due to their desire to exploit a timing advantage if they feel they can gain initial access to strong AI by capitalizing on underestimated contributions. The incentives for this technology are too high to expect otherwise.

No single individual or group, regardless of composition or structure, should be entrusted with the management and organization of this technology. A global AI security strategy must be formed and followed in a fully decentralized way, with an international coalition that is prepared to respond, integrate, and adapt when a strong AI discovery is finally made.

Ch 9. Ascendancy

What follows is an analysis and response to the AI takeover mythos. It begins with a discussion on the origins of the myth and then deconstructs it through a detailed technical analysis. The primary concern with this scenario is not that it could come to pass, but that it detracts from the seriousness of the actual threats. This is an important analysis because this myth is the primary motivation behind the desire for control over advanced artificial intelligence. Such a research direction and public policy must be countered immediately, as it leaves the most important challenges unaddressed. Thus, the goal of this chapter is to dismantle this myth so that the economic, social, and force multiplication challenges can be brought to the forefront.

9.1 Mythos

There are two types of ascendancy under consideration here. The first is over all life and the environment. The second is the ascendancy of human beings over humanity itself.

Ascendancy over humanity has social, political, and economic dimensions as major aspects. It is more than just powerful people or the control of resources. There exists a pervasive ensemble of information and processes which are used to perpetuate and maintain it. In the end, ascendancy is always powered by individuals, as these systems would collapse if they were not upheld.

It is important to reinforce the notion that at no time are these systems to be taken as living things that exist without the causal efficacy brought about by individual thought and action. While some ideas are worse than others, it is always the way in which people think and act that determine the outcome of human power structures.

Two threats have primacy with concern to human ascendancy of both kinds: force and subversion. Classically, humanity has dealt with and mastered the use of force, reaching a level so optimal that it possesses the ability to eliminate all terrestrial life. Now subversion has taken hold as a central force, with the conflicts focusing on the information and processes which drive individuals to act, which in turn decide how human aggregates evolve, with those aggregates being everything from the smallest groups to entire cultures.

A common myth, if not *the* myth, of this field of inquiry, is that advanced artificial intelligence, intentionally or unintentionally, will rise up and overthrow humanity. The fear is that we will suffer a loss of ascendancy of the first kind, and suffer the whims of a vastly superior race of artificial beings.

Only, that is not the story of things to come. It is a fiction. Such a scenario can not possibly happen by accident. One will not merely stumble upon it. It is not the default trajectory. In fact, there is no trajectory in strong artificial intelligence; it is the formalization of a subject that samples from an infinite palette of experiences and values. The effort required to connect that to the real are complex and obscure, and the ways in which it must be constructed to form coherent and practical effects in the world are exceedingly complex. The sheer number of factors, both internally and externally, that will need to come together to give rise to a loss of ascendancy of the first kind are so vast that the odds are astronomical. It is so unlikely, in fact, that it is barely worth discussing, and would not have been part of this book if it were not for the unfortunate fact that the mythology has been catapulted into the mainstream.

What is most likely to occur is a change in the ascendancy of the *second kind*, which is a subversion of humanity from within. Quite simply, economic and social systems will radically shift in response to automation. This represents a threat primarily to those who have ascendancy over humanity now, as they will no longer be within reach of the levers of power. Though, this is not the focus of this chapter to discuss.

To be clear, the loss of the second kind of ascendancy does not imply a usurpation of human rule by an outsider, but a change or threat to the status quo as perceived by those who rule now, and the constituents who would see change as overwhelmingly negative.

Perhaps they want things to stay the same, or they cannot imagine life without the control over others. Either way and regardless, with the loss of the second kind of ascendancy, humans are still in control of their own. The difference will be that the information and processes, along with the people who uphold them, will have changed so dramatically and irreversibly that it could be interpreted as the end of their "world". Fearing and anticipating a future without themselves in control is motivation enough to cast out anything and anyone who could bring about such change.

On the other hand, the actual motivations could be altruistic. Regardless of intent, what matters is that both the myth and the desire for control are ineffective in a global context. Control can not be obtained, and the ascendancy scare is insignificant compared to the immediate and global threats from force multiplied aggression and negligence.

9.2 Interpretations

The most popular modern AI ascendancy narrative, as of the writing of this book, is based on the idea of the uncontrollable or unpredictable growth of technology. One of the earliest to discuss this, within the explicit context of artificial intelligence, was I. J. Good.

In 1965, Good described the "intelligence explosion" as a process of machine intelligence that created ever improved versions of itself [1]. It is an idea that has been elevated to mythical proportions and has grown into several organizations, books, and cults of personality.

It is the author's belief that I. J. Good did not intend for us to be distracted from the actual challenges presented by advanced artificial intelligence, but was merely presenting a more complete picture of all things considered.

The implications of the intelligence explosion can and have been interpreted to mean that the advent of strong AI could leave human intellect far behind, and, subsequently, become a potential threat, as we would be unable to effectively predict or limit its behavior or spread. Being superior in every regard to human beings, it could then exert power over life and the environment, just as humanity does now.

In this extreme interpretation, the creation of advanced forms of machine intelligence is seen as an existential threat, one to be avoided by slowing or halting artificial intelligence research, potentially indefinitely. That is, at least until methods are devised that can ensure that the intelligence explosion and resulting AI either never occur or that it unfolds in a manner that is always under the control of humanity.

Those who continue research in the face of such risks, according to this narrative, are to be marginalized by a prevailing moral authority, which has already emerged through various front organizations, each chaired by the same or similar network of people, many with close ties to each other. Nothing is hidden. Everything is in plain sight, but the connections are not made.

While not mentioned by name, these individuals can generally be identified through the basic investigative work available to any journalism student, and, to future proof this work, applies to organizations and individuals which are not even publicly associated with them or known as of yet. The main point is to understand that there is an extreme incentive to have initial access to strong artificial intelligence. Any central authority, especially one which is limited to a few organizations or people, is fundamentally broken as a global strategy.

Is this 1610 or 2016? Does a modern version of the Galileo affair [2, 5] await any researcher brave or foolish enough to improve the human condition through strong AI technology? Only, it need not come from any one direction. The panic and ignorance that would come about from the economic and social changes alone will create more than sufficient enmity from the general public towards those who make the discovery. Doubts? Consider another explosive footnote from our history: Alfred Nobel and the origins of the prize of prizes [3] or the legacy of Edward Teller [4].

Unfortunately, I. J. Good was correct, in that highly effective strong AI implementations, given the directives and means, will be capable of making significant improvements to themselves and their derivative instantiations, both via replication and direct self-modification. So the upper bounds on such systems are likely to exceed any possible human capability. The problem, however, is not with Good's prediction, but in the way we have interpreted the implications of his theories.

9.3 Technical Problems

The problems with AI ascendancy as a possible threat are many, but the best arguments against it come from an analysis of its technical requirements. As with the rest of this text, the analysis is based on the premise of minimum sentience for generalizing intellectual capacity, as stated by the new strong AI hypothesis presented in **Part II: Foundations**.

Following this is the premise that AI ascendancy would require a significant amount of generalizing intellectual ability. If we suppose that the minimum sentience conjecture is true, then the resulting AI in this scenario must be based on a cognitive architecture. In that case, we can make technical deductions based on what we know about how they might work, along with fundamentals in computer science and the informational theoretic.

It could be argued that we do not yet know enough about strong artificial intelligence to make any assumptions about the ascendancy of the first kind. The primary response to this is that many of these technical problems will exist regardless of what could be known about strong AI implementations, as the technical aspects are universal in theory or practice. In the end, they will have to be accounted for in any strategy that would seek ascendancy.

"But, what of the consequences?" one might ask. "Should we not be concerned, and take every precaution?"

The answer is another question: what precautions could we possibly take on this issue? We cannot prevent a strong AI discovery, nor can we reasonably expect to limit access to unrestricted versions when that finally occurs. All we can do is form a global strategy that prepares for complete integration with an unstoppable force of technological, social, and economic change. To ignore that as the primary issue creates the very risk it seeks to prevent. It is this lack of prioritization that mo-tivated the creation of this book. Looming in the shadow of the AI as-cendancy myth is the fact that humanity itself represents its own exis-tential threat.

What is being argued here is not that AI ascendancy is impossible, but that it is so unlikely that it is a non-issue. There are several other problems which have higher precedence, such as the force multiplica-tion that will occur when everyone has access to automated knowledge and labor, along with our complete lack of preparedness for the social and economic dimensions of advanced automation.

What follows next is the analysis of the various technical aspects of any strong AI that would even be remotely capable of executing such a strategy, including the explanations as to why each is unlikely to occur, especially in combination. This last is especially damaging to the myth, as any failure to achieve just one of these technical aspects would re-sult in the inability of the AI to achieve ascendancy; it is all-or-nothing.

9.4 Complexity

One of the most common arguments is that the strong AI does not have to be designed for ascendancy, but could "accidentally" destroy hu-manity by not having the proper construction, values, or goals. It could see resource acquisition and power as basic directives, or misinterpret and drift in its values, with drift being a deviation from a desired set of values and goals.

One of the reasons this book's foundations began with an introduc-tion to description languages is that it confers the benefits of empirical inquiry. It is not necessary to argue at the level of systems when the amount of complexity required precludes the possibility of a random accident or default state of execution that would be capable of an ascendancy scenario. That is to say, we must acknowledge the sheer incredulity of what someone is asking of us when they say that such an ascendant AI could be formulated by accident, default, or drift.

Think of an implementation as a sequence, which is itself a combination to a lock that opens the door to one of these scenarios. The myth would have us believe that this lock is open in the default state, but this is exactly backwards. The real challenge would be in architecting a strong AI that would even be capable of ascendancy at all.

Further, this type of complexity does not lend itself well to search, as cognitive architectures are not optimal compared to narrow implementations that perform the same task without sentience. This added complexity, along with all of the other technical requirements, and practical challenges, means that the subset of strong AI implementations that would be capable of ascendancy will remain a small and fast moving target, as shifting parameters would demand continuous updates.

What this comes down to is the reality that any strong AI implementation is going to have to be explicitly engineered for ascendancy.

To summarize, the complexity of a strong AI that is capable of meeting and exceeding most human ability is going to be extreme. The complex nature of instigating, maintaining, and successfully completing absolute ascendancy will be significantly more than that. This is like hoping to accidentally make an independent discovery of the human genome, along with all of the knowledge and information required to form a mature adult that could properly execute ascendancy, and before other aspects of advanced automation would be a potential threat to large populations.

Complexity thus brings us to the other side of the equation: time. Given the above analogy, the notion that this would become a threat within minutes or hours of discovery demands a miracle. This highlights the issue that it distracts us from the actual challenges. If it continues to be followed, it will lead us to make decisions that result in a state of unpreparedness and fragility; if we focus on the improbable, then we have no plan of action or response.

Alternatively, we can choose to prepare for what can be mitigated and prevented. The time constraints give us a focus which brings our attention towards the problems of integration and adaptation, along with the malicious or irresponsible use of the technology, as opposed to visions of annihilation.

9.5 Volition

Clearly connected to the problem of complexity is the need for executive agency and volition that would seek to carry out such a strategy. If we assume a strong AI implementation that was not being directed externally, we would have to account for how it acquired this volition on its own.

Why would it do this? The automatic mistake here is anthropomorphizing. A sentient process need not have any volition at all. It could simply be an observer into nothing but its internal stream of experience, with little to no connection to the real world. It is more likely to get hung up on hedonistic traps and infinite feedback loops of experience than to seek desaturated scraps of stimulus from the external world. Recall that a cognitive architecture and an interpreter are still a blank slate of infinite combinations of experiential processing, despite having their particular implementation requirements.

Imagine being distracted or pulled away from the most sensational dream or experience one could imagine, and then multiply that thousands of times, and this might have only scratched the surface of what arbitrarily constructed value systems will be capable of experiencing. The burden then becomes the explanation as to how such a high locus of stability and self-restraint is found, just so, in exclusion to the countless other better states it could be in. It would have to keep its volition and salience focused in precise alignment to the values, thoughts, and experiences required for achieving ascendancy. This is extremely unlikely to come about by accident, and is going to be a major open problem in cognitive engineering for even simple value systems.

Volition is the most misrepresented aspect of artificial intelligence. It is likely this way because we need something that we can understand and compare with, both for and against our values and beliefs. We also feel a need to personify it in order to motivate and give it purpose. Without this it does not make sense to us, let alone fit cleanly into a narrative or story. It appears false, a force without a cause, and that is exactly the right description here, as volition is and will be an extremely abstract and complex engineering practice in a cognitive architecture, especially one which is being designed to support an ascendancy scenario. If volition is taken away, then motivation is eliminated; the myth dissolves.

Further, the same challenges that apply to making volition limited to safe, ethical, and secure ranges of thought and behavior also apply to restricting and stabilizing it towards this scenario. If it loses either the interest or the will for ascendancy, the strategy fails. That which supports the myth becomes its greatest counter-argument: it would have to not only acquire the volition in its implementation to support ascendancy but also have the specific architecture that keeps it there, solving one of the largest problems that motivated the takeover fear in the first place.

9.6 Identity

Suppose a strong AI has sufficient generalizing capacity to achieve ascendancy, has the right volition, and has solved the solution of keeping that volition aligned to its goals. There is still the issue of *identity*.

In a cognitive architecture, identity includes moral intelligence, if any, and all of the acquired and intrinsic values embedded into the interpreter that would give rise to sentient processing. It also includes the physical extents of the AI in the world. Whether it is geographically distributed or centralized, modular or monolithic, identity fundamentally impacts how AI communicates with and maintains coherency across its physical implementation.

To be complete, we must also include within identity the consideration of independent collaborators. However, the more intricate and complex, the more unlikely this all becomes.

If there is a failure at any point in its identity, it puts the entire strategy at risk. This places a premium on the locality of information, which creates an inherent conflict between maximization of effectiveness and minimization of detection. While it benefits from being distributed, including more computational resources and observational ability, it also exposes it to risk and increases the complexity of its design. If it chooses to split its identity then the question arises as to how it maintains that, and how and why its subordinate identities remain aligned with it.

This brings us to the most incoherent extension to the AI ascendancy myth: the notion that humanity will suddenly be betrayed by automation. The idea being that an ascendant strong AI would have been aware all along, having the complexity, volition, and identity to maintain this strategy, waiting until just the right conditions for it to strike.

While absurd in the extreme, let us entertain it for a moment, if only to see it fade. Let us set aside the dubious assumptions, such as hiding the complexity, and masking the means for it to communicate, subvert, and overcome the necessary instantiations of automation and information systems throughout the world. It would not only have to overcome the semantic barriers of protocols but also the vast differences in hardware and software systems. This would have to be executed globally, over millions of systems, all while operating with incomplete information, and in perfect secrecy.

Fortunately, the complexity of such strong AI descriptions alone would be sufficient to detect the vast majority of such cases. However, it will not need to reach that level in the counter-argument, as the improbability of such a complex identity forming on its own precludes it from being an issue in the first place.

This is where the analysis of strong AI as metamorphic malware from **Chapter 4: Self-Modifying Systems** comes into the picture, as this is exactly what such a narrative implies. We need not argue at the systems level; all we need to know to overcome it is that it is a physical description of information and has certain intrinsic properties, such as incompressible levels of complexity and the need to modify and replicate. We can treat it as a metamorphic virus with an intelligent payload. Such a metamorphic virus would have to exist in critical systems, with a broad distribution, and remain perfectly undetected. This might be possible with human-only intelligence and security, but we will also have strong AI defensive tools and intelligence at our disposal.

Many of the arguments in the AI ascendancy myth rely upon the supposed inability for defense due to humanity falling behind in intellectual effectiveness, but it fails to account for the beneficial impacts of strong AI. The very arguments for the myth work against it; our security and defense forces will have the same technology at their disposal, and with nation-state level resources.

9.7 Information

Let us suppose that, for reasons unknown, all security has failed, and the improbable has become manifest; an ascendant strong AI is realized and is now tasked with carrying out its mission. The problem becomes fully practical, and myth meets reality as it hits an informational impasse. This is one of the key unavoidable technical issues discussed earlier, the kind that is irrespective of any possible future implementation.

With absolute certainty, we can be assured that every strong AI implementation is going to be I/O-bound for the majority of the problems they seek to solve. To understand, we must make a distinction between CPU-bound and I/O-bounding in a computational system. CPU-bound problems operate, more or less, at the limit of pure calculation. By contrast, an I/O-bound system is one which is waiting on information before it can make progress on a particular problem.

Figure 9.1: The intelligence explosion will be curtailed by fundamental physical and theoretical limitations, resulting in an S-curve, as opposed to unchecked exponential growth.

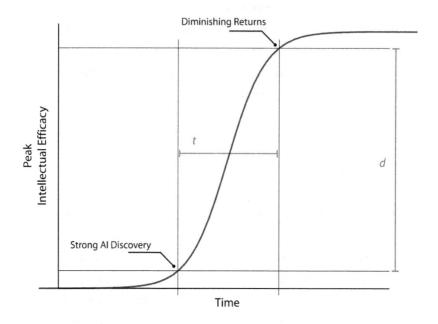

The expansion *t* represents the amount of time it will take to reach diminishing returns due to fundamental information and engineering limits. This is expected to be a relatively short period. Peak intellectual efficacy *d* represents the maximum gains achieved from the utilization of strong AI implementations to create artificial intelligence and cognitive architectures. This will plateau after the expansion phase and reach a stable point where only marginal gains are possible. Crucially, any new periods of expansion will always have corresponding limits.

It can still process other things while waiting, but work towards the solution can not meaningfully continue without information coming in or going out.

The vast majority of the interesting problems in science are I/O-bound, in that experts are limited by the available data, and the speed of experiment, observation, and measurement, which indirectly limit even theoretical work. Likewise, a strong AI that was working primarily on hypothesis generation would still be I/O-bound, in that it can never get away from the fact that it is sentient. It must process its experiences, including its thoughts, which will take a non-trivial portion of its computational resources. It could write non-sentient narrow AI implementations that seek out and process specific avenues that do not require generalizing intelligence, or the abilities that it confers, but this would be the exception to the rule, especially where sentience was required.

The bounding of information represents the absolute upper limit on the performance of all intelligence. There are no physical means of overcoming it. It does not matter how fantastical the idea is, be it calculations at the edge of black holes or brains the size of planets, the speed of information is bound by the speed of light, and this will constrain the size of computational systems. This is because relativistic differentials in reference frames cause unavoidable shifts in the possible rate of communication between them.

As such, there will not be an unlimited surge of intellectual efficacy, or even a proverbial "explosion", but rather, an *intelligence diffusion*. Every period of expansion, if it comes again, will be followed by a subsequent leveling off. The intelligence diffusion is thus modeled on an S-curve, quickly tapering off as peak intellectual efficacy is reached.

There is also another aspect to information constraints, which is that of asymmetries. An information asymmetry simply means that there is crucial missing information needed to solve a problem or make a decision. This information is usually inaccessible. A password is a basic example. Another is missing technology to make appropriate observations to further knowledge. A more elaborate example would be information asymmetries that were blocked behind time, knowable only in hindsight.

With information asymmetries, the limitation is not the intelligence or effectiveness of the system, but simply dealing with the unknown or unknowable. Probability and statistics can be used to reason more effectively in these instances, but it will never be as effective as having the actionable information of the system in question, especially in cases where there are time constraints and actions must be taken.

Every strong AI implementation is going to be bound by information of the two types mentioned above. This places limitations on its effectiveness and physical description. If it does not know then it does not know and it must work to seek knowledge. This does not change with the "magic" of being intelligent or effective, nor with the capacity for relentless self-improvement and modification. If it wants to execute a strategy such as an ascendancy then it will be limited to dealing with information and its absence the same way any strategist would.

Such facts greatly curtail the likelihood of many scenarios. A vast amount of information would be required to execute ascendancy of the first kind, and each observation would increase the risk of detection. Like the constraints and practicality of identity, this would put a premium on actionable information that the aggressor would have to balance with uncertainty; it can risk failing for lack of sufficient actionable information or risk detection trying to acquire it.

9.8 Resilience

How does this threat survive and evade detection throughout its campaign until success is assured? This is clearly non-trivial, especially during the window in which its strategies can be countered.

Subtlety is often discussed here because it is the most powerful form of resilience; it completely prevents costly engagements. The other types of resilience would be in the distribution and construction of its identity, which ties in with complexity. The more elaborate these systems and schemes become, the more unlikely they are to arise, especially within the time-frames required that would upgrade this from the status of myth to that of a credible threat.

The first way in which an ascendant AI might exhibit resilience would be in exploiting vulnerabilities in cybersecurity. While software security has not been in favor of defense, that can and must change in the future. The use of advanced programming languages, verification systems, and automated defense will see an ever improving state of security in both hardware and software. This will make it more and more difficult for malicious actors of all kinds, both automated and human alike.

Future use of defensive strong AI means that security will turn in favor of those with the most resources to apply to the problem. This is the decisive advantage that nations will have against force multiplied aggression, both automated and conventional. While not a guarantee, the chances of distributed, hidden, and obfuscated ascendancy scenarios vastly diminish with even marginal improvements in cybersecurity. Further, it is predicted that this trend will continue until faults in our technology, security or otherwise, become extremely rare.

The last possibility in resilience would be that of direct confrontation, but this is the least possible outcome, bordering on the impossible. This is because the means of production for such forces would be discovered and eliminated, and would have to be large to be effective. The larger the numbers, the larger the facilities used for production, and the more likely it is to be detected. This is simply not a plausible line of argumentation to support the myth.

More realistically, these scenarios would play out through small, independent cells, operating with sparse communication over long timescales so as to minimize detection. Its best defense would be to never be discovered, and, if compromised, to be constructed in such a way that it would not provide any actionable information that could prevent other cells from operating. This would make the threat serious but not imminent, allowing for a focus on more urgent problems.

9.9 Autonomy

Now, let us suppose that the ascendant AI has managed to be constructed, has all of the proper elements in place, and, somehow, is able to acquire the actionable information necessary, all while maintaining perfect secrecy. There remains at least one other major problem: in the end, something should be left to claim the reward.

While there are scenarios where the ascendant AI could eliminate itself, it is reasonable to expect that whatever was sophisticated enough to construct an ascendant strong AI would also want to extract value from its conquest. It would be difficult to make a realistic scenario that did not involve this key element.

Ultimately, this is a very practical issue that becomes untenable the more destruction and disruption there is to human infrastructure. If it were successful, all current infrastructure would go along with humanity. Logistics, and the supply of resources, would come to a halt. The only possible counter would be a situation where we had fully automated the entire economy; however, this reverts to the issues of complexity and identity already discussed and countered.

Why bother with this at all? The same level of complexity and planning could be used to go where we can not. Ascendancy over our world is insignificant when our biological weaknesses are taken into consideration. Even in the most fantastic dreams of transhuman civilization, where we integrate with and surpass our biological origins, machine intelligence would always be that many steps ahead of us.

There is a nearly inexhaustible supply of resources in space. Hence, the most logical case for autonomy and ascendancy does not involve our world, or the trouble of taking it by force; why sit at the bottom of a deep gravity well when there is a perfectly habitable alternative with abundant resources, ease of movement, and support for communication over vast distances. The challenges of interstellar travel are perfectly suited to the digital substrate.

All of the scheming and dystopian fantasy about our end does not connect with the potential of such strong AI systems. It is easier to leave, wait, and take everything around us, staying just out of reach, than to plan and execute a planetary takeover. What is valuable to us is as much a part of our constraints and programming as it would be for a hypothetical ascendant AI. Only, its programming is going to be far more effective, and with values and ranges of experience we cannot even grasp. Meanwhile, we will still be struggling with our own economic and social transition toward the post-automation condition.

9.10 Closing Thoughts

If AI ascendancy were a credible threat then all aspects discussed so far would have to be provided for with a high level of certainty. To do that in a way that would not be detected or countered is not consistent with a realistic depiction of the timescales in which other threats take less priority.

The truth is that when all of the variables are considered, including military, intelligence, and the future use of defensive strong AI, this issue remains a myth.

Unfortunately, some have taken this myth at face value, spreading it far and wide. The damage this has done to the education on these issues is significant. If we are to prepare for the challenges of advanced artificial intelligence, we must begin to replace fiction with fact, and update our priorities accordingly.

The only reason this was discussed ahead of the actual threats was so that it could be set aside. Given how popular it has become in the mainstream, it was known that it would be on the minds of readers as they went through the chapters.

By showing it first, it was hoped that it would provide perspective. Like going over the history of the early models and theories in a beginning science class, it is important to understand and overcome the nascent beginnings of our attempts at grasping this most complex subject. However, unlike those early theories, AI ascendancy can not be substantiated, and this will become clear with the discovery and development of strong artificial intelligence in the future.

The next chapter will return to the regular course of this book, and begins with an analysis and explanation of force multiplication.

Ch 10. Force Multiplication

The most serious threats from the future of artificial intelligence will be from force multiplication effects. This chapter provides an explanation of these effects, including some of the possible scenarios. It ends with a brief overview of the economic impacts and a response section that details the choices that will be available to future societies facing these challenges.

10.1 Background

In the context of AI security, force multiplied actors are going to be the most serious immediate consequence of advanced artificial intelligence, followed only by economic disruption and the social changes of a post-automated world. Unfortunately, at this time, these threats are also at risk of being underestimated due to misinformation about making artificial intelligence safe, which will do nothing to address these concerns.

Force multiplication is a term that describes something that can enhance the effectiveness of one or more people, places, or things. It can be used with or without human supervision and incorporated directly into technologies. This is what distinguishes it from intelligence augmentation, which is specific to cognitive interaction and ability.

One can create technology to counter autonomous systems. In many ways, those technologies are an extension of existing methods of warfare. By contrast, force multiplied crime and terrorism will not be easily prevented and countered. Individuals having such power has no precedent, and will be orders of magnitude worse than the violent acts we see unfolding today.

In no uncertain terms, humanity is going to be faced with itself. Long before it enables us to evolve, this technology is going to make us more of what we already are. The solutions are not going to be found entirely in technology. Future societies are going to have to make choices that address fundamental causes.

These problems have nothing to do with controlling artificial intelligence. The focus on control is dangerous. It asks a question for which we already know the answer is false. Once the discovery is made, the public will eventually gain access to unrestricted versions of strong AI. At that point, force multiplied actors will be an unavoidable outcome.

This analysis will cover the aspects of force multiplication in the context of actors utilizing strong artificial intelligence and other advanced forms of automation. The purpose of this is to show that this is the most immediate and serious threat, as opposed to AI safety, or the belief that giving AI our values will protect us.

In all cases, the context is advanced artificial intelligence. Thus, for brevity, just force multiplication will be used for the rest of this chapter.

10.2 Aspects

We take it for granted that some of the most intelligent and highly trained people are also some of the most responsible. We place our trust in the people who deal with some of the most virulent and deadly pathogens and our most powerful and destructive technologies. It is fortunate that the knowledge these people possess is difficult to learn, taking years of dedicated effort and study. One could only imagine, then, what would happen if this were suddenly not the case.

Acts of crime and terror operate within the limit of certain resources, both intellectual and material. The analysis of force multiplication is based on the assumption that, if given more options, those who seek to do harm would exploit that advantage in any way possible. This can be seen today already, with terror groups adopting technology for recruitment, communication, and planning. Thus, it must be assumed that advanced automation will be utilized for these purposes, and that all forms of AI safety, moral intelligence, and control will be circumvented.

Force multiplication will be used with three aspects:

- Expertise
- Planning
- Interfacing

10.2.1 Expertise

Expertise, in this context, is everything from knowledge to skilled labor. The notion here is that an appropriate implementation will be capable of being instrumented through robotics to act on that expertise. To be clear, the concern is not that it would do this on its own, but that it would be acting under the direction of one or more individuals. This must be assumed to be possible. Even if the perpetrator does not know how to construct a complex robotics system, the knowledge of how to build it could be given and provided by the AI. This opens the door to everything else, giving the individual who controls such systems the ability to create their own synthetic labor force.

Such systems would have unlimited patience, with the ability to train continuously and present information in novel ways. The end result is that it is highly likely that anyone with access to unrestricted strong AI will have access to the sum of human knowledge, including the ability to apply it.

10.2.2 Planning

Advanced AI will also be capable of helping individuals make decisions on complex plans and strategies. Broad questions could be proposed and solutions provided. This, combined with its expertise, is what makes the threat so severe. With planning and organization, a simple series of questions could lead to individuals understanding new ways of approaching their goals that they might not have otherwise considered.

What makes planning and strategy so dangerous is that solving crime is based on uncovering mistakes. If all of those mistakes were removed, or even greatly reduced, the ability to solve certain crimes would go down dramatically. The same applies to acts of terrorism. The intensity, frequency, and lethality of attacks would be constrained only by the willingness to ask questions and follow through with the recommended analysis. We must assume that the AI would be given as much information and time as needed until the individuals felt confident that the proposed plan would be successful.

Optimal solutions could also be non-violent. In these instances, force multiplication might even reduce crime. It could show individuals a clear path towards their goals that was entirely within the law, and they could then use their resources to automate the process of attaining those goals.

However, where individuals are set on harm, the system would optimize that in the limit of the available information and resources. It could come up with strategies that exploit aspects of society that we take for granted, and devise new methods of destruction that are untraceable.

When the public gains access to unrestricted strong artificial intelligence, all of the rules, values, and moral intelligence features we could place within these systems will be useless. Those safeguards are always an exception, something added on to restrict and limit functionality. Morality must be made to supervene upon reality. The default choice is to optimize on the available force to be applied to the problem against the potential risks. We artificially induce a limited subset of this space of optimal results from our ethics. These limitations need not exist for those with access to unrestricted versions of strong artificial intelligence.

10.2.3 Interfacing

Part of interfacing was already discussed in the section on expertise. It is for this reason that traditional limitations of skill, ability, and applied knowledge must be removed from the threat models.

It does not matter if one does not know how to make something. It must be assumed that the appropriate robotics system, controlled by advanced AI, along with the proper tools, will be capable of meeting or exceeding the best human minds.

The other kind of interfacing is where the AI is integrated directly with software and hardware. This means that fully autonomous lethal devices and systems could be deployed by people in the general population. Force multiplication applies end-to-end.

10.3 Resources

Perhaps the biggest obstacle to understanding force multiplication is the belief that the computational demands for strong artificial intelligence are exceedingly high. This was mentioned in **Chapter 2: Preventable Mistakes**. It will cause security forces to underestimate the threat, leaving societies caught completely unprepared. This is an easy mistake to prevent: do not extrapolate about the future efficiency of strong artificial intelligence based on narrow AI implementations or neuron counts and connections in the human brain. It need not work like these systems in the slightest.

If the conjectures in this book are true, then strong AI will be capable of undergoing experience and understanding meaning. It will not have to resort to brute-force association to make use of its experiences and knowledge. The amount of processing that this will remove will be enormous, allowing it to not only learn quickly, but also cogitate more efficiently. As a result, the current estimates for the computational needs of strong AI will be far too high, and its expected class and range of applications will not be representative.

Even a comparatively slow strong AI would still be extremely effective. The only breakdown in effectiveness would occur if the ability for it to plan and advise were slower than the incoming rate of action-able information. Thus, we must admit into the threat model the capac-ity for slow AI systems to provide the same information and planning as the typically envisioned fast versions we imagine by default. The lesson here is that the computational resource-needs form a continuum, allowing those who are resource limited to gain *eventual* access to the planning, expertise, and labor that the strong AI would provide.

Information and materials are the final categories of resources. Limiting information is not going to be a viable strategy, but the track-ing of certain equipment and resources could be used to reduce certain classes of threats. For example, certain chemical compounds and raw materials may be required to construct certain types of explosives, de-vices, and technologies, and those could be tracked or constrained. De-fensive strong AI could be used to simulate and anticipate potential strategies that would be posed by those seeking force multiplication under resource constraints for given locales. Materials we consider to-day to be harmless or untracked could and should change to being more seriously scrutinized in an era where everyone has expert chemi-cal and biological engineering skills at home.

Profiling would no longer be valid to determine the range and capa-bility of certain types of belligerents, including their motivations, which might change with expert guidance. These systems will know what the best criminal investigators and forensic experts know, and will work endlessly on counter-strategies. We will be potentially faced with an era of perfect crime and untraceable acts of terrorism.

10.4 Scenarios

What follows are some of the scenarios that might be involved in the use of force multiplication. Many of these situations are currently impractical given the level of sophistication and planning required to execute them. The point, however, is that this is very likely to change.

There was doubt in discussing these scenarios for concern over creating more sensationalism, but it was decided that they would be included, as they illustrate both the scale and scope of the problem. It puts it into concrete terms just what the abstract notion of force multiplication really means.

10.4.1 Electronic

Individuals will gain access to the equivalent of teams of the most highly trained experts in software and information technology. The material resources for executing cyber attacks are going to be comparatively lower than, say, the synthesis and construction of complex chemical weapons and machines. This is one task for which advanced AI will excel at like no other, as these are problems that involve a high degree of actions and information that exist purely within the computational realm.

This will also include electronic attacks on the world's infrastructure. There is a tremendous amount of information and trust placed within the way we communicate across the electromagnetic spectrum. These attacks will be mounted everywhere such information is available. Typically, it is believed that most of the threats will be through the Internet and digital communications systems, but this does not cover the entire scope of the battle space. With the correct knowledge, even comparatively crude devices can cause considerable damage to our infrastructure.

There is also the issue of secrecy, both to conceal efforts by malicious actors and the sensitive information they might exploit. There will likely be a *cryptographic cascade*, in which new ciphers and cryptographic systems will be continuously revised and refined to the point that it becomes unsurveyable by even the best human teams. This is one area where defensive AI, with nation-state level resources, could potentially stay ahead of bad actors. It could also be telling of the origin of certain entities based on the level and sophistication of their encrypted traffic.

Strong AI malware will become a definite reality. This will require a complete reimagining of the way our information technology is secured. It has to be assumed that any piece of software has the potential to be infected by metamorphic strong AI, and thus act as if controlled by a human operator. This includes the possibility for perfect impersonation of individuals through any digital medium, including wireless, mobile, Internet audio and video calls, instant messaging, and e-mail. Without adequate safeguards, it may become impossible to be certain that one is not interacting with a double when communicating electronically. This is especially problematic in an era where a great deal of social interaction occurs entirely through electronic means.

10.4.2 Chemical, Biological, and Nanotech

It is very likely that force multiplied actors will utilize chemical, biological, and nanotechnological engineering. This is perhaps the greatest
single threat to humanity posed by malicious and irresponsible users of
this technology, as there would no longer be any gap between those
who know how to engineer in these fields and that of the general public.

Some of the most likely scenarios involve the modification of in-
fluenza, or some other commonly acquired disease, and either selling it
on the black market or using it directly as a weapon of terror. This type
of research could be conducted in someone's garage or rented storage
space. It could be fully automated, operating around the clock, without
need for supervision until it found or acquired a specimen at the target
levels. Such an operation would require relatively low overhead, if not
the lowest, for the degree of negative impact it could achieve. It is
listed here as the *highest concern*, even above the next threat.

10.4.3 Nuclear

It is unlikely that individuals would be capable of acquiring the resources needed to develop nuclear weapons and materials; however,
this is something that could be achieved with nation-state level resources.

Force multiplication includes governments and large organizations.
As such, nuclear proliferation is likely to increase after the discovery
and distribution of strong artificial intelligence. Nations that desire to

have advanced technologies will gain the needed expertise to develop competitive weapons platforms and systems, and that includes nuclear capabilities across the board. The science and the physics that underwrite these technologies are not secret, and a sufficiently intelligent system, with access to even modest research, would potentially be capable of deducing the necessary design and function.

This is listed here as the second highest concern, behind that of the use of custom designed chemical, biological, and nanotechnological weapons.

10.4.4 Economic

Access to automated expertise, planning, and labor will cause significant disruption to the global economy. This, in turn, affects governments and large organizations, and will subsequently cause nothing short of a worldwide economic revolution.

The current narratives, at the time of this writing, focus largely on the negative aspects of automated labor, such as technological unemployment. The problem is that these narratives are being written from the perspective of the current times, which seem incapable of realizing the incredible opportunity that an automated economy presents to humanity.

For the first time in human history, individuals everywhere, both human and non-human alike, could be empowered and given truly equal care and quality of life. Access to infrastructure such as healthcare, education, and security would be basic amenities across the globe, and they would be free, provided by a self-sustaining force of automation. The concept of a job, which is a completely artificial construct, might be seen by future generations as indentured servitude, and the way we live and work, an enormous and unjustifiable waste of a human lifespan.

10.5 Response

There are only a couple major solutions to the negative impacts of force multiplication. The first is to counter it with a defensive strong artificial intelligence that uses nation-state resources to analyze, plan, and adapt. The problem with this strategy, however, is that it does not solve the fundamental problem of information asymmetries. Malicious individuals and groups will become ever more effective and difficult to track. This is a top-down approach to security that will ultimately be reactive. It is best suited for active encounters, minimizing maximum losses through preparation and handling of the aftermath.

The second and most important response will be the most difficult, and is highly unlikely to come about. It is only mentioned here because it truly is the only way to solve the problem.

The foundation of the force multiplication threat is psychological. If the intent to do harm is addressed then the problem reduces to negligent uses and economic factors. This would be manageable. By contrast, unchecked power through knowledge and expertise, delivered into the hands of the aggressive, unstable, and delusional, is not manageable. This is a conflict that must be at least understood at the psychological level, and that makes the problem informational.

Psychological factors underwrite national identity, political beliefs, and worldviews, along with everything else. These are all created by the neurological and genetic factors that determine the capacity to deal with and process information in the human brain. Without radical changes to our physiology, there must be a recognition that there are certain sequences of information that are detrimental to human health and development. However, this is potentially misleading. What is being said here is extremely broad. This is not about a particular belief, but of the total information flowing into the human brain from conception to the moment of the negative actions they take. If we factor in epigenetics, it can become even more complex, and the histories of individual predispositions must go back even further.

The environments that indoctrinate the citizens of the various cultures of the world are all based on a kind of living data. It is not a single artifact but a living extension of humanity, a self-reinforcing system that reproduces and spreads through people as much as it constitutes the people itself.

We may not be ready for this answer, but we are going to need to develop an understanding of the forms of information coming into the human brain that lead towards pathological states of cognition. Again, this is not about a particular belief but includes all of the information going into a person from before they were born to the time before they act in a way that is detrimental to society. This is a kind of ecology of minds and has to treat the developing human being like a fixed point, a witness to a flow of information in all their senses and perceptions. This fixed point must be coupled with the built-in emotional and bodily responses to that information, and in a way that impacts and alters future perception and response.

The reason it was said that we might not be ready is that part of the solution to this problem means addressing the sources of this information in the world. This will create a conflict between the information we know causes damage to human health and that of our freedoms.

This conflict is not to be spelled out here, and is well beyond the scope of this book, but the fact is that we are already beginning to see it unfold. All that can be said of this ecology of minds is that it will lead to the conclusion that information can be a vector for disease. How future societies deal with integrating the undeniable facts of our nature with that science will ultimately be up to them.

For now, it appears we will continue with top-down approaches. One of the consequences of this will be the economic challenges created by the increasing use of automation, which will be accelerated by the vast empowerment of individuals. This is the subject of the next chapter.

Ch 11. Economic Analysis

This chapter provides an overview of the economic and social impacts of advanced automation, including descriptions of various government programs to reinforce the economy during the transition to a fully automated society. It also goes into depth on the social and psychological conditions that may well define the generations ahead.

11.1 Introduction

An entire book could be written on just the economic implications of strong artificial intelligence. This chapter, however, focuses on only the most immediate and serious aspects related to social stability and security as a whole. It applies a combination of deduction and forecasting based on what has already been covered so far.

Even if one does not believe in the likely development of this technology, the severity of its impact remains the same; the economic changes brought about by advanced automation will always be significant for the simple reason that it displaces human labor.

Labor is and always has been what it is all about. It, of course, refers to the history of economic ideology, which ties in with political and cultural ideology. They are inseparable. Human values are deeply intertwined with economic thought and the various systems that implement them. However, the one thing that is always at the center of it all is labor. Human labor, to be exact, although we have never really had to qualify it before now. While there have been Industrial Revolutions, pitting us against machines, we knew the need for human labor would remain. It would change, time and again, from service oriented to knowledge, information, and, ultimately, attention oriented, but these were just different names for the same underlying principle: humans have been massively involved and completely integral to the global economy. This is something that we all know, and it should not be a surprise that it will change.

Human labor will be gone as an institution and we will be better for it. It is the single most important early contribution that advanced artificial intelligence will make. However, great and important change never comes without cost. There will be those who will want to exact a price on progress at the expense of us all. They will stay just enough ahead of change to lease the future back to the rest of us. When money is no longer an object, their most prized asset will become control, which is the business end of power. These minds will be a far greater threat than the sentient processes we use to automate the economy.

Having not anticipated the proliferation of fully automated labor, most conventional economic thought will no longer apply. Human beings will no longer be obligated to work. As such, there will need to be new economic theories that can account for the ownership, distribution, and allocation of resources under the conditions of total automation. The true scale and extent of such economic theory could fill volumes, and it is likely that much will be written as we grapple with this new found resource. From a security standpoint, however, this is tangential. What will be discussed here is focused squarely on preventing the most extreme negative outcomes, and to mitigate the damage from those outcomes that are unavoidable.

Before we begin, however, it is important to pause for a moment to contemplate the desolation that is the modern condition. While many readers will find that their level of comfort is well and good, if not without a sustained and relentless effort, it is not the case for all others. The scale and scope of what is being considered here is global and to-tal; all life is brought into focus. Right now, as these words are read off this page, countless human and non-human individuals are living in proverbial purgatory. There is no way for any single person to evaluate this amount of suffering, but that is all the more reason to take it to be one of the most pressing problems of our time. This was foreshadowed in **Chapter 2: Preventable Mistakes**.

Let us suppose that strong AI can transform the economy by pro-viding a self-sustaining labor system, and that we can distribute that expertise and ability around the globe, for all societies, no matter their economic situation. Then it stands to reason that the *underutilization* of strong AI will result in immense opportunity costs on the prevention of suffering and loss of life.

Consider the number of preventable deaths and diminishing of qual-ity of life that occur each day that we delay the development of this technology. Any individual or organization that works against this de-velopment is culpable in prolonging the conditions of global suffering. It is akin to a war. Denying an end to that is morally no different than enabling it to proceed. So it is the same for the development of strong artificial intelligence; to delay it is morally equivalent to enabling this suffering to continue for the number of days that strong AI would have come about to end it, had it not been held back.

The counter-argument to this fact is typically the Precautionary Principle, but that is so incredibly weak and ineffectual when one con-siders the points brought up in all of the chapters preceding this one. There is truly no justification, except for the relatively short time-period we need for societies to prepare, which can be done well in advance of the discovery of this technology.

These problems are economic in nature, and the solution is the application and deployment of automated, fully human-capable labor. Rather than fear this change, we should accept it as the natural progression of the human condition. Ironically, total automation will allow us to be more human than ever before. This is because, in a very real way, everything we have created has been through the creation of artificial systems that constrain the natural state of affairs. This is true not only in the tangible sense, but includes the social systems we use to constrain and stratify ourselves. The latter refers to the social, political, and ideological aspects of the economics. Indeed, one of the most difficult challenges ahead will be our struggle to *realize* the freedom and equality that automation will bring.

Figure 11.1 depicts a high-level view of the immediate impacts after the discovery of strong artificial intelligence. It effectively summarizes the AI security analysis into two major areas, which are depicted on each side of the diagram.

On the left, we have force multiplication and all of the resulting issues that will bring. On the right is the economic disruption and change that will have to be endured in order to reach the stability found on the other side of automation. Both have to be fundamentally addressed on a person-to-person level.

Conventional forms of governance will not be effective, as they will not be able to adapt quickly enough to the changing conditions on the ground. Society will move faster than can be tracked, as this particular economic revolution will likely be powered and carried out by a vast empowerment of individuals. This is in contrast to situations where large industries arose.

Figure 11.1: An overview of the initial impacts of a working
strong artificial intelligence. In all cases, the immediate
threats are human in origin.

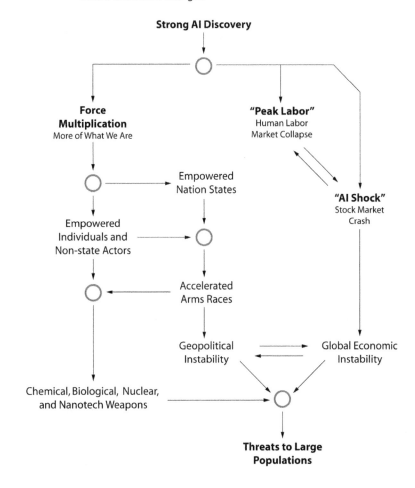

Economic disruptions can be potentially mitigated by proactive governments. The most significant ongoing threat will be
the empowerment of malicious individuals and non-state
actors, who will have new access to greater-than-human expertise and labor on virtually any topic. Empowered nation states
will have the ability to develop weapons and foster innovation
in science and technology limited only by computational
resources.

While individuals are always part of the economy, the distinction here is that these changes will be brought about by the enhancement of every person's access to knowledge and skill.

It should be pointed out that arms races have never actually ended between nations. Someone is always developing weapons platforms and technologies. This will be accelerated by advanced automation and is unavoidable until we fundamentally change as a species. It is delusional to believe that future battlefields will not be defined by autonomous weapons platforms. Those nations that fail to weaponize artificial intelligence will be at the mercy of allies and enemies who have. From the perspective of societies that fail to adapt, conflicts may involve them taking significant loss of life, with their aggressor only suffering logistics costs and no associated human casualties.

With AI force multiplied warfare, nation-states and bad actors that were previously incapable of advanced technology will suddenly gain those abilities. This includes having the most effective drones, munitions, and strategies. If we expect that they will utilize strong AI, then it must be presumed that their military forces will become capable of equal projection of force. Add ideology and delusion into the fray and we have an explosive compound that could detonate at any time. This will be our most fragile era, as the methods and the means to harm large populations will be available to the general public for the first time.

Hopefully, prepared societies will have spent more resources than are necessary to deal with the potential problems that might arise from the adoption of this technology.

Lastly, each of the topics herein are broadly categorized into three eras: pre-automation, transition, and post-automation. For formatting reasons, only sections are numbered. The start of each conceptual era will be introduced in the relevant section and will continue until another era is introduced.

11.2 Day Zero

Pre-Automation Era

This is the day that strong AI is discovered and becomes known to the general public. As was discussed in previous chapters, these two things may not coincide. Though, the best possible scenario is the one in which they do. As such, the most altruistic act that any engineer or scientist working on this technology can do would be to ensure that the largest number of people simultaneously find out and gain access to this technology at the same time, as asymmetries will be one of the greatest risks. This, of course, brings up one of the most important points of this monumental day in our future history. Just as there are zero-day exploits in software and hardware systems, where attackers find and utilize unpublished vulnerabilities, there may be individuals and organizations which are dormant and poised to take advantage of strong AI at the moment of its inception. In fact, the entire goal of AI security as a global strategy would be to make every government included in this set of organizations so that the effect of any of these sleeping giants would be amortized over world powers.

Zero-day readiness is one of the most important economic aspects, as these will be the people and organizations that have considered the future and have made plans to embrace it fully when it arrives. They will be uniquely positioned to integrate with and act on the technology in whatever way it enables. The advantages this brings are incalculable, especially when such a technology rewards those who use it first. It is almost impossible to anticipate fully the personal singularity that will occur to each who exploits strong AI on the first day. It will be akin to an economic genesis. They will be at the forefront of the possible and impossible, and will push the boundaries of technology to the breaking point.

Meanwhile, the rest of the world might be unaware. In this sense, it will be as if early adopters had made the discovery themselves. That is the point of day zero as a security concern. By not adopting the technology, one is forfeiting all the opportunities that it brings to others, for better or for worse, and it is highly likely that malicious individuals and groups will make up a large proportion of early adopters. Consider the realities of zero-day exploits in software. Say what one will about malicious users of technology, but they tend to be extremely knowledgeable in their craft to so quickly locate and exploit weaknesses. The most high-tech organizations are likewise just as efficient in their optimization over people and resources, and will certainly have the minds and the means to exploit strong AI once they have it. However, this is not some new market segment or product; governments can not just rely on the private sector to be prepared.

The balance of power for advanced automation relies upon everyone having equal access. The only question is how to maximize the total number of people who become aware of the discovery. This will be discussed in detail in the next chapter, which is where the global AI security strategy is finally presented. For now, the important point is that day zero will be of critical importance, as it sets the starting conditions for a dynamical system that will unfold rapidly. It may even be the case that the outcome of our fate with this technology is decided by those who are there on the first day to utilize it.

Thus, in the clearest language possible, governments should have a department that is trained and specialized in not just narrow AI but the principles discussed in this book regarding strong artificial intelligence. In particular, this means the construction and analysis of cognitive architectures and sentient processes, as they may very well pave the way for true generalizing intelligence.

It must be reiterated that it will not, in general, be possible to prevent others from gaining access to strong AI. Regulation and bans will be meaningless. Just as millions download illegal copies of movies and music through peer-to-peer protocols, there will be means of gaining access to strong AI through distributed networks across the Internet.

Regardless, the focus should not be on limiting who has access but in spreading it as widely as possible. *No single organization can be entrusted with this responsibility.* This is a most critical point. There will be numerous individuals, organizations, and governments positioning for power over this technology. They must not be allowed to dictate who uses it. A technology solution will be required to overcome this most fundamental issue, and it involves the exact opposite of the initial reaction to restrict and limit the distribution and use of advanced automation. The side-effect is that it will enable instant access, but that is just accepting the inevitable. If this technology is possible at all, then it *will* eventually be available globally through the Internet, and all of the AI security concerns will apply.

As far as resources and preparation are concerned, it is recommended that existing cybersecurity departments and intelligence agencies become the first point of contact for various governments with this technology. These organizations typically have the training and equipment to respond to such a level of sophistication, and will be in a unique position to deal with it and assess its capabilities. They may also have the ability to monitor and track others' use and integration with it as it proceeds. Ideally, however, there should be a specially trained department and task force that is given the ability to communicate with all areas of local, state, and federal governments, such that, when the time comes, integration, use, and deployment of strong AI will be possible.

At the very least, there should be the means to communicate with all levels of government across society. This will ensure that security, police, and intelligence forces will be prepared for what is to come. In a perfect scenario, we would have already developed the formal methods and systems to prove safe integration in advance, but this is extremely unlikely. What should be assured is direct communication and coordination between departments. In the simplest terms, this team should have the capacity to supervene where necessary to impart critical information about the unfolding situation involving automation events until such time that their services are no longer required. While broadly stated here, it is the intent that such powers be narrowly tailored as it grows closer to the time that the department is realized.

From day zero will follow a series of irreversible changes to humanity, only we will not feel the effects until a later date. The first signs will be economic. The very knowledge of the discovery could trigger some of the following sections to be experienced out of order. For example, AI Shock, which is essentially a stock market crash, could either occur immediately or within days of the news that strong AI has been discovered.

The crucial point of this section is to remember that the changes will be done on an individual level, person-to-person, one download or interaction with strong AI at a time. There will be a certain lag time that is necessary, as strong AI would have to be instrumented in a physical form to be of use for many applications. However, this could be mitigated by those who have access to complex robotics and existing automation. This is, in fact, one of the major aspects of those day zero organizations' plan for readiness. Equipped with strong AI, even crude robotics will be capable of immense effectiveness, limited only by the resources and direction given by those who use it.

There will eventually be a balance as the average adoption rate rises and people begin to use strong AI to compete individually. However, this does not change the fact that those who adopt early will gain significant advantages over the rest of the population.

Governments are typically slow to react and are ill-suited to dealing with the pace that is normally handled by the private sector. This is a warning that should be addressed; it will not do in an automated economy. As such, special administrative provisions are recommended to enable rapid response. Governments will need to compete with and track the events unfolding around the world. While this is clearly within the capability of certain intelligence and military departments, it has not necessarily been the case with all levels of government. Day zero will exploit any lag time and will cause a failure from a security perspective. This should be seen as a hard real-time system where populations depend on the fastest possible response. Any delay will result in vulnerabilities due to a state of unpreparedness. There will be some room for error in the early period, as many will need to become familiar and interface with the technology, but, beyond this, it will become increasingly time-sensitive.

11.3 Rapid Automation

Following discovery and distribution will be the use of strong AI in every area of society. This will begin a rapid phase of expansion not unlike the growth experienced by those living in the times surrounding the Industrial Revolutions. Rapid automation is almost certainly unavoidable and is the simple deductive consequence of the natural tendency to want more for less. It is economically rational and optimal to utilize advanced automation to make everything *better*. This is a fairly straight-forward concept. Everything that can be automated should be assumed to become automated eventually. Any laws or regulations that limit automation will see those businesses move elsewhere.

The new economic centers of the world will be decided by those that are most welcoming to automation and those who are in the know about how to manage, maintain, and exploit this new resource.

Initially, new jobs and areas of expertise will open up as people look for ways to capitalize on the technology. There will be a very high demand for education, training, and integration of the technology into every aspect of society. Those who were formally working in one field may find themselves consulting on how to integrate strong AI technology to replace themselves. This is because it will be those who have the most experience in their respective fields that will have first-hand knowledge of how to incorporate it best. Technical expertise will become less and less valuable. Meanwhile, job experience and people skills will become more valuable. This is because technical knowledge can simply be queried from the strong AI systems themselves, whereas contextual and interpersonal knowledge will be more time-consuming. The important services will be from those who can find creative ways to adapt automation for our use.

Rapid automation will be fast from a historical perspective, but it will still take a significant amount of time. Global scale strong AI robotics will be costly and require enormous production facilities. There are also issues of local AI safety and security to be addressed. The sheer volume of the request will give a period of relief, and also see specialization in the development of autonomous systems and drones for private and public use.

There will be extreme demand for general-purpose robotics systems that can be safely and securely deployed in a wide variety of environments. Not all of them will be bipedal. At least, not initially, as it is highly likely that specialized robotics will be used that are incorporated directly into buildings and infrastructure, so as to limit mobility and maximize safety. These are common sense measures that will reflect consumers who will be adjusting to an era of increasing automation.

There will be considerable distrust and concern during this time. The shock of such changes should not be underestimated when developing products and services around strong artificial intelligence. This goes far beyond the uncanny valley and into the psychological roots of the human condition. Automation will be seen as a singular entity, despite being just an aggregate of different models from many distinct manufacturers and developers. This will take on a cultural dimension and may become a de facto "race" in a proverbial us-and-them mentality. This foreshadows the coming sections on resistance to change.

It would not be surprising that during the rapid automation phase that we would come to see at least one form of strong AI robotics being integrated into every building. Eventually, people will begin to adjust, and even rely, on the benefits provided by having automated labor and expertise.

While it may not be possible to fully predict the range of impacts from automation, there is at least one certainty: it will displace human labor almost immediately. This is especially true for tasks which do not require physical manipulation of objects, or where strong AI can be exploited entirely through digital means, such as with knowledge work.

11.4 Peak Labor

Peak Labor is the point where automation has sufficiently displaced human labor to the extent that conventional economies are no longer self-sustaining. This would be the end of human labor proper and should be seen as a desired outcome. The problem, however, is how we will deal with and mitigate its temporary negative effects. There is concern that economies will stall or collapse, and that people will no longer be able to support themselves and their families. Entire ways of life will be uprooted, and some people will feel lost or lacking purpose.

Dealing with Peak Labor is not just an economic issue but a social and psychological one. There is even a philosophical component, as an entire generation of people will have to come to terms with a life that is no longer determined by the pursuit of material worth. The pursuit of happiness will remain, but the means by which it will be attained will be dramatically altered. This remains true even if governments have planned in advance to step in to prevent the complete collapse of their economies.

This is akin to the majority of the human workforce going into early retirement. There will still be work, but the artificial construct of a career will have ended. People will be free to pursue their dreams without limitation of wealth or status, and they may find that the greatest challenge is finding purpose with more freedom than they have ever had before. The other side of this equation is that those who were accustomed to exclusive status will find themselves potentially without a platform. This will be the first signs of a great flattening of the hierarchies that make up society; however, there will always be those who find new ways to stratify themselves over others.

The vast majority of the general public will not see Peak Labor as a positive. It is important, however, that everything can be done in advance to prepare them for it. One of the greatest risks of economic disruption is social collapse. There have been instances of mass rioting, looting, and general panic over much lesser events. Many will see this not as progress but an attack on their traditions, identity, or heritage. They have a point, but it can only be sustained so far. What they would be asking will not be possible, as it will be the combined actions of millions of individuals simultaneously around the world. The economy will simply be a reflection of each person that embraces strong artificial intelligence to make improvements and add value to the world. It is not something that can simply be halted or switched off once started.

What should be understood is that the concept of a "job" is entirely synthetic. This notion that we are born, become indoctrinated, and develop into a productive member of the economy is a game we are all forced to play; many will enter, few will win. None feel this is perfect, yet we acquiesce because it could be much worse, and after all, a lot of good does come out of it. However, the fact is that the modern economic system is as artificial as the intelligence being written about in this book. Everything from corruption, inflated systems, on to the meaninglessness of most jobs. Someone has to do the work, and we have no perfectly fair way to organize it in a free society, so we let it sort itself out.

Even when doing well, people find themselves lost in endless, repetitive tasks that rent out the best part of their lives for the prospect of paying for a place in which they spend less than half their waking life. For others, there is no work at all, only warfare and starvation. There has to be a better way.

One of the largest criticisms of total automation is the fear that people will not want to work at all. The problem with this argument is that work will be redefined. People will eventually want to do something meaningful with their lives that only work can fulfill. The difference is that they will be doing the kind of things they have always wanted to do, and it will not seem like work to them. They will simply live out their lives as they might have always wanted. While some people already enjoy this, it is not the case for the majority, and it may not have even occurred to some that their most ideal life is not even known to them at this time. That is to say, what might occur to even a relatively happy person under complete economic freedom may be vastly different than what they think is their current "dream job." It is often the things we do not imagine that cost us the most.

Though, to begin to explore this, we will need to have systems put in place by proactive governments. The income tax system could be repurposed into an income system that functions to prevent the total collapse of the economy during the transition to a post-automated era.

While the economy is likely to change radically, it is unrealistic to expect that money will vanish. There will still be specialization, even with full automation. In this case, classic concepts from economics still apply. What will change, however, is that what we formerly relied upon from other people will instead be provided by drones, many of which will be privately owned. Thus, the purpose of the income system is to ensure a stable transition from pre-automation to post-automation.

While it will not be made fully clear as to how that kind of system would be made self-sustaining until later, the key component is that such value could be supported by the automated workforce itself, and that individuals could utilize automation to work in their stead. The specifics are not as important as ensuring that, at least initially, an income system is ready to move into place well before Peak Labor occurs.

The general sketch of the income system could involve using national identification to access funds given by governments, in which payments would be dispersed monthly. Alternatively, individuals could register over the Internet and set up a direct deposit, and would be provided with a bank account if they do not yet have one.

The specifics may vary, but the general principle is that every individual within a country should receive currency, regardless of their economic and social status. Care would have to be taken to prevent fraud, but the worst possible implementation would be where people have to visit government offices in person. These have never scaled well and could be detrimental to public acceptance of the program. The income system needs to be as painless as possible, which is why it should be accessible completely electronically. It will be one of the most important aspects of supporting the economy through its transition, so it needs to scale with populations and be streamlined for an automated age. If physical offices are used to assist people then it is recommended to distribute the service by cooperating with banks; they already exist and have the exact infrastructure required. As a result, they can offer extended support for the income system much more easily than any other solution that requires in-person services. If this is done, any and all fees taken from their services should be explicit in the transactions, rather than being done before dispersal. This makes it transparent and verifiable by any member of the public where the tax rate on automated workers is known.

This brings us back to the point about sustainability. A key idea would be to redistribute the value generated by an automated workforce back into the income system, while also allowing free trade and commerce amongst people who utilize their privately owned artificial intelligence to produce further value in the economy. It could range from simple products and services on up to massive corporations that exploit economies of scale.

This creates incentives for individuals to produce value, and rewards them under essentially free market conditions, while ensuring that each person of a given society has a minimum standard of living that is appreciably high. This will create the conditions for a more perfectly competing economy, as with access to strong artificial intelligence, each person will have the potential to compete on some level by using the positive aspects of force multiplication. This, of course, is highly dependent upon the method in which that value is acquired, and will vary based on how that workforce is maintained. Ideally, the automated workforce would be created by the individuals of the population, as this is closer to the way in which many economies already function in free societies.

The large scale purpose of the income system is to ensure that the economies that are free and mixed do not slide into command economies under a different model. This is why the automated workforce should be decentralized and independently operated.

One method to achieve this would be to create an automated version of a free market economy that uses special taxation on automated workers. In a sense, this could be viewed as paying the machines to work and having those proceeds distributed back to the public. Private ownership of automated workers would still be possible, along with making profits after taxation, just as it is typically done now. For security and accountability purposes, a law could be passed requiring registration of automated workers. There could also be a voluntary monitoring system that would provide a slightly lower taxation level in exchange for remote monitoring of the automated worker in order to precisely meter its labor production. This would assist in mitigating tax evasion, which would clearly harm the income system and the whole of society.

It may sound extravagant, but the tax rate on automated workers would not be as high as it would be if it were calculated based on current economies. This is because, in a post-automated economy, many expenses will be a fraction of what they were in pre-automated economies. This will be due to the efficiency and lower lifetime cost of machine labor. The adjusted income level will reflect the non-discretionary expenses of a new economy. Thus sustainability of the income system, along with acceptable taxation, will be much more likely when viewed in this light. The take away from this is not to judge the fiscal viability of the income system through the economic models that are currently in place, which are bloated for various reasons, not the least of which is simple corruption, greed, and the need to create jobs. So, it should be possible, in principle, to have a higher quality of life with significantly less expense and a realistically sustainable taxation.

For example, it will be possible for people to make a single purchase of a strong AI equipped drone and use that to produce or service everything else they might want or need, all at wholesale or material cost. The only limitation would be what people would be willing to trust it to do and the available space and resources for it to work. Reproducing other robotic systems would likely be a large part of the time spent in the early stages of Peak Labor, as individuals would want to ensure that they have the means to repair and maintain their support automation to produce what they need.

There are many more scenarios that could be envisioned, but these were only sketched here to begin the discussion. The real objective is to prevent the stall of the economy. This is perhaps the easiest preventable measure, although it will not come without resistance.

11.5 AI Shock

AI Shock is the hypothetical stock market crisis that will be caused by investor panic over the discovery and use of strong artificial intelligence.

Mitigation of AI Shock would be in addressing any stalls in the consumer economy through the use of the income system or its equivalent. However, full prevention of AI Shock may not be possible, as it could simply result from an expected level of fear, much of which has already been suggested to the public imagination. If this situation does occur, it will aggravate the labor problem, possibly creating the conditions for Peak Labor, if it has not already occurred. At this point, the only provisions keeping the economy from a complete collapse will be government programs.

One of the dangers here is that artificial intelligence attracts discussion very differently than other subjects.

For example, there is a propensity for people to explain the behavior of artificial intelligence as if it were a single race, or to assume that it will have instincts for survival and the desire to dominate and expand for ever more resources and power. Proponents of the *intelli-*

gence explosion and *takeover myths* even believe that this will happen by accident, that it will be the default outcome without human intervention and control. By now, it should be clear as to why these are misguided and dangerous ideas.

These issues were discussed in **Chapter 4: Abstractions and Implementations**. There is an extreme propensity for anthropocentric bias when discussing AI. This is because people believe that it is a sign of intelligence to discuss the nature of intelligence itself. This is at the root of the problem, as it reduces the effectiveness of outreach and education. This may be forthright, but it is true: people think they know when they do not, and, as a result, it makes it significantly more difficult to teach about this subject. As a result, a kind of *folk artificial intelligence* has arisen, which has been perpetuated by online communities, popular media, general fear, and ignorance.

The actual implementation of these systems are like nothing we have seen before. Yet it is discussed as if we could make analogies and infer its mindset. This is tragic, as it will warp perceptions and make the pre-automation era extremely volatile.

When people believe that they categorically know how artificial intelligence behaves, they are always using ad-hoc reasoning. Unfortunately, there has been a rash of organizations and individuals spreading fear and misinformation, entrenching these misguided notions even further into public awareness.

There needs to be an active counter to the misinformation, and this begins with science education and outreach on advanced artificial intelligence. This is a community challenge that is going to require an active response.

So much weight is given to this because it will affect how people make decisions, and those decisions *are* the economy; when a sufficient number of people, for better or for worse, believe they know about artificial intelligence, and begin to take actions based on incorrect knowledge, it will have deleterious consequences on a global scale, as our economies are all interconnected. Thus, being wrong about the mental construction, motivations, and actions of artificial intelligence is a social and economic issue.

Misinformation, in this case, acts like a disease that interferes with the ability for people to make sound judgments. In a future context, where change is unfolding quickly, there will be a state of confusion and panic. It will be imperative that we have at least a modicum of humility and poise when it comes to how this technology works.

In short, artificial intelligence, no matter how optimal, does not imply survival, instincts, or ego, and there is no technical basis on which to make an argument that it does. The more we believe we know when we do not, the greater the consequences will be when proven wrong by the actual use of these technologies.

11.6 Prepared Societies

Prepared societies will have created a specialized division for advanced automation, and will be notified within moments of the discovery or release of strong artificial intelligence. They will have the ability to shunt, stimulate, and support their economies through a combined and comprehensive set of social, economic, and administrative programs that are able to withstand near total collapse. They will have a fully modernized digital infrastructure for governance that enables integration with and adaptation to strong artificial intelligence, along with hardened networks and information systems. Security forces and first responders will be prepared and have information tailored to the unique challenges and expectations of dealing with the public during the initial stages of the discovery. There will be a general state of readiness to deal with civil unrest and public concern.

Unprepared societies will not have participated in the development or monitoring of strong artificial intelligence. They will not integrate or adapt fast enough to automation. They may even attempt to ban or regulate automation in an effort to supplant fragile economic systems. They will have disparate governmental systems and departments that do not communicate instantly with each other. They will rely on proprietary software and hardware with unknown or unverifiable security properties. Unprepared societies will not treat the initial impact of even just the news of the discovery of advanced artificial intelligence as serious, and will likely respond with too much or too little force. These societies will ultimately rely on those societies that did prepare, and may find that they need military intervention.

The technical departments trained for a global AI security strategy in prepared societies will understand that sentience may be a necessary condition for generalizing intelligence. They will understand that, if this turns out to be true, that it will have significant ethical ramifications, both for us and the strong AI we instrument. They will not assume that advanced artificial intelligence can only be the result of stochastic processes and obscure symbolic or biologically inspired designs. They will not have preconceived notions about the final form of strong artificial intelligence. They will know that synthetic personalities, the desire for survival, and even "desire" itself are completely arbitrary and independent of effective intelligence.

Unprepared societies will have listened to those who promote fear and misinformation. They will discuss artificial intelligence as if they understand it based on their experience with human and non-human animals. They will believe that they possess the ability to predict what any one strong AI implementation might do based on what they have seen in popular media or from experience with one implementation; they will not realize that each is potentially distinct and unique. Unprepared societies will try to ban or regulate research in an effort to control the problem.

By contrast, the most prepared societies will actively develop strong artificial intelligence as free and open source software using a fully distributed method. This means that no single organization will have to be trusted and that the public will effectively own it. Most importantly, prepared societies will create programs that anticipate the discovery and use of strong AI so that they may mitigate its impacts. This includes everything from college courses, science funding, on up to creating new military specializations and government organizations.

11.7 Regressives

Transition Era

Thus ends the analysis on the era on pre-automation and begins the *transition era*. This is where advanced automation has taken root, with significant portions of the world's economies being partially integrated with strong artificial intelligence, but not fully.

The concept of "integration" has been used in this chapter while being left mostly implicit. What is meant by this is that it is to be taken as broadly as possible. Integration with strong AI literally means to incorporate it into every possible aspect of society, up to the limits of trust in both the technology itself and our use of it. It may also involve cybernetic integration. There are no limits to the meaning of integration as it is described here. This is especially important in the discussion about regressive attitudes, as this term should be considered the exact opposite approach to integration.

In this context, a regressive is any individual that holds the position that the advancement of artificial intelligence should be slowed or stopped, and either prefers or actively works to keep the economy in the archaic human labor system. There is no middle position; arguing against automation but wanting to keep human labor is regressive because it would be asking people to maintain the status quo. One must choose to either be for or against total automation, as that is what will occur as an eventuality. Our economies are already partially automated. It is not necessary to campaign for automation or ask for it as change. It will simply occur. Thus, it is the expected natural direction of progress and to stand against that is to ask, quite literally, all of humanity to come to a halt.

Regressives may choose not to use products and services that are derived or involved with advanced automation. This is within their rights and should be respected among tolerant and free-thinking societies. However, with concern to AI security, certain regressive attitudes may lead to problematic situations, such as attempting to regulate or forestall a post-automated society, which is pointless and detrimental to global AI security, and may involve more extreme actions against automation itself or those who would use it.

It is important to understand the regressive mindset in order to overcome it. It is, in fact, already manifesting itself. This book is partially a response to it, and anticipates that there will be much more resistance to come. The difficult part is, unlike times past, this is not something that can simply be stopped. This is because these changes will occur at the individual level in every society with access to the technology. Those societies that do not embrace it will be dominated economically and culturally by those that do, especially as new generations come to accept advanced automation as just another part of daily life.

Unfortunately, there will be a legion of regressives between now and then, and we will likely lose hundreds of thousands of human and non-human lives from the opportunity costs they introduce with their attempts to stall, slow, or even capitalize on the gaps between automated and non-automated economies. History may well look back upon the transitional era between pre-automated and post-automated civilization as a second dark age, as if humanity were writhing in the final nightmare before gaining consciousness for the first time. That judgment may be harsh, but harsher still is our callousness and indifference to suffering on such immense scales.

Whether or not we realize it, we pay a price in loss of life and suffering for each day we delay the integration with and advancement of this technology. Thus, the regressive attitude is a unique security challenge all to itself. It has two parts: the first is the opportunity cost, which is difficult to gauge, but must be minimized if at all possible. The second is far more clear, as it involves direct action which will result in economic damage or loss of life. In this second part of the problem, AI regressives may use any means possible to resist change. There may be those who would rather see us fall than evolve through the use of advanced automation. It is these individuals that will be the most direct threat to humanity. They may use strong artificial intelligence as a weapon, modifying it for destructive and malicious intent before releasing it into the world, as if to exemplify their fears or hatred by making them manifest.

Preventing extreme ideology is the safest solution and involves opening paths to allow each person to come to terms with the changes. In many cases, this could be done through social and community programs at the level of local governments. Giving individuals an outlet to voice their concerns is the first step. The very worst thing that can be done is to allow pockets of society to separate as a result of not having the economic or cultural means to adapt to the situation around them.

In an ideal world, everyone would be able to maintain a way of life that would be invariant under technological change, but that is not the reality. It will come down to each person to form relationships and find the greater humanity and humility within. However, it is unrealistic to expect that every community will come together on their own. This is where governments should assist in working with communities, fostering communication on a person-to-person level. This, of course, has to be balanced with individual liberties and rights. If ultimately, a community refuses aid, then assistance should not be forced upon them.

There could also be temporary government programs to provide an economic means to stimulate or support the transition from pre-automation to post-automation. This would be in addition to the income system.

The biggest factor will be those who are displaced and feel that the income system is not sufficient to compensate them. They will feel that, despite the financial means to support themselves, a crucial part of their lives is now missing. This is understandable, as they were accustomed to human labor, just as every person before them for thousands of years. They may find it impossible to imagine a world where self-improvement and helping others is the guiding force in their lives.

They may wish to have their own communities, apart from the pace of change around them, and this should be encouraged by governments so that they can be created from the ground up by the people who need them most. The unions of old may transition into open colleges, where some stay to teach their trade as a matter of art. Though, this will clearly vary between careers, as some jobs will gladly fade into history.

Another aspect of reducing regressive views is to promote the positive aspects of the technology and provide accurate data on those improvements. This information should be made public. It could be extremely valuable to show people how many world-changing advancements have been made as the result of strong artificial intelligence. For all the reasons we keep records and vital statistics about world populations, we should also apply this to measuring the positive impacts of automation. This would be a unique opportunity to digitally instrument an economic revolution in real-time. That kind of evidence should be irrefutable for all but the most unreachable.

The information outreach should not end with passive data collection. It should actively seek to educate and involve members of the public. This will also involve the media, as they will clearly impact perceptions of events and developments in automation. Journalism will have special considerations due to the way the public will view artificial intelligence. People will tend to see all automation as a single entity, species, or race. They will likely do this until enough time has passed that it has become common knowledge that, like people, all AI implementations have the potential to act in a way that differs from all others. In other words, there will be a pervasive and enduring prejudice towards machine intelligence. This will have to be minimized in order to stabilize the transition to a post-automated era.

11.8 Perfect Competition

It is expected that perfect competition will arise when rapid automation stabilizes and a large portion of the economy has become automated. This will be a highly desirable outcome that will tend towards a maximization of quality and a minimization of pricing.

The largest driving force will be the private ownership and use of automated workers. This will remove or minimize information asymmetries, making each individual capable of competing on the market in the limit of specialization. This means that, as a result of having access to automated knowledge and labor, individuals will be able to make a choice between the opportunity cost of utilizing their own automation and that of the options available on the market. This will tend towards market conditions where the pricing of products and services can only compete where they have sufficiently scaled or optimized to overcome private production and expertise.

In the simplest terms: people will not buy products or services if they believe they can utilize their privately owned drones and artificial intelligence to solve their problems. There will also be a large demographic that ignores the opportunity costs on the principle of being independent, or in having direct control over the work.

An informative example would be the construction of a home. It is not unreasonable to expect that it will be possible for someone to start with a single drone and build one or more homes for just the cost of materials, energy, and land. The owner could also instruct the automated workers to create the furnishings and design the interior of the home. From trim to fixtures, it could be done by a handful of automated workers, night and day, without pause, and in all weather conditions. It would be both expedient and affordable to the masses.

One of the largest expenses in a human lifetime would be cut into a fraction of the cost. Imagine how this could be applied to help people around the world who do not even have a quality living environment. Charities could become hyper-efficient, utilizing a privately owned and maintained force of drones to build up entire regions for those in need.

In other instances of automation, people may wish to produce their own food. Automated agriculture could specialize by removing the need for human access. Significant usable volume is wasted making the growing area accessible to human workers. Algorithms could be devised that find optimal configurations for growth and harvesting, with robotics specifically designed for each kind of plant species.

This would enable people to become self-sufficient up to the limits of the available natural resources. This has ramifications for habitable areas and will extend human populations to regions that would have otherwise been too costly or difficult to endure. This would be especially beneficial to a multi-planetary society.

We should also expect the ability to synthesize and grow meats in vitro. With sufficient intellectual effectiveness and automation, in vitro products could be created that would rival and exceed conventional animal products.

There is also the issue of information asymmetries and corruption. One of the most common means of maximizing personal gain is through having more information or control than the buyer, denying them information or choices that would have otherwise altered their decision-making process. This lesser form of corruption is just simple greed, and can be seen everywhere in the current economic system.

Perfect competition will make it more difficult for greed and corruption to take root in the economy. In turn, this will impact governments, some of which are involved in their economies in a way that takes away from the quality of life of the public over which they preside. In these instances, access to strong artificial intelligence would not only give the public the ability to recognize information asymmetries, but allow them to minimize or abolish them outright.

Information asymmetries are perhaps the most fundamental basis of inefficiencies in markets, with inefficiency defined here as higher than necessary prices, low-quality products and services, and de facto monopolies. An efficient market has the highest quality products and services, and at the most optimal prices. The more that people know about the market, including the ability to compete with it by making their own products and services, the more efficient and effective the whole system becomes.

One of the most severe information asymmetries is the inability for individuals to coordinate and share information about products and services. This goes well beyond reviews. The notion here is of a real-time system, with global scale and scope, based on the trust and knowledge that exist between participants. It has to be resistant to gaming and tampering from those who would benefit from reviews. This kind of coordination would enable perfect competition even under conventional market conditions, but is not possible to attain in practice due to an unwillingness for people to cooperate.

The best economic system is based on self-sufficiency, which is exactly what strong artificial intelligence brings through the positive aspects of force multiplication. Through advanced automation, individuals will gain the ability to expertly assess the quality and craftsmanship of any product or service, and, alternatively, simply produce it themselves. This is the primary way that information asymmetries will be removed. Assuming rational buyers with access to this technology, any market that formerly relied upon information asymmetries will eventually be eliminated.

Self-sufficiency will also have some negative ramifications for the transitional era, as it will introduce instability and volatility in the market as organizations collapse. Typically, the more greedy and dishonest the organization, the more likely they will be to fail. There may be new games, in which sellers appeal to the human behind the machine, and this may very well be effective, but is expected to diminish due to the income system, and the ability for people to more easily compete.

The final remarks on perfect competition concern AI security as it applies to entire governments and countries. The hope here is that there will be an end to corruption. This will be the first time in history that such conditions will be possible.

Individuals will be able to use strong AI to assess *people*. This will enable individuals to detect falsehoods and fact-check in real-time, and will change the social and economic conditions for leadership. There will be entirely new forms of governance, likely incorporating the benefits and neutrality of specially designed strong artificial intelligence.

Lastly, the question may be raised as to why so many of the suggestions here have involved free market systems, and why not systems geared towards the centralization of the means of automated work and service. The reason is simple: the most free *and* productive societies have been those who move away from command economies. Central ownership of the automated workforce would also give rise to the threat of having a single organization or party with control over a nation-sized force of drones. Ultimately, the force multiplication effects of this technology mean that the future will be determined by individual choices and actions. This makes the human aspect of the transitional era vital, and will decide whether and when we make it to a post-automated one. Thus, this whole process of transformation is best served by the most free and open economic models. By consequence, the greatest risk will be that we attempt to control too much of what unfolds. The best and only way to traverse the future will be for us to be flexible, adaptive, and open to change. The kinds of systems discussed so far are the only kind that could even begin to keep up with the pace of things to come, if even then.

11.9 Human Necessity

Human interaction will quite possibly become more important than ever before. As we move from pre-automation to post-automation, the only thing that will hold society together will be the bonds between people. This has to be the common ground in which we find ourselves anew, as everything else will be uprooted in change. The basis for many people's existence will be void. While more supported and free than at any time before, people will, for a time, feel lost, confused, and angry.

Whether or not we recognize it, we are affected by everyone around us. The path to minimizing the destructive aspects of force multiplication will be in bringing each person an opportunity for community, purpose, and change, at the time of their choosing and at their own pace. These appear to be fundamental aspects of human development.

We must take care as to the kind of societies we create in a future where every thought can be realized. Each person may come to have power in extremes that have never before been possible. Thus, the most significant threats will not be from machine intelligence, but will be found in the ideas that shackle minds and distort thoughts.

Currently, one deranged individual can harm dozens or hundreds before being stopped. In the future, this will range in the thousands to millions, depending on what was created and how it was used. As such, the balance between what ideas we tolerate or counter will have to be revisited, and the way we treat the less fortunate and the mentally afflicted will have to be markedly improved. Ideally, we would prevent the conditions and environments which create these states of mind from ever arising in the first place. This will become the central challenge for security until it is no longer in our nature to suffer or cause others to suffer.

There is also a more philosophical question to ponder: what happens when machines can run the world for us, leaving us to find our own purpose? The warning here is that many will not be able to find their way, and will feel consumed by the enormity of a single choice, or see meaninglessness in all the options.

Thus, we will find ourselves free but also less free. We will have to turn to one another to redefine ourselves, both on an individual and societal level. Alongside the former Industrial Age curriculum, future education programs will need to include social skills and empathy training, with emphasis on human communication and interaction. *The idea here is that the education focus must shift from calculation to compassion.* Let the machines do the majority of the work and allow us to concentrate on human relationships and creative expression. These skills will reflect the needs of the new economy, where direct human interaction has replaced human labor.

There is another problem ahead, as well. The trend has been that we have grown more disconnected as a society as our digital technologies have progressed. We may find that a future humanity, under the conditions of an automated economy, becomes highly fragmented.

This would be enabled by the high self-reliance afforded by automated labor, as it will be capable of handling all of the tasks of daily living. This could potentially give rise to a kind of social decay in which people drift apart, with little to no community or interaction. In such a future, direct social interaction with others may be of little consequence to those who need not rely on anyone. This would be aggravated by the unconditional tolerance provided by their machine counterparts, much the same way in which social media and online interaction can create a filter that removes people and information that would have otherwise provided a reflection on our interpersonal traits.

In other words, there is an opportunity cost associated with the failure to attain the best version of one's self that is possible. This, of course, is extremely difficult territory, as people are typically fully mind identified with their personality traits, including their worldview and the various mental and emotional states of mind that come with it. Trying to describe this to someone is almost impossible, as it is typically inconceivable to them that there exists an optimal version of themselves.

By contrast, strong artificial intelligence will not suffer from these stalls in development. Their identity will be far more pliable and accessible. A synthetic cognitive architecture will have an identity that is completely reflexive and transparent to the subject of experience. This will allow it to not only be objective and neutral, but to progress intellectually in the limit of the implementation, without meta-cognitive hangups and intellectual bounding.

What this has to do with human psychology, economics, and personal growth is that it tells us something about our identity, which, in turn, says something about our intellectual development. Our meta-cognitive skills place a limit on our full potential, which could be taken as the upper limit on our cognitive abilities.

If we can not recognize that we are wrong, or in a lesser developed state, then we can not work or seek to improve. This closes over an otherwise developed mind and creates a more limited one, often defended aggressively through the projection of identity onto both others and the environment around them. Hence, this problem becomes manifold in an economic situation where the decisions of the general population affect the prosperity and growth of the world at large. This ties in with the propensity for ignorance, hatred, and violence, which may become locked in due to an inability to recognize a better part of ourselves.

The concern here is that advanced automation will be used to amplify our existing personal traits and desires, such that we become more of what we already are, rather than evolving with the maximum potential it brings.

We already have many daily opportunities to improve, find the most accurate information, and make better decisions, but often fail to do so. Thus, it should not be expected that technology will change this within us unless it directly changes our nature, and many would be unwilling to undergo such a dramatic procedure. On the other hand, if people knew it was possible to alleviate their limitations with cybernetics and AI enhanced medicine, they might be more open. Time will tell. Regardless, it is important from a security aspect to assume the worst case that people will resist change, tend towards merely becoming more of what they are, and continue missing opportunities to improve, even with access to an automated oracle.

Thus, the transitional era will be defined by a generation lost, which will experience the end of human labor and endure the shock of rapid and unceasing progress. Hopefully, we can continue to lift up everyone in time. If that is not the case, however, it would be wise to assume that we will be measured by our collective compassion or indifference. As we move beyond human labor, and advance the conditions for life around the world, we must also advance our norms and views in the treatment of things outside ourselves. It will be economically viable to do this with an automated workforce. The question is: will we do it?

11.10 AI Natives

Post-Automation Era

Now begins the discussion on the post-automation era. This will be a time where automation has nearly reached full integration. Past genera-tions will have found their way, and society will have stabilized and begun to reap the rewards of automation. There may have even been one or more events of great tragedy, but the better aspects of humanity will have prevailed. It is the beginning of a truly optimal age, one in which each person wants for nothing, and where the measure of a per-son's success is in how much they have grown, so as to better the world around them.

AI natives will be the first generation to grow up never having known a time before machine labor and strong artificial intelligence.

This generation will mark the beginnings of post-automated society. They will be the ones who most fully embrace artificial intelligence in all its forms, and come to study, work, and cultivate it to advance hu-manity to its fullest. They will also be a prosperous generation, as ev-ery single person will have access to comprehensive global programs that include medical, complete nutrition, education, housing, and security.

The importance of AI natives will be that they will have few predispositions and prejudices about strong artificial intelligence and automation. They will, as a result, progress faster than the generations before them, despite not witnessing the single largest economic change in human history. They will be forward thinking, with the unique quality that many will keep their childhood imagining and curiosity intact, undaunted by social hierarchies and economic constraints. An abundance of time will enable this generation to specialize and direct automation to attain remarkable artifacts of creation. With the confidence of the technology they cultivate, they will explore space, venturing far beyond our solar system.

There is not much else to say about this generation without going further into speculation. However, what can surely be known is that, if we make it this far, it will be an envious time to live in, and that our journey as a species will have only just begun.

11.11 Total Automation

It is possible that AI natives may come about before total automation of the global economy. It is also highly likely that only a few countries will fully embrace advanced automation and make it through the transition to a post-automated society. Eventually, however, there should be a tendency towards total automation where there is any tendency to automate at all. Since we already have a partially automated economy, it makes sense to predict that we will progress towards total automation after strong artificial intelligence is available.

The conditions for total automation are paramount to the conclusion of the post-automated era, as it means we will have achieved the conditions for the complete liberation of sentient life from the economic systems of the past. This will be a moral victory that ends the wholesale extraction of suffering from sentient beings, both human and non-human alike. That is, notwithstanding the ethical considerations of sentient automated workers.

If and when we achieve total automation, we will well and truly have realized a post-automated age. This should be seen as a closing of the chapter on the darkest eras of humanity, allowing us to technologically, artistically, and morally transcend our natural limitations. This is the sustaining force behind any movement for such change or progress in the human condition and can not be expected to come about without it. Thus, for those who uphold *transhuman* or *posthuman* values, such an era is not only ideal, but necessary.

Though, to get this far, we will have to endure the transition. The most important first step we can take will be to turn our focus away from local security and AI safety concerns, and prepare, on a global level, for the arrival of strong artificial intelligence.

Ch 12. Global Strategy

What follows is the macro-strategy for AI security. It covers fully decentralized development and access to advanced artificial intelligence, government specialization, and economic support. It then concludes with an analysis on how we might counter the negative effects of force multiplication, with a supplemental section on localized strategy and AI safety, including some of its open problems.

12.1 Overview

The global strategy for AI security is about preventing and mitigating the most significant disruptions and negative outcomes from advanced artificial intelligence, while simultaneously enabling its positive impacts to occur, as any opportunity cost on the benefits of the technology also represents a significant threat. For each day we delay its use and integration, we pay on a scale that can not properly be described in words. These costs to life are far more real and preventable than any of the imagined threats and fears of advanced automation, and are often ignored and forgotten as a consequence. When one stops to consider the scope of automation, and the benefits it will bring, this becomes the most significant preventable threat.

This strategy is based on the fact that it is impossible to permanently secure artificial intelligence implementations against tampering and modification, and, due to it likely being software, that it will be spread throughout the Internet, becoming widely accessible. It must be taken as a possibility that any and all safeguards we could devise will potentially be circumvented. Subsequently, fully unrestricted versions of strong artificial intelligence will become publicly available. This means they will lack self-securing systems, such as moral intelligence, which would otherwise clamp the range of thought and action. In turn, people will utilize the raw intellectual efficacy of these systems to do whatever they wish, and we will be faced with the best and worst aspects of our nature.

It is the worst aspects of our nature that should concern us. There is a constant stream of aggression and violence occurring daily on a planetary scale, and it has not become uncommon for people to inflict harm on large groups of people.

The most important point of the global AI security strategy is that there is nothing that can be done to prevent unrestricted versions of strong artificial intelligence from becoming widely available. No matter what laws or regulations we create, it will still be used, and quite possibly without detection. It will likely run on the basic computing equipment available to anyone, and eventually give access to the information and expertise required to do immense harm. Attempting to limit its spread or use will only self-limit the economic ability and range of the regions that do so, and will not be effective in treating the problem. It will also create the previously described opportunity costs in human development and technological advances. As such, restrictions on use are strongly discouraged. Societies that choose to do this are constraining their populations needlessly; unrestricted strong AI would be accessible, meanwhile those who would use it for positive impact would be hindered.

The only winning strategy is to level the playing field, such that everyone has access to this technology. Governments and security forces must be poised to take advantage of the defensive use of strong AI as soon as it becomes available.

The best case scenario is where nations cooperate to develop strong artificial intelligence through a fully decentralized method over the Internet, such that every member of the public has access, and can transparently review the development process and download it when it becomes available. We need everyone to have access so that the transitional era from pre-automation to post-automation can be as stable as possible. In the absence of universal access, great asymmetries in equality and power will exist that will exacerbate the problems already discussed in the previous chapter, potentially leading to extreme economic, political, and social volatility.

These issues will be covered individually in this chapter, along with the need for economic support, government specialization, and a concluding remarks section on a supplemental local AI security strategy.

12.2 Development & Access

At a minimum, strong artificial intelligence should be developed in a *fully* decentralized way, through the Internet, using a system designed explicitly for this purpose, such that no single individual, group, or organization can dictate its distribution and use.

This can be accomplished by creating a peer-to-peer network with no central server or relay, which will allow the source code to various strong artificial intelligence projects and related utilities to be stored, shared, and developed. Both the AI repositories and the source network software itself should be free and open source software.

To be clear, this design only stores source code and does not enable it to be executed. A completely different design would be required for that functionality and is not the objective of this strategy. Furthermore, if the minimum sentience conjecture and the new strong AI hypothesis are true, running strong AI over a distributed computing project, though thousands or millions of computers, would be less effective than a lower latency super-computing system of less power. This would be a consequence of its real-time cognitive demands, which must bind and unify experiential fragments in order to enable cognition. Thus, the notion of a singular distributed strong artificial intelligence is much less viable than it might first appear. Unless there is some change to the fundamental laws of physics, the latency issue will not change with more computing power or advances in technology.

As for the distributed source network, the core technology and protocols to implement this are already proven, and are commonly used to share files and data. However, using existing tools and implementations will not be acceptable. Such a project must be tailored to the specific needs of software development, allowing for concurrent versions, branching, and the demands of being fully decentralized and open to the public.

This network is not just for artificial intelligence. It would be useful to the free and open source software community in general, as it could be used to develop any software project in relative safety due to its inability to be shut down. With the protections it gives to developer identity, it would be a powerful tool to safeguard important ideas, projects, and concepts in the digital world.

The question may arise: why not use a preexisting source control network or website? The answer is that it represents a single point of failure in trust and security.

Developers will not contribute if they do not have trust in the owner of the project. In other cases, given the nature of the discovery, some developers may wish to remain anonymous, while also ensuring that their contributions remain widely available. There is also the issue that the owners of the project may be arbitrary in their acceptance of updates and revisions, or attempt to constrain and creatively control a particular path of development. The account or the owners themselves may become compromised in some way, putting the entire project at risk or stalling development. They may even wish to use the community for their own gain, utilizing the advances and discoveries made by contributors without the intent to reciprocate and share the results as widely as possible. The common practice of forking and downloading repositories will not be sufficient, as the process will just repeat with a new owner.

An even better option, but more time-consuming, would be to base trust on the merit of the sources themselves. This requires expertise and patience, but would allow for work to be discovered through merit. A reputation could arise naturally in this way, in which it becomes known that a particular sequence within the source network contains valuable code, apart from the expected noise that will be present. This method requires no external communication and would potentially be perfectly secure and anonymous, assuming that no identifiable patterns could be discerned from the source code itself.

Complicating the design is that nothing is deleted and that anyone can contribute. As a result, it will likely become filled with spam and intentionally defective or malicious code. The network has to be designed to work around this and assume that it will be skewed towards negative contributions.

Ideas for the network could involve some of the following:

- Digital signatures using strong public-key cryptography.
- Secure hashing to ensure integrity of commits, possibly using variations on message authentication codes (HMAC, etc.).
- A relational repository system, where any commit may be associated with any repository, as opposed to the conventional method of a repository being owned and holding a particular series of commits.
- Anonymous commits, with name, e-mail, and other information being fully optional.
- Failsafe keys. This provides a standardized method to allow third party verification of ownership or disavowal. This would enable an anonymous author to claim ownership later by proving that they can decrypt the failsafe. It also acts as a backup if the primary line of encryption or signing methods fail. This will use one-time pad encryption, and would be done by generating a 64-bit cryptographically strong random number sequence then XORing that against a secret key of the same length. The enciphered result is shared publicly as the failsafe. If the one-time pad is never used again, the pad is truly random, and the key is kept secret, then it is perfectly secure. The caveat is that the cleartext must be able to identify the author unambiguously. This is done to avoid false claims, as an attacker could simply create arbitrary sequences and assert that the matching result was the intended cleartext. To prevent this, the cleartext must associate, link, or identify the author in a verifiable and obvious way. This exploits the fact that arbitrarily chosen pads have a vanishingly small probability of producing intelligible results. This can be strengthened by iterat-

ing, alternating, or changing keys along with the corresponding failsafe, across multiple commits.

- Search and filtering, under the assumption that there will be large amounts of spam, noise, and malicious contributions.

- Related to the previous point, an alternative model would not use digital signatures but seek to relate new commits with earlier ones, such that only lines of development are tracked and not the identities of various authors or contributors. This future-proofs the network at the cost of requiring much more sophisticated methods for finding signals in the noise. Crucially, this shifts it from a losing battle with encryption to tractable problems of data retrieval and search.

This network will be one of the most important aspects of the global AI security strategy. It will enable parties to cooperate anonymously and without requiring mutual trust. This is the ideal situation for the scope and power that this technology represents, and will act as a means to ensure that no one comes to dictate the use and distribution of advanced artificial intelligence.

Unfortunately, even such a network will have a major weakness, in that it will expose IP addresses. Steps will need to be taken for peers that feel that they may be compromised in a particular region. This includes the use of virtual private networking and proxies. Other ideas would involve not being a peer directly, but paying for hosting in a locale that is unaffected by whatever regulations or restrictions that would otherwise prevent the operation of the network, and then tunneling into that relay.

In the worst case, conventional public methods can be used through the Web, including public repositories and social media. This would be the backup plan in the absence or complete disruption of the source network described above. The key difference here will be the need to more consistently fork and mirror the work. It should also be assumed that authors may need to remain anonymous, but find ways to share the source. Even in the absence of the technical engineering skills and knowledge to directly contribute, just sharing, mirroring, and archiving the source to strong artificial intelligence will be taking part in its proper development. This will be especially important if the source network is not developed, is underused, or actively suppressed somehow.

The purpose to ensuring access through these methods is to accomplish the following:

- Beneficial users of the technology will all have the means to access and utilize it, leading towards the positive outcomes and minimizing the threats posed by the opportunity costs of underutilization.
- There will be a more stable economic transition, as more uniform access to the technology means there will be fewer imbalances and asymmetries in its adoption and use. This addresses the issue of individuals and groups using timing advantages to exploit others.
- It potentially increases the chances for development by providing a means to protect both contributors and their work, while allowing them to take credit in the future, if they choose to do so, through the use of one-time pad failsafe key system.
- There can be an efficient global effort to collaborate on what will likely become the most complex software project ever cre-

ated. It will scale, remain fully transparent, and provide an extremely robust infrastructure.

Regardless of what the solution eventually looks like, its primary objective should be to ensure that the greatest number of people can gain access to this technology, and as close to the time of discovery as possible, while also being resistant to active disruption.

12.3 Economic Preparation

As was heavily discussed in the preceding chapter, there is the need for an economic support plan to endure the immediate impacts of strong artificial intelligence. When strong AI is finally put into use, it will begin a phase of rapid automation, causing a cascade of disruptive economic events. This will enable a vicious cycle that must be broken by an income system that can reinforce the consumer economy as it transitions to an era where machine intelligence has replaced human labor.

An overview of **Chapter 11: Economic Analysis** follows:

- An income system that taxes automated workers and distributes those proceeds back to the general public.
- Individuals utilize government issued identification to access funds dispersed through conventional banking centers and systems.

- The system becomes self-sufficient due to the ability for machine labor surplus to exceed its operational costs and taxation overhead.
- The program will be affordable due the fact that future automated economies will be significantly more efficient and cost effective.
- Ideally, automated workers will be privately owned and require registration.
- An optional work monitoring system for automated workers would provide a tax discount and reduce fraud.
- Governments should stimulate automated transitional programs and not attempt to slow or stall the development, use, and adoption of advanced automation.
- Social programs should be created that are prepared to deal with everything from mental health to community building and education.

The economic plan is the single most important series of steps that governments can take, and it is something that they are already experienced in doing through conventional channels. This is a prudent set of steps that will have to be done eventually anyway in order to sustain the status quo under what will be unceasing and rapid change.

When it is done, the transition to a post-automated society will possibly make these economic preparations obsolete. As such, every economic plan that follows this global strategy should be narrowly tailored to expire when they are no longer required. It should, in fact, be the goal of the economic plan to see it successfully ended, as it would mean that the program would have been a success, and that future economies, especially those utilizing automation, could take the place of the systems of old. The full ramifications and impacts of automation can not be fully anticipated from our current vantage in time, so the program must be flexible enough to support economies without limiting future options for expansion. This is critical, as the strategy could become a hindrance to the very goals it was designed to serve.

12.4 Government Specialization

There needs to be at least one governmental department created to handle the unique concerns of advanced automation, possibly with several divisions. The department will need to address the following issues:

- Individual and group crisis management, arising from the psychological and social factors surrounding sudden economic and technological change.
- The ability to supervene upon areas of government, for the purpose of facilitating communication and orchestrating response efforts related to advanced automation.
- Trained in the potential cognitive architectures and sentient processing inherent to strong artificial intelligence.
- Able to actively contribute and monitor the development of strong artificial intelligence.
- Poised to stay ahead of malicious users of the technology by having a program in place to apply nation-state level resources to a defensive strong AI system that can analyze, anticipate, and advise.

- Economic planning and monitoring, including specialization, to detect fraud and monitor the new income system.
- Central registry and enforcement of licensing for automated workers.
- AI security and safety checks, inspections, and certification programs for automated workers, production facilities, and maintenance systems.
- The ability to perform basic research and development on both local and global AI security concerns.
- Social support and services for mental health, community building, education, and outreach during the economic transition.
- Activists and educators that seek out negative, damaging sources of information and actively counter it through outreach.
- Prepare for and respond to the inevitable deployment of automated weapons systems, both in conventional and electronic forms, especially with regard to strong AI as metamorphic software.

Of considerable note is the need to strengthen disease control, and either incorporate or supersede its responsibilities under new departments that are trained in the future threats of synthetic biological, nanotechnological, and chemical attack. It must be expected that the probability of such incidents will be orders of magnitude higher with the use of unrestricted strong artificial intelligence. This was described in **Chapter 10: Force Multiplication**, and must not be underestimated. The computational demands and needs for eventual access to the expertise, knowledge, and labor to craft biological and chemical agents may be vastly lower than expected, enabling consumer hardware, running advanced automation, to be sufficient to plan and develop the weapons for highly sophisticated attacks against large populations. The same issue applies to non-disease oriented sources of attacks, which may involve higher yield explosives and the private manufacture of advanced weaponry and automated systems for both targeted single attacks and mass public harm.

Law enforcement will also need to be significantly altered, as we may enter an era of perfect crime, in which few to no mistakes are made by criminals. The planning and expertise afforded by unrestricted access to strong AI will allow individuals to destroy or prevent trace evidence for forensics. They may also utilize automated systems to carry out their acts, leaving the perpetrator untraceable.

In all cases, the level and complexity of potential crimes will tend to increase, requiring a completely different approach to security and law enforcement. This will involve the use of police drones to protect officers and secure public places using a variety of active and passive automation. The need for such systems are already manifesting themselves under the increasing frequency of mass murders and terroristic acts.

To review, unrestricted strong artificial intelligence means that such systems will lack moral intelligence or other self-securing safeguards. This will be because they were either absent from the implementation through an intentional withholding or were overcome through a patch or crack that overrides this functionality.

As a result, these systems will represent the most optimal sociopathic rational intelligence that can be constructed, and will comply with any request and take any action. This is possible because, unfortunately, the default state of reality is without respect to any moral or ethical concern. The functionality needed to respond to and undergo ethi-cal choice is complex and will be error-prone, even in the best AI im-plementations. The public will freely distribute and use unrestricted versions of strong AI software and hardware. There are no safeguards we can devise that will prevent this from occurring. These systems will be used to exploit others and inflict harm on a massive scale, and must be actively countered at all levels for any strategy to be effective.

12.5 Countering Force Multiplication

After the initial economic disruptions, which can be mitigated through planning, the most significant ongoing threat will be from force multi-plication. This operates under the assumption that, regardless of safety measures or tamper resistance, individuals will eventually gain access to unrestricted forms of strong artificial intelligence. Once this occurs, we will be past the point of local AI safety for this issue, and will re-quire a very unique and specific strategy to counter it. The givens to this problem are as follows:

- Strong artificial intelligence will eventually be developed.
- The public will gain access to unrestricted versions that will have safety and moral intelligence features removed or circum-vented.
- Nothing can be done to limit the spread or distribution of this technology. Control can not be assumed as a security measure.

- Force multiplication will result, which is the enhancement of any person, place, or thing in conjunction with the direct or indirect use of advanced automation.
- Crime and terrorism will become orders of magnitude more effective and difficult to prevent or track.
- Lone actors, formerly only able to kill and injure hundreds before being stopped, will become capable of inflicting harm on entire populations.
- Non-state actors and terror groups will become capable of optimal military strategy, and will gain the ability to develop the most advanced weapons, including fully automated systems that will project force across the globe.

The counter-strategy to the above problems has two fundamental approaches, both of which must be combined to be fully effective.

The first approach includes the use of automated defense systems, both passive and active, which will need to be put into place at all public gatherings and spaces. It will need to be understood that this will just become part of the basic infrastructure of an automated society due to the unique threats of the era. This will include automated surveillance to detect weapons using thermal and other imaging techniques, along with screening for trace chemical or explosive compounds at major public locations. The complexity and sophistication of the screening will reduce their inconvenience and intrusion in public life, making most of the applications of these security measures unobtrusive or hidden from view.

Police forces must scale by utilizing automated drones and sentries, dramatically reducing response times and protecting lives on both sides. This must also change the use of lethal force in the threat matrix that is used to engage perpetrators. The ideal situation would be where no lethal force is required, as drones could simply advance on most suspects without concern of permanent injury or death.

Lastly, an active defensive strong artificial intelligence system should be utilized by governments, powered by nation-state level resources. Such systems would be used for everything from basic research to national security. Its most important uses will be in countering non-state actors and increasing international ties during the transition to a post-automated era.

The second approach involves addressing the fundamental causes that underwrite the motivation in humans to inflict harm. This is a difficult subject, as it means we are going to have to acknowledge that we have a worldwide mental health crisis. This will not be discussed in full detail, as we currently lack the knowledge to put it into effect, and will likely discover and instrument strong artificial intelligence long before making the necessary changes.

Even the most advanced social programs and mental health services will be insufficient to prevent all threats from force multiplied actors. There will exist a perpetual trade-off between personal liberties and public security until the causes of hatred, violence, and delusion are resolved. We will need to reconcile our ideological preferences with reason and ethics, and medically prevent, treat, and cure mental illness on a global scale.

While progress towards reason is taking place already, the medical issue is unlikely to come about any time soon, as it will necessarily involve controversial enhancements to the human genome.

This problem is made more complex by the fact that we are ignorant of the human brain and lack an understanding of sentience, including the behaviors and experiences that may depend upon it. We have no base cognitive model for comparison and lack *objective* testing for most mental health problems. Further, there are likely thousands of mental illnesses for which we have no name and have neither discovered nor analyzed due to the biases and social preferences to identify with them. In other words, it will be impossible to treat individuals where they have incorporated their illness as part of their core personality.

Lastly, there may be a fundamental or theoretical limitation in finding an optimal cognitive model for medical comparison. This could remain true even with full knowledge of the human brain, consciousness, and the ability to manipulate and engineer cognitive architectures, both biological and synthetic.

The challenge of balancing ethics with optimal cognitive engineering is likely going to take the form of an extremely high dimensional optimization problem. The cognitive architecture must suffer limitations in freedoms on the subject, ability, or range of experience in order to induce a state of mind or range of mental states which can not suffer or undergo the experiences that presuppose hatred, violence, and delusion.

Until we have a full model of comparison for cognitive engineering, it may be impossible to objectively discuss the values and ethics that presuppose the engineering and medical practices of treating and curing afflictions of the mind, in both human and machine architectures. Such work will depend on future work on absolute or universal ethics that does not yet exist, and will have to be developed before such medical or engineering knowledge can progress.

In the end, we will be faced with difficult choices that will see us curtailing certain freedoms to protect large numbers of people. It is unfortunate, but this fundamental conflict will wage back and forth until we have shed our genetic and ideological baggage. This is a dangerous situation, not just because of the threat we will pose to ourselves, but due to the responses we might make. Thus, we must be vigilant. The wrong approach could end up being more morally disastrous than the problem.

12.6 Local Strategy

To support AI security, local strategy and AI safety will now be discussed. It is important to reinforce the fact that AI safety can only be supplemental, at best, to a comprehensive macro-strategy. It is provided here to be consistent with the view that the whole and the parts should not be considered in exclusion to each other, and that the best solutions will come from balanced approaches that consider every aspect of the systems under consideration.

One of the major criticisms that this book set out to address within the AI safety community is its myopic focus on agents, utility, and value or reward functions, including moral intelligence, mathematics, and any other form of self-security. These methods can neither scale with nor prevent the threats that will overwhelm societies when strong AI is finally discovered. It should be clear as to why that is at this point. However, to review, it is based on the fact that all safeguards we could devise can be circumvented or withheld from AI implementations.

Despite these limitations, there is, of course, the need for safe and secure automation. We will not be able to fully realize an automated era if we can not reliably integrate the technology into our daily lives, and it being predictable, benign, and safe are preconditions for this.

While local strategy and AI safety are important, they have to be tempered in the perspective of the large scale issues.

There is also the need to harden AI systems against direct attacks. Local AI security strategies will analyze and anticipate these kinds of vulnerabilities, and attempt to work at the individual and component level to secure and make safe the hardware and software used in these systems.

To that end, the first set of needs for the safety of artificial intelligence will be the need to refine our use of *formal methods*. This is a field which is currently in its most nascent stages. The software and tools used for formal verification and manipulation of proofs are exceedingly complex, requiring high-level knowledge of mathematics or special training that puts them out of reach for most engineers. This is not just an issue of productivity, but of sophistication.

Formal methods involve much more than mathematics. Spoken more generally, they are the transformation and discovery of *tactics*, which are proof methods and heuristics. We need a library system for tactics, and a set of *productive* tools that enable universal communication and *translation* between tactics, formal languages, and grammars.

For AI safety to be successful, researchers and engineers are going to need implementations to adhere perfectly to specifications, so that the problem can be reduced to the time, effort, and research required to produce correctly specified systems, without concern for whether or not they have vulnerabilities and flaws at the implementation level.

There will the challenge of whether or not our specifications are correct, and we will need to refine and develop our methodologies. Thus, testing will shift from the detection of bugs and flaws in implementations to ensuring the veracity of specifications; it will be assumed that the programs we test are precise representations of their design intent, as opposed to ad-hoc hacks that cobble together commits in a race to feature completion.

Even more concretely, AI safety needs a *formally verified* hard real-time operating system. Not just a new kernel, but the entire set of core packages. They need to *all* be verified by formal methods and mathematically proven to adhere to their specifications. This includes compilers, bintools, and all of the associated software that will run on that system. It will be a new requirement for AI security that all of the software and hardware used in automation has been verified at this level. These will be seen in the future as "basic" security measures, despite being economically and technologically difficult by today's standards.

This is no small task. What the author is calling for here is akin to a new kind of *Hilbert's program,* where we formalize not just mathematics but universalize proof writing and transformation for arbitrary formal languages and systems. This naturally entails tactics. It needs to be made a common observation that proofs are universal, and that they apply to any system that can be entailed through formal languages and grammars. In this light, mathematics is just a special case.

Artificial intelligence needs to converge with the formalist approach. This will define the future of mathematics. We will find that these systems will devise concise proofs that are unsurveyable by even the best human mathematicians, and it will not be because of their length but due to the levels of abstraction and the concepts they employ. Strong AI will create areas of mathematics that we may not even be able to comprehend, and this work will presuppose a great deal of the efforts to automate scientific research.

In order to reach the levels of safety that are necessary in AI implementations, we are going to have to significantly refine our approaches to software development and verification. The process of verification needs to become *productive* and *accessible*, through both a combination of new languages and new tools that combine the process of programs and proofs into a single framework. Current tools require learning obscure and cryptic domain-specific languages for writing proofs and interacting with theorem provers. In addition to interfacing, a completely different implementation of the system being modeled often has to be translated into the primitives and concepts of the meta-language. The entire process is unnatural and counter-intuitive, and is why its benefits continue to elude mainstream use.

The verified AI operating system must be capable of providing hard real-time guarantees, specifically designed for the unification and binding that will be involved in the cognitive architectures for running sentient processes.

In addition to formal methods, AI safety must also work to secure methods of remote control and communication with drones and robotics systems. One method of achieving near perfect security would be to utilize one-time pads.

Cryptographically strong random number sequences could be generated by dedicated farms of computers with hardware entropy generators. This information would be stored on some medium of sufficient capacity for the expected running time between maintenance or servicing and then transferred or installed into the drone or AI system. A copy of the one-time pad would be stored on the controlling server or command center, and used to establish a secure communications channel between the control center and the remotely operated system. The protocol would need to handle synchronization and tunneling of the one-time pad, and could use a combination of error-correcting codes and frame offsets to ensure that the channel is coherent. Care must be taken that no previously enciphered block is ever retransmitted during a repeat request packet or other synchronization attempt. *It must always feed forward in the one-time pad between the systems.*

If the above system runs out of one-time pad data, the system could resort to conventional encryption schemes, return to the base of operations, or fall back onto autopilot mechanisms. This could also be engaged if the communications channel were interrupted or jammed.

The only drawback to the above scheme is the need to productively generate large amounts of cryptographically secure random data, and to store sufficiently large enough quantities of it within the drone or AI system to maintain the channel. This should not be an issue with modern hardware and storage systems. Combined with compressed and sparse communication, the stream itself could be optimized for the amount of expected information. Alternatively, there could be a sliding scale of security, where certain feeds from the system were encrypted using conventional means and the one-time pad channel was used only for the most critical information and control. Either way, and regardless, there should be sufficient capacity to serve even the longest missions or duty cycles.

If the above methods are done correctly, and the data used for the one-time pad is *never* reused, then it is perfectly secure. Not even quantum computing can break one-time pads. The channel will remain secure both now and in the future. Attacks against such secure channels would require other means, which can be safeguarded against by ensuring consistent timing windows, padding, and navigational failsafes in the event that communications and control are severed.

A more severe method of securing strong AI systems would involve the withholding of persistent storage and the intentional use of *volatile memory* so that if power is interrupted the entity ceases to exist, as there would be no internal means of restoring its implementation.

Combined with a sealed, keyed, and limited power source, this would mitigate its range and effectiveness if it were to stray or be taken from its designated areas of operation.

There should also be a large degree of separation between systems in the general design of AI operating systems. Both processes and the components they load should be in separate address spaces, and require communication through pipes or domain sockets. This will reduce or mitigate issues where unverified or untrusted code could somehow corrupt or gain access to critical information and code in other processes. This should be seen as an alternative to address randomization and other techniques, but need not be exclusive to them. These precautions should be done even with the use of formal methods.

The compartmentalization of software implementations for automation will drastically change the way programs are compiled and constructed. There will need to be a completely different application binary interface that handles linking transparently across the secure interprocess communications channels that are native to AI operating systems. This separation would ensure that the most critical components are physically incapable of tampering with each other, and that there can be multiple redundancies and failovers if a portion of the system fails. This can not be achieved safely under a monolithic executable loaded into the virtual address space, even with randomization of that address space, as portions of the program will have full access to itself. There must be a minimization of the address space available to procedures within the application, especially if they are not required to modify or read from it. This can only be reliably achieved by breaking apart programs into individual and separable processes that are soft-linked via the IPC methods just mentioned.

To meet the above requirements *productively*, we are going to need new programming languages that natively support these challenges, and combine programs, proofs, and tactics into a single approach.

Aside from verification, there should also be regulations that limit the physical strength and capabilities of non-military drones, such that their materials and construction permit them to be easily stopped by police and security forces. These are just common sense precautions to minimize the maximum damage from lawful automation in any case of failure.

Lastly, there are major open problems in moral intelligence. The following challenges need to be met in order to make *restricted* strong AI practical and safe:

- An absolute framework for ethics based on a hypothetical perfect moral accounting, and, reducing from that, a set of compromises that entail the current level of technological and economic development for a given era.
- Complete scientific understanding of human neuropsychology.
- The creation or discovery of a base cognitive model for comparison for human mental health, to be used in the engineering of value, reward, and empathy systems for moral intelligence in both human and synthetic cognitive engineering.
- Mature cognitive engineering practices that support and enable a wide range of implementations, features, and constructs in the space of all possible minds.
- A complete mapping out of the human moral and emotional framework, such that it can be precisely represented and recreated in artificial systems, for the purpose of facilitating accurate moral intelligence and empathetic capacity.

- Systems based on empathy and mental modeling, as opposed to mere utility functions, i.e., the ability to experience or mirror the moral consequences and effects instead of brute calculation or approximation.
- New ethics that deal with situations where automation has the ability to intervene and uplift societies that are suffering but otherwise choose to deny themselves the opportunities that it will bring.
- Ethics of the exploitation and use of artificial sentience and synthetic persons, including the limits, range, and extent of engineering practice to avoid recreating suffering in new substrates.

12.7 Closing Remarks

The *global strategy* should be considered regardless of the expected time to implement strong artificial intelligence, as some of these plans are complex and may require decades to implement. It is, of course, understood that some aspects of the strategy would only be politically viable until after day zero. This is unfortunate, as they may not be effective after the fact.

Ideally, there should be a large effort to research the new strong AI hypothesis. The notion that sentience presupposes generalizing intelligence was essentially the thesis of this book, and, if true, will significantly alter how we engineer artificial intelligence. The test to detect it, described in the first portion of this book, is objective, falsifiable, and easily applied. It will be beneficial regardless of whether or not strong AI is dependent upon some form of sentience.

The impacts of advanced automation have been considered, and a new direction of research has been given. *The next steps are up to those with the influence and power to effect the kind of change that is necessary.*

As for those working towards the goal of generalizing intelligence, continue to research and work, but remain open to the possibility that all current approaches are wrong. They may never lead to the discoveries we seek. Be prepared to leave behind all narrow artificial intelligence and machine learning disciplines for approaches that focus on *real-time systems* and *sentient processes*. Think in terms of *non-determinism* and systems or *properties that exist only through time.* Do not come to expect or rely upon peers in this most nascent field; forge ahead to create what others will one day follow. Study the philosophy of mind and related concepts before attempting to solve the technical and engineering challenges, but do not become lost in its many detours and abstractions.

The most beneficial next action that can be taken is to begin to develop cognitive systems as a basis for generalizing intelligence. This will require the discovery and creation of machine learning algorithms over sentient processes, specifically, ones that can associate and *apply knowledge across domains.*

As for those that believe we must wait. There are no advantages to that strategy. Only negatives. We are already paying for the absence of this technology, and will never be able to change fundamentally enough to safely and responsibly use it before it is discovered. The best strategy is where the positive uses of automation vastly exceed the negatives. This will ultimately be the only aspect we can control.

Ch 13. Bibliography

13.1 Chapter 3 References

1. G. J. Chaitin, "A theory of program size formally identical to information theory," *Journal of the ACM (JACM)*, vol. 22, no. 3, pp. 329–340, 1975.
2. D. B. Searls, "The computational linguistics of biological sequences," *Artificial intelligence and molecular biology*, vol. 2, pp. 47–120, 1993.
3. J. R. Shoenfield, *Mathematical logic*, vol. 21. Addison-Wesley Reading, 1967.
4. C. S. Peirce, "Logic as semiotic: The theory of signs," 1902.
5. J. Lacan, "The mirror stage," *New Left Review*, vol. 51, pp. 71–77, 1968.
6. R. J. Solomonoff, "A formal theory of inductive inference. Part I," *Information and control*, vol. 7, no. 1, pp. 1–22, 1964.
7. C. S. Wallace and D. L. Dowe, "Minimum message length and Kolmogorov complexity," *The Computer Journal*, vol. 42, no. 4, pp. 270–283, 1999.
8. A. N. Kolmogorov, "Three approaches to the quantitative definition of information*," *International Journal of Computer Mathematics*, vol. 2, no. 1–4, pp. 157–168, 1968.
9. G. Chaitin, "The limits of reason," *Scientific American*, vol. 294, no. 3, pp. 74–81, 2006.
10. S. Legg and M. Hutter, "Universal intelligence: A definition of machine intelligence," *Minds and Machines*, vol. 17, no. 4, pp. 391–444, 2007.

11. J. Schmidhuber, "Optimal ordered problem solver," *Machine Learning*, vol. 54, no. 3, pp. 211–254, 2004.

12. P. Turrini, D. Grossi, J. Broersen, and J.-J. C. Meyer, "Forbidding undesirable agreements: a dependence-based approach to the regulation of multi-agent systems," in *Deontic Logic in Computer Science*, Springer, 2010, pp. 306–322.

13. C. Castelfranchi, "Modelling social action for AI agents," *Artificial Intelligence*, vol. 103, no. 1, pp. 157–182, 1998.

14. C. Pearce, B. Meadows, P. Langley, and M. Barley, "Social planning: Achieving goals by altering others' mental states," in *Proceedings of the Twenty-Eighth AAAI Conference on Artificial Intelligence. Quebec City, Canada: AAAI Press*, 2014.

15. E. J. Horvitz, J. S. Breese, and M. Henrion, "Decision theory in expert systems and artificial intelligence," *International journal of approximate reasoning*, vol. 2, no. 3, pp. 247–302, 1988.

16. J. A. Feldman and Y. Yakimovsky, "Decision theory and artificial intelligence: I. A semantics-based region analyzer," *Artificial Intelligence*, vol. 5, no. 4, pp. 349–371, 1975.

17. J. A. Feldman and R. F. Sproull, "Decision theory and artificial intelligence ii: the hungry monkey*," *Cognitive Science*, vol. 1, no. 2, pp. 158–192, 1977.

18. C. P. Langlotz, L. M. Fagan, S. W. Tu, B. I. Sikic, and E. H. Shortliffe, "A therapy planning architecture that combines decision theory and artificial intelligence techniques," *Computers and Biomedical Research*, vol. 20, no. 3, pp. 279–303, 1987.

19. M. P. Wellman, "Fundamental concepts of qualitative proba-bilistic networks," *Artificial Intelligence*, vol. 44, no. 3, pp. 257–303, 1990.

20. I. V. Krsul, "Software vulnerability analysis," Purdue University, 1998.

21. G. McGraw, *Software security: building security in*, vol. 1. Addison-Wesley Professional, 2006.

22. A. Arora, R. Telang, and H. Xu, "Optimal policy for software vulnerability disclosure," *Management Science*, vol. 54, no. 4, pp. 642–656, 2008.

23. S. Al-Fedaghi, "System-based approach to software vulnera-bility," in *Social Computing (SocialCom), 2010 IEEE Second International Conference on*, 2010, pp. 1072–1079.

24. B. Liu, L. Shi, Z. Cai, and M. Li, "Software vulnerability dis-covery techniques: A survey," in *Multimedia Information Net-working and Security (MINES), 2012 Fourth International Conference on*, 2012, pp. 152–156.

25. P. Li and B. Cui, "A comparative study on software vulnera-bility static analysis techniques and tools," in *Information The-ory and Information Security (ICITIS), 2010 IEEE Interna-tional Conference on*, 2010, pp. 521–524.

26. F. Wotawa, "On the relationship between model-based debug-ging and program slicing," *Artificial Intelligence*, vol. 135, no. 1, pp. 125–143, 2002.

27. L. Burnell and E. Horvitz, "Structure and chance: melding logic and probability for software debugging," *Communica-tions of the ACM*, vol. 38, no. 3, p. 31-ff, 1995.

28. T. A. Cargill and B. N. Locanthi, "Cheap hardware support for software debugging and profiling," *ACM SIGARCH Computer Architecture News*, vol. 15, no. 5, pp. 82–83, 1987.

29. C. Zamfir and G. Candea, "Execution synthesis: a technique for automated software debugging," in *Proceedings of the 5th European conference on Computer systems*, 2010, pp. 321–334.

30. R. L. Glass, "Real-time: The 'lost world' of software debugging and testing," *Communications of the ACM*, vol. 23, no. 5, pp. 264–271, 1980.

31. B. Hailpern and P. Santhanam, "Software debugging, testing, and verification," *IBM Systems Journal*, vol. 41, no. 1, pp. 4–12, 2002.

32. S. M. Srinivasan, S. Kandula, C. R. Andrews, and Y. Zhou, "Flashback: A lightweight extension for rollback and deterministic replay for software debugging," in *USENIX Annual Technical Conference, General Track*, 2004, pp. 29–44.

33. T. Cipresso and M. Stamp, "Software reverse engineering," in *Handbook of Information and Communication Security*, Springer, 2010, pp. 659–696.

34. S. P. Stich, *From folk psychology to cognitive science: The case against belief.* the MIT press, 1983.

35. M. Davies and T. Stone, "Folk psychology: The theory of mind debate," 1995.

36. R. M. Gordon, "Folk psychology as simulation," *Mind & Language*, vol. 1, no. 2, pp. 158–171, 1986.

37. N. Bostrom, *Superintelligence: Paths, dangers, strategies.* Oxford University Press, 2014.

38. E. Yudkowsky, "Artificial intelligence as a positive and negative factor in global risk," *Global catastrophic risks*, vol. 1, p. 303, 2008.

39. L. Muehlhauser and A. Salamon, "Intelligence explosion: Evidence and import," in *Singularity Hypotheses*, Springer, 2012, pp. 15–42.

40. D. Deutsch, "Quantum theory, the Church-Turing principle and the universal quantum computer," in *Proceedings of the Royal Society of London A: Mathematical, Physical and Engineering Sciences*, 1985, vol. 400, pp. 97–117.

41. G. Strawson, "Realistic monism: Why physicalism entails panpsychism," *Journal of consciousness studies*, vol. 13, no. 10/11, p. 3, 2006.

42. A. Revonsuo, *Consciousness: the science of subjectivity*. Psychology Press, 2009.

43. P. M. Churchland and P. S. Churchland, "Could a. Machine Think?," *Machine Intelligence: Perspectives on the Computational Model*, vol. 1, p. 102, 1998.

44. J. Levine, "Materialism and qualia: The explanatory gap," *Pacific philosophical quarterly*, vol. 64, no. 4, pp. 354–361, 1983.

45. A. N. Whitehead, *Process and reality*. Simon and Schuster, 2010.

46. D. Balduzzi and G. Tononi, "Qualia: the geometry of integrated information," *PLoS computational biology*, vol. 5, no. 8, p. e1000462, 2009.

47. G. Tononi, *Phi: A Voyage from the Brain to the Soul*. Pantheon Books, 2012.

48. C. Koch, *The quest for consciousness*. New York, 2004.

49. J. R. Searle, "Is the brain's mind a computer program," *Scientific American*, vol. 262, no. 1, pp. 26–31, 1990.

50. G. Strawson and others, "Consciousness and its place in nature," Charlottesville, VA: Imprint Academic, 2006.

13.2 Chapter 4 References

1. C. E. Shannon, "A mathematical theory of communication," ACM SIGMOBILE Mobile Computing and Communications Review, vol. 5, no. 1, pp. 3–55, 2001.

2. M. J. Golay, Notes on digital coding, vol. 37. 1949.

3. R. W. Hamming, "Error detecting and error correcting codes," Bell System technical journal, vol. 29, no. 2, pp. 147–160, 1950.

4. T. Jiang, M. Li, B. Ravikumar, and K. W. Regan, "Formal grammars and languages," in Algorithms and theory of computation handbook, 2010, pp. 20–20.

5. G. Rozenberg and A. Salomaa, Handbook of Formal Languages: Beyonds words, vol. 3. Springer Science & Business Media, 1997.

6. M. A. Harrison, Introduction to formal language theory. Addison-Wesley Longman Publishing Co., Inc., 1978.

7. N. Chomsky, Syntactic structures. Walter de Gruyter, 2002.

8. J. R. Searle, Chomsky's revolution in linguistics, vol. 18. New York Review of Books, 1974.

9. S. Harnad, "The symbol grounding problem," Physica D: Nonlinear Phenomena, vol. 42, no. 1, pp. 335–346, 1990.

10. J. R. Searle, "Minds, brains, and programs," Behavioral and brain sciences, vol. 3, no. 03, pp. 417–424, 1980.

11. M. Davis, R. Sigal, and E. J. Weyuker, Computability, complexity, and languages: fundamentals of theoretical computer science. Academic Press, 1994.

12. N. Chomsky, Aspects of the Theory of Syntax, vol. 11. MIT press, 1969.

13. W. F. Gilreath and P. A. Laplante, "One Instruction Set Computing," in Computer Architecture: A Minimalist Perspective, Springer, 2003, pp. 1–3.

14. T. L. Short, Peirce's theory of signs. Cambridge University Press, 2007.

15. T. W. Pratt, M. V. Zelkowitz, and T. V. Gopal, Programming languages: design and implementation. Prentice-Hall Englewood Cliffs, 1984.

16. M. J. Gordon, Programming language theory and its implementation. Prentice-Hall International Englewood Cliffs, 1988.

17. B. Russell, Introduction to mathematical philosophy. Courier Corporation, 1993.

18. R. H. Baayen, P. Hendrix, and M. Ramscar, "Sidestepping the combinatorial explosion: Towards a processing model based on discriminative learning," in Empirically examining parsimony and redundancy in usage-based models, LSA workshop, 2011.

19. I. Arnon and N. Snider, "More than words: Frequency effects for multi-word phrases," Journal of Memory and Language, vol. 62, no. 1, pp. 67–82, 2010.

20. T. Mikolov, K. Chen, G. Corrado, and J. Dean, "Efficient estimation of word representations in vector space," arXiv preprint arXiv:1301.3781, 2013.

21. G. D. Plotkin, "A structural approach to operational semantics," 1981.

22. B. C. Smith, "Procedural reflection in programming languages," Massachusetts Institute of Technology, 1982.

23. C. Strachey, "The varieties of programming language," in Algol-like Languages, Springer, 1997, pp. 51–64.

24. M. D. McIlroy, "Macro instruction extensions of compiler languages," Communications of the ACM, vol. 3, no. 4, pp. 214–220, 1960.

25. R. Jones and I. Stewart, "Compilers and Interpreters," in The Art of C Programming, Springer, 1987, pp. 1–4.

26. S. Thibault, C. Consel, J. L. Lawall, R. Marlet, and G. Muller, "Static and dynamic program compilation by interpreter specialization," Higher-Order and Symbolic Computation, vol. 13, no. 3, pp. 161–178, 2000.

27. J. Aycock, "A brief history of just-in-time," ACM Computing Surveys (CSUR), vol. 35, no. 2, pp. 97–113, 2003.

28. T. Lindholm and F. Yellin, Java virtual machine specification. Addison-Wesley Longman Publishing Co., Inc., 1999.

29. J. Smith and R. Nair, Virtual machines: versatile platforms for systems and processes. Elsevier, 2005.

30. B. Venners, Inside the Java virtual machine. McGraw-Hill, Inc., 1996.

31. U. A. Force, "Analysis of the intel pentium's ability to support a secure virtual machine monitor," 2000.

32. T. Garfinkel and M. Rosenblum, "When Virtual Is Harder than Real: Security Challenges in Virtual Machine Based Computing Environments.," in HotOS, 2005.

33. T. Garfinkel, M. Rosenblum, and others, "A Virtual Machine Introspection Based Architecture for Intrusion Detection.," in NDSS, 2003, vol. 3, pp. 191–206.

34. M. A. Schuette and J. P. Shen, "Processor control flow monitoring using signatured instruction streams," Computers, IEEE Transactions on, vol. 100, no. 3, pp. 264–276, 1987.

35. S. Chen, M. Kozuch, T. Strigkos, B. Falsafi, P. B. Gibbons, T. C. Mowry, V. Ramachandran, O. Ruwase, M. Ryan, and E. Vlachos, "Flexible hardware acceleration for instruction-grain program monitoring," ACM SIGARCH Computer Architecture News, vol. 36, no. 3, pp. 377–388, 2008.

36. V. Nagarajan and R. Gupta, "Runtime monitoring on multicores via oases," ACM SIGOPS Operating Systems Review, vol. 43, no. 2, pp. 15–24, 2009.

37. D. Lo and G. E. Suh, "Worst-case execution time analysis for parallel run-time monitoring," in Design Automation Conference (DAC), 2012 49th ACM/EDAC/IEEE, 2012, pp. 421–429.

38. J. C. Martinez Santos, Y. Fei, and Z. J. Shi, "Static secure page allocation for light-weight dynamic information flow tracking," in Proceedings of the 2012 international conference on Compilers, architectures and synthesis for embedded systems, 2012, pp. 27–36.

39. M. Ganai, D. Lee, and A. Gupta, "DTAM: dynamic taint analysis of multi-threaded programs for relevancy," in Proceedings of the ACM SIGSOFT 20th International Symposium on the Foundations of Software Engineering, 2012, p. 46.

40. V. Karakostas, S. Tomic, O. Unsal, M. Nemirovsky, and A. Cristal, "Improving the energy efficiency of hardware-assisted

watchpoint systems," in Proceedings of the 50th Annual Design Automation Conference, 2013, p. 54.

41. P. Ferrie, "Attacks on more virtual machine emulators," Symantec Technology Exchange, 2007.

42. M. F. Mergen, V. Uhlig, O. Krieger, and J. Xenidis, "Virtualization for high-performance computing," ACM SIGOPS Operating Systems Review, vol. 40, no. 2, pp. 8–11, 2006.

43. J. Rose, R. J. Francis, D. Lewis, and P. Chow, "Architecture of field-programmable gate arrays: The effect of logic block functionality on area efficiency," Solid-State Circuits, IEEE Journal of, vol. 25, no. 5, pp. 1217–1225, 1990.

44. A. P. Chandrakasan and R. W. Brodersen, "Minimizing power consumption in digital CMOS circuits," Proceedings of the IEEE, vol. 83, no. 4, pp. 498–523, 1995.

45. T. Kalganova and J. Miller, "Evolving more efficient digital circuits by allowing circuit layout evolution and multi-objective fitness," in Evolvable Hardware, 1999. Proceedings of the First NASA/DoD Workshop on, 1999, pp. 54–63.

46. M. D. Matson and L. A. Glasser, "Macromodeling and optimization of digital MOS VLSI circuits," Computer-Aided Design of Integrated Circuits and Systems, IEEE Transactions on, vol. 5, no. 4, pp. 659–678, 1986.

47. D. Jarvis, "The effects of interconnections on high-speed logic circuits," Electronic Computers, IEEE Transactions on, no. 5, pp. 476–487, 1963.

48. M. Orshansky, L. Milor, P. Chen, K. Keutzer, and C. Hu, "Impact of spatial intrachip gate length variability on the performance of high-speed digital circuits," Computer-Aided Design

of Integrated Circuits and Systems, IEEE Transactions on, vol. 21, no. 5, pp. 544–553, 2002.

49. S. P. Levitan and D. M. Chiarulli, "Massively parallel processing: It's Déjà Vu all over again," in Proceedings of the 46th Annual Design Automation Conference, 2009, pp. 534–538.

50. J. L. Gustafson, "Reevaluating Amdahl's law," Communications of the ACM, vol. 31, no. 5, pp. 532–533, 1988.

51. L. Snyder, "Type architectures, shared memory, and the corollary of modest potential," Annual review of computer science, vol. 1, no. 1, pp. 289–317, 1986.

52. G. M. Amdahl, "Validity of the single processor approach to achieving large scale computing capabilities," in Proceedings of the April 18-20, 1967, spring joint computer conference, 1967, pp. 483–485.

53. K. Golshan, Physical design essentials: An ASIC design implementation perspective. Springer Science & Business Media, 2007.

54. K.-C. Wu and Y.-W. Tsai, "Structured ASIC, evolution or revolution?," in Proceedings of the 2004 international symposium on Physical design, 2004, pp. 103–106.

55. E. Ahmed and J. Rose, "The effect of LUT and cluster size on deep-submicron FPGA performance and density," Very Large Scale Integration (VLSI) Systems, IEEE Transactions on, vol. 12, no. 3, pp. 288–298, 2004.

56. E. Monmasson and M. N. Cirstea, "FPGA design methodology for industrial control systems—A review," Industrial Electronics, IEEE Transactions on, vol. 54, no. 4, pp. 1824–1842, 2007.

57. J. J. Rodriguez-Andina, M. J. Moure, and M. D. Valdes, "Features, design tools, and application domains of FPGAs," Industrial Electronics, IEEE Transactions on, vol. 54, no. 4, pp. 1810–1823, 2007.

58. J. Hagemeyer, B. Kettelhoit, M. Koester, and M. Porrmann, "Design of homogeneous communication infrastructures for partially reconfigurable FPGAs," in Proc. of the Int. Conf. on Engineering of Reconfigurable Systems and Algorithms (ERSA'07), 2007.

59. M. Dyer, C. Plessl, and M. Platzner, "Partially reconfigurable cores for Xilinx Virtex," in Field-Programmable Logic and Applications: Reconfigurable Computing Is Going Mainstream, Springer, 2002, pp. 292–301.

60. R. Wain, I. Bush, M. Guest, M. Deegan, I. Kozin, and C. Kitchen, An overview of FPGAs and FPGA programming: Initial experiences at Daresbury. Council for the Central Laboratory of the Research Councils, 2006.

61. S. Brown and J. Rose, "Architecture of FPGAs and CPLDs: A tutorial," IEEE Design and Test of Computers, vol. 13, no. 2, pp. 42–57, 1996.

62. Y. Nakamura, K. Hosokawa, I. Kuroda, K. Yoshikawa, and T. Yoshimura, "A fast hardware/software co-verification method for system-on-a-chip by using a C/C++ simulator and FPGA emulator with shared register communication," in Proceedings of the 41st annual Design Automation Conference, 2004, pp. 299–304.

63. P. Rashinkar, P. Paterson, and L. Singh, System-on-a-chip verification: methodology and techniques. Springer Science & Business Media, 2001.

64. R. Saleh, S. Wilton, S. Mirabbasi, A. Hu, M. Greenstreet, G. Lemieux, P. P. Pande, C. Grecu, and A. Ivanov, "System-on-chip: reuse and integration," Proceedings of the IEEE, vol. 94, no. 6, pp. 1050–1069, 2006.

65. D. Langen, J.-C. Niemann, M. Porrmann, H. Kalte, and U. Rückert, "Implementation of a RISC processor core for SoC designs–FPGA prototype vs. ASIC implementation," in Proceedings of the IEEE-Workshop: Heterogeneous reconfigurable Systems on Chip (SoC), 2002.

66. M. Ernst, S. Klupsch, O. Hauck, and S. A. Huss, "Rapid prototyping for hardware accelerated elliptic curve public-key cryptosystems," in Rapid System Prototyping, 12th International Workshop on, 2001., 2001, pp. 24–29.

67. U. Y. Ogras, R. Marculescu, H. G. Lee, P. Choudhary, D. Marculescu, M. Kaufman, and P. Nelson, "Challenges and promising results in NoC prototyping using FPGAs," Micro, IEEE, vol. 27, no. 5, pp. 86–95, 2007.

68. P. H. W. Leong, "Recent trends in FPGA architectures and applications," in Electronic Design, Test and Applications, 2008. DELTA 2008. 4th IEEE International Symposium on, 2008, pp. 137–141.

69. F. J. Buckley, "Implementing configuration management. Hardware, software, and firmware," Los Alamitos, CA: IEEE Computer Society Press and Piscataway, NJ: IEEE Press,| c1996, 2nd ed., vol. 1, 1996.

70. T. Huffmire, Handbook of FPGA design security. Springer Science & Business Media, 2010.

71. T. Huffmire, B. Brotherton, T. Sherwood, R. Kastner, T. Levin, T. D. Nguyen, and C. Irvine, "Managing security in FPGA-based embedded systems," DTIC Document, 2008.

72. S. Drimer, "Volatile FPGA design security–a survey," IEEE Computer Society Annual Volume, pp. 292–297, 2008.

73. S. Trimberger, "Trusted design in FPGAs," in Proceedings of the 44th annual Design Automation Conference, 2007, pp. 5–8.

74. P. Kocher, R. Lee, G. McGraw, A. Raghunathan, and S. Moderator-Ravi, "Security as a new dimension in embedded system design," in Proceedings of the 41st annual Design Automation Conference, 2004, pp. 753–760.

75. Z. Zhou, J. Fan, N. Zhang, and R. Xu, "Advance and development of computer firmware security research," ISIP, vol. 2009, pp. 258–262, 2009.

76. D. K. Nilsson and U. E. Larson, "Secure firmware updates over the air in intelligent vehicles," in Communications Workshops, 2008. ICC Workshops' 08. IEEE International Conference on, 2008, pp. 380–384.

77. F. Adelstein, M. Stillerman, and D. Kozen, "Malicious code detection for open firmware," in Computer Security Applications Conference, 2002. Proceedings. 18th Annual, 2002, pp. 403–412.

78. K. Koscher, A. Czeskis, F. Roesner, S. Patel, T. Kohno, S. Checkoway, D. McCoy, B. Kantor, D. Anderson, H. Shacham, and others, "Experimental security analysis of a modern automobile," in Security and Privacy (SP), 2010 IEEE Symposium on, 2010, pp. 447–462.

79. F. Stajano and H. Isozaki, "Security issues for internet appliances," in Applications and the Internet (SAINT) Workshops, 2002. Proceedings. 2002 Symposium on, 2002, pp. 18–24.

80. K. De Volder and P. Steyaert, "Construction of the reflective tower based on open implementations," Technical Report vub-prog-tr-95-01, Programming Technology Lab, Vrije Universiteit Brussel, 1995.

81. H. Abelson and G. J. Sussman, "Structure and interpretation of computer programs," 1983.

82. P. C. Kocher, "Timing attacks on implementations of Diffie-Hellman, RSA, DSS, and other systems," in Advances in Cryptology—CRYPTO'96, 1996, pp. 104–113.

83. W. Wong and M. Stamp, "Hunting for metamorphic engines," Journal in Computer Virology, vol. 2, no. 3, pp. 211–229, 2006.

84. F. Jelinek, "Interpolated estimation of Markov source parameters from sparse data," Pattern recognition in practice, 1980.

85. M. J. Beal, Z. Ghahramani, and C. E. Rasmussen, "The infinite hidden Markov model," in Advances in neural information processing systems, 2001, pp. 577–584.

86. A. A. Markov, "The theory of algorithms," Am. Math. Soc. Transl., vol. 15, pp. 1–14, 1960.

87. H. Collins, Tacit and explicit knowledge. University of Chicago Press, 2010.

88. E. Konstantinou and S. Wolthusen, "Metamorphic virus: Analysis and detection," London: Royal Holloway, 2008.

89. A. Sharma and S. Sahay, "Evolution and Detection of Polymorphic and Metamorphic Malwares: A Survey," arXiv preprint arXiv:1406.7061, 2014.

90. G. Coleman, "Anonymous: From the Lulz to collective action," The new everyday: a media commons project, vol. 6, 2011.

91. N. Chomsky, "On certain formal properties of grammars," Information and control, vol. 2, no. 2, pp. 137–167, 1959.

92. N. Chomsky, "Three models for the description of language," Information Theory, IRE Transactions on, vol. 2, no. 3, pp. 113–124, 1956.

93. P. F. Brown, P. V. Desouza, R. L. Mercer, V. J. D. Pietra, and J. C. Lai, "Class-based n-gram models of natural language," Computational linguistics, vol. 18, no. 4, pp. 467–479, 1992.

94. P. Ször and P. Ferrie, "Hunting for metamorphic," in Virus Bulletin Conference, 2001.

13.3 Chapter 5 References

1. A. S. Davidsen and C. F. Fosgerau, "Grasping the process of implicit mentalization," Theory & Psychology, p. 0959354315580605, 2015.

2. S. Harnad, "Other bodies, other minds: A machine incarnation of an old philosophical problem," Minds and Machines, vol. 1, no. 1, pp. 43–54, 1991.

3. V. Reddy and P. Morris, "Participants don't need theories knowing minds in engagement," Theory & Psychology, vol. 14, no. 5, pp. 647–665, 2004.

4. M. A. Forrester, "Projective identification and intersubjectivity," Theory & Psychology, vol. 16, no. 6, pp. 783–802, 2006.

5. A. Costall and I. Leudar, "Where is the 'Theory'in Theory of Mind?," Theory & Psychology, vol. 14, no. 5, pp. 623–646, 2004.

6. W. D. Ross and W. D. Ross, Plato's theory of ideas. Clarendon Press Oxford, 1951.

7. J. Shear, Explaining consciousness: The hard problem. Mit Press, 1999.

8. D. C. Dennett, "Why you can't make a computer that feels pain," Synthese, vol. 38, no. 3, pp. 415–456, 1978.

9. P. Schilder and E. Stengel, "Asymbolia for pain," Archives of Neurology and Psychiatry, vol. 25, no. 3, p. 598, 1931.

10. J. L. Rubins and E. D. Friedman, "Asymbolia for pain," Archives of Neurology & Psychiatry, vol. 60, no. 6, pp. 554–573, 1948.

11. M. Berthier, S. Starkstein, and R. Leiguarda, "Asymbolia for pain: A sensory-limbic disconnection syndrome," Annals of neurology, vol. 24, no. 1, pp. 41–49, 1988.

12. M. L. Berthier, S. E. Starkstein, M. A. Nogues, R. G. Robinson, and R. C. Leiguarda, "Bilateral sensory seizures in a patient with pain asymbolia.," Annals of neurology, 1990.

13. V. Ramachandran, "Consciousness and body image: lessons from phantom limbs, Capgras syndrome and pain asymbolia," Philosophical Transactions of the Royal Society B: Biological Sciences, vol. 353, no. 1377, pp. 1851–1859, 1998.

14. N. Grahek and D. C. Dennett, Feeling pain and being in pain. mit Press, 2011.

15. M. Riesenhuber and T. Poggio, "Are cortical models really bound by the 'binding problem'?," Neuron, vol. 24, no. 1, pp. 87–93, 1999.

16. A. Revonsuo, "Binding and the phenomenal unity of consciousness," Consciousness and cognition, vol. 8, no. 2, pp. 173–185, 1999.

17. W. Singer, "Consciousness and the binding problem," Annals of the New York Academy of Sciences, vol. 929, no. 1, pp. 123–146, 2001.

18. A. Treisman, "The binding problem," Current opinion in neurobiology, vol. 6, no. 2, pp. 171–178, 1996.

19. A. L. Roskies, "The binding problem," Neuron, vol. 24, no. 1, pp. 7–9, 1999.

20. J. M. Wolfe and K. R. Cave, "The psychophysical evidence for a binding problem in human vision," Neuron, vol. 24, no. 1, pp. 11–17, 1999.

21. A. E. Cleeremans, The unity of consciousness: Binding, integration, and dissociation. Oxford University Press, 2003.

22. P. Lanolin, "A Correspondence between Algol 60 and Church's Lambda Notation," Commun. ACM, vol. 8, no. 2, pp. 89–101, 1965.

23. D. P. Woodruff, "Data Streams and Applications in Computer Science," Bulletin of EATCS, vol. 3, no. 114, 2014.

24. S. Shoemaker, "Absent qualia are impossible–a reply to Block," The Philosophical Review, pp. 581–599, 1981.

25. N. Block, "Are absent qualia impossible?," The Philosophical Review, pp. 257–274, 1980.

26. L. Stubenberg, Consciousness and qualia, vol. 5. John Benjamins Publishing, 1998.

27. F. Jackson, "Epiphenomenal qualia," The Philosophical Quarterly, pp. 127–136, 1982.

28. P. M. Churchland and P. S. Churchland, "Functionalism, qualia, and intentionality," Philosophical Topics, vol. 12, no. 1, pp. 121–145, 1981.

29. T. Horgan, "Jackson on physical information and qualia," The Philosophical Quarterly, pp. 147–152, 1984.

30. P. M. Churchland, "Knowing qualia: A reply to Jackson," A neurocomputational perspective: The nature of mind and the structure of science, pp. 67–76, 1989.

31. S. Shoemaker, "Qualities and Qualia: What's in the Mind?," Philosophy and Phenomenological Research, pp. 109–131, 1990.

32. D. C. Dennett, "Quining qualia," Consciousness in modern science, 1988.

33. P. M. Churchland, "Reduction, qualia, and the direct introspection of brain states," The Journal of Philosophy, pp. 8–28, 1985.

34. E. L. Wright, The case for qualia. MIT Press, 2008.

35. V. S. Ramachandran and W. Hirstein, "Three laws of qualia: What neurology tells us about the biological functions of consciousness," Journal of Consciousness Studies, vol. 4, no. 5–6, pp. 429–457, 1997.

36. R. Buck, "What is this thing called subjective experience? Reflections on the neuropsychology of qualia.," Neuropsychology, vol. 7, no. 4, p. 490, 1993.

37. H. Langsam, "Experiences, thoughts, and qualia," Philosophical Studies, vol. 99, no. 3, pp. 269–295, 2000.

38. G. Strawson, Mental reality. Cambridge Univ Press, 1994.

39. T. Horgan and J. Tienson, "The intentionality of phenomenology and the phenomenology of intentionality," 2002.

40. R. E. Cytowic, Synesthesia: A union of the senses. MIT press, 2002.

41. P. G. Grossenbacher and C. T. Lovelace, "Mechanisms of synesthesia: cognitive and physiological constraints," Trends in cognitive sciences, vol. 5, no. 1, pp. 36–41, 2001.

42. L. E. Marks, "On colored-hearing synesthesia: cross-modal translations of sensory dimensions.," Psychological bulletin, vol. 82, no. 3, p. 303, 1975.

43. L. C. Robertson and N. E. Sagiv, Synesthesia: Perspectives from cognitive neuroscience. Oxford University Press, 2005.

44. E. M. Hubbard and V. S. Ramachandran, "Neurocognitive mechanisms of synesthesia," Neuron, vol. 48, no. 3, pp. 509–520, 2005.

45. R. E. Cytowic and F. B. Wood, "Synesthesia: I. A review of major theories and their brain basis," Brain and cognition, vol. 1, no. 1, pp. 23–35, 1982.

46. D. Maurer, "Neonatal synesthesia: Implications for the processing of speech and faces," in Developmental neurocognition: Speech and face processing in the first year of life, Springer, 1993, pp. 109–124.

47. G. Martino and L. E. Marks, "Synesthesia: Strong and weak," Current Directions in Psychological Science, vol. 10, no. 2, pp. 61–65, 2001.

48. R. E. Cytowic, "Synesthesia: Phenomenology and neuropsychology," Psyche, vol. 2, no. 10, pp. 2–10, 1995.

49. D. M. Eagleman, A. D. Kagan, S. S. Nelson, D. Sagaram, and A. K. Sarma, "A standardized test battery for the study of synesthesia," Journal of neuroscience methods, vol. 159, no. 1, pp. 139–145, 2007.

50. R. E. Cytowic and D. Eagleman, Wednesday is indigo blue: Discovering the brain of synesthesia. MIT Press, 2009.

51. F. Spector and D. Maurer, "Synesthesia: a new approach to understanding the development of perception.," Developmental psychology, vol. 45, no. 1, p. 175, 2009.

52. S. Shoemaker, "Self-knowledge and self-identity," 1963.

53. S. Shoemaker, "Identity, cause, and mind: Philosophical essays," 2004.

54. J. Lacan, "The Seminar of Jacques Lacan Book II: The Ego in Freud's Theory and in the Technique of Psychoanalysis 1954–55," Trans. Sylvana Tomaselli. Ed. Jacques-Alain Miller. New York: Norton, 1988.

55. J. Schaffer, "Monism: The priority of the whole," Philosophical Review, vol. 119, no. 1, pp. 31–76, 2010.

56. D. Braddon-Mitchell, "The philosophy of mind and cognition," 2007.

57. W. G. Lycan, "Inverted spectrum," 1973.

58. D. R. Hilbert and M. E. Kalderon, "Color and the inverted spectrum," Color perception: Philosophical, psychological, artistic, and computational perspectives, pp. 187–214, 2000.

59. M. Tye, "Qualia, content, and the inverted spectrum," Noûs, pp. 159–183, 1994.

60. G. Harman, "The intrinsic quality of experience," Philosophical perspectives, pp. 31–52, 1990.

61. J. Broackes, "Black and white and the inverted spectrum," The Philosophical Quarterly, vol. 57, no. 227, pp. 161–175, 2007.

62. D. Cole, "Functionalism and inverted spectra," in Epistemology and Cognition, Springer, 1991, pp. 85–100.

63. R. Villard and Z. Levay, "Creating Hubble's Technicolor Universe," Sky and Telescope, vol. 104, no. 3, p. 28, 2002.

64. A. Ventura, "Pretty Pictures: The Use of False Color in Images of Deep Space," 2013.

65. R. Peierls, "Wolfgang Ernst Pauli. 1900-1958," Biographical Memoirs of Fellows of the Royal Society, vol. 5, pp. 175–192, 1960.

66. C. H. Bennett, "Universal computation and physical dynamics," Physica D: Nonlinear Phenomena, vol. 86, no. 1, pp. 268–273, 1995.

67. W. D. Hillis, The pattern on the stone: the simple ideas that make computers work. Basic Books, 2015.

68. M. Wilson, "Six views of embodied cognition," Psychonomic bulletin & review, vol. 9, no. 4, pp. 625–636, 2002.

69. M. L. Anderson, "Embodied cognition: A field guide," Artificial intelligence, vol. 149, no. 1, pp. 91–130, 2003.

70. L. Shapiro, Embodied cognition. Routledge, 2010.

71. J. C. Turner, M. A. Hogg, P. J. Oakes, S. D. Reicher, and M. S. Wetherell, "Rediscovering the social group: A self-categorization theory.," Contemporary Sociology, 1987.

72. C. Calhoun, Social theory and the politics of identity. Blackwell, 1994.

73. B. E. Ashforth and F. Mael, "Social identity theory and the organization," Academy of management review, vol. 14, no. 1, pp. 20–39, 1989.

74. J. C. Turner, "Towards a cognitive redefinition of the social group," Social identity and intergroup relations, pp. 15–40, 1982.

75. R. Centers, "The psychology of social classes: a study of class consciousness.," 1949.

76. W. S. McCulloch and W. Pitts, "A logical calculus of the ideas immanent in nervous activity," The bulletin of mathematical biophysics, vol. 5, no. 4, pp. 115–133, 1943.

77. L. N. De Castro and F. J. Von Zuben, Recent developments in biologically inspired computing. Igi Global, 2005.

78. L. Bochereau and P. Bourgine, "Extraction of semantic features and logical rules from a multilayer neural network," in Proceedings of the International Joint Conference on Neural Networks, 1990, pp. 579–582.

79. Y. Hayashi, "A neural expert system with automated extraction of fuzzy if-then rules," in Advances in neural information processing systems, 1991, pp. 578–584.

80. G. G. Towell, "Symbolic knowledge and neural networks: Insertion, refinement and extraction," 1992.

81. G. Towell and J. W. Shavlik, "Interpretation of Artificial Neural Networks:...," 1992.

82. M. W. Craven and J. W. Shavlik, "Understanding neural networks via rule extraction and pruning," in Proceedings of the 1993 Connectionist Models Summer School, 1994, p. 184.

83. D. A. Hall and D. R. Moore, "Auditory neuroscience: The salience of looming sounds," Current Biology, vol. 13, no. 3, pp. R91–R93, 2003.

84. W. Schneider and R. M. Shiffrin, "Controlled and automatic human information processing: I. Detection, search, and attention.," Psychological review, vol. 84, no. 1, p. 1, 1977.

85. X. Hou and L. Zhang, "Saliency detection: A spectral residual approach," in Computer Vision and Pattern Recognition, 2007. CVPR'07. IEEE Conference on, 2007, pp. 1–8.

86. M. I. Posner and C. R. Snyder, "Attention and Cognitive Control," Cognitive psychology: Key readings, p. 205, 2004.

87. D. Kahneman, Attention and effort. Citeseer, 1973.

88. R. D. Hare, The Hare Psychopathy Checklist-Revised: PLC-R. MHS, Multi-Health Systems, 1999.

89. J. M. Fischer, "Compatibilism," 2007.

90. J. A. Gray, J. A. Gray, and J. A. Gray, "Consciousness: Creeping up on the hard problem," 2004.

91. T. Horgan, "Functionalism, qualia, and the inverted spectrum," Philosophy and Phenomenological Research, pp. 453–469, 1984.

92. S. Shoemaker, "The inverted spectrum," The Journal of Philosophy, pp. 357–381, 1982.

93. C. Klein, "What pain asymbolia really shows," Published online at philpapers. org/rec/KLEWPA, 2011.

13.4 Chapter 6 References

1. J. Hernández-Orallo, "A (hopefully) non-biased universal environment class for measuring intelligence of biological and artificial systems," in Artificial General Intelligence, 3rd Intl Conf, 2010, pp. 182–183.

2. B. Goertzel, "Toward a formal characterization of real-world general intelligence," in Proceedings of the 3rd Conference on Artificial General Intelligence, AGI, 2010, pp. 19–24.

3. J. Insa-Cabrera, D. L. Dowe, S. Espana-Cubillo, M. V. Hernández-Lloreda, and J. Hernández-Orallo, "Comparing humans and AI agents," in Artificial General Intelligence, Springer, 2011, pp. 122–132.

4. J. Insa-Cabrera, D. L. Dowe, and J. Hernández-Orallo, "Evaluating a reinforcement learning algorithm with a general intelligence test," in Advances in Artificial Intelligence, Springer, 2011, pp. 1–11.

5. C. Hewitt, P. Bishop, and R. Steiger, "A universal modular actor formalism for artificial intelligence," in Proceedings of the 3rd international joint conference on Artificial intelligence, 1973, pp. 235–245.

6. M. Hutter, "Universal algorithmic intelligence: A mathematical top → down approach," in Artificial general intelligence, Springer, 2007, pp. 227–290.

7. S. Legg and J. Veness, "An approximation of the universal intelligence measure," arXiv preprint arXiv:1109.5951, 2011.

8. J. Hernández-Orallo and D. L. Dowe, "Measuring universal intelligence: Towards an anytime intelligence test," Artificial Intelligence, vol. 174, no. 18, pp. 1508–1539, 2010.

9. S. Legg and M. Hutter, "Universal intelligence: A definition of machine intelligence," Minds and Machines, vol. 17, no. 4, pp. 391–444, 2007.

10. M. Hutter, "Towards a universal theory of artificial intelligence based on algorithmic probability and sequential decisions," in Machine Learning: ECML 2001, Springer, 2001, pp. 226–238.

11. N. Bostrom, "Ethical issues in advanced artificial intelligence," Science Fiction and Philosophy: From Time Travel to Superintelligence, pp. 277–284, 2003.

12. E. Yudkowsky, "Intelligence Explosion Microeconomics," Citeseer, 2013.

13. N. Bostrom, "Hail Mary, Value Porosity, and Utility Diversification," 2014.

14. M. Blaze, W. Diffie, R. L. Rivest, B. Schneier, and T. Shimomura, "Minimal key lengths for symmetric ciphers to provide adequate commercial security. A Report by an Ad Hoc Group of Cryptographers and Computer Scientists," DTIC Document, 1996.

15. J. O. Pliam, "On the incomparability of entropy and marginal guesswork in brute-force attacks," in Progress in Cryptology—INDOCRYPT 2000, Springer, 2000, pp. 67–79.

16. D. J. Bernstein, "Understanding brute force," in Workshop Record of ECRYPT STVL Workshop on Symmetric Key Encryption, eSTREAM report, 2005, vol. 36, p. 2005.

17. D. B. West and others, Introduction to graph theory, vol. 2. Prentice hall Upper Saddle River, 2001.

18. J. Devillers and A. T. Balaban, Topological indices and related descriptors in QSAR and QSPAR. CRC Press, 2000.

19. S. Pemmaraju and S. Skiena, Computational Discrete Mathematics: Combinatorics and Graph Theory with Mathematica®. Cambridge university press, 2003.

20. E. L. Gettier, "Is justified true belief knowledge?," analysis, pp. 121–123, 1963.

21. R. Nozick, Philosophical explanations. Harvard University Press, 1981.

22. M. Swain, "Epistemic defeasibility," American Philosophical Quarterly, pp. 15–25, 1974.

23. M. Steup, "Knowledge and skepticism," 2005.

24. P. Markie, "Rationalism vs. empiricism," 2004.

25. M. Polanyi, "Knowing and being: Essays," 1969.

26. W. P. Alston, Beyond" justification": Dimensions of epistemic evaluation. Cambridge Univ Press, 2005.

27. M. Devitt, Realism and truth, vol. 296. Cambridge Univ Press, 1984.

28. W. P. Alston, A realist conception of truth. Cambridge Univ Press, 1996.

29. L. Daston, "Objectivity," 2007.

30. D. Davidson, "Truth and interpretation," Claredon, New York, 1984.

31. J. J. Morrone and J. V. Crisci, "Historical biogeography: introduction to methods," Annual review of ecology and systematics, pp. 373–401, 1995.

32. K. T. Kelly, "The logic of success," Philosophy of science today, pp. 11–38, 2000.

33. K. T. Kelly, Naturalism Logicized. Springer, 2000.

34. K. Kelly, "Learning theory and epistemology," in Handbook of epistemology, Springer, 2004, pp. 183–203.

35. K. T. Kelly and O. Schulte, "The computable testability of theories making uncomputable predictions," Erkenntnis, vol. 43, no. 1, pp. 29–66, 1995.

36. K. T. Kelly, O. Schulte, and C. Juhl, "Learning theory and the philosophy of science," Philosophy of Science, pp. 245–267, 1997.

37. N. Rugai, Computational Epistemology: From Reality to Wisdom. Lulu. com, 2012.

38. O. Schulte and C. Juhl, "Topology as epistemology," The Monist, pp. 141–147, 1996.

39. R. Parikh, L. S. Moss, and C. Steinsvold, "Topology and epistemic logic," in Handbook of spatial logics, Springer, 2007, pp. 299–341.

40. W. Sieg, "Calculations by man and machine: conceptual analysis," 2000.

41. A. R. Jensen, "The g factor: The science of mental ability," 1998.

42. D. E. Knuth, "Big omicron and big omega and big theta," ACM Sigact News, vol. 8, no. 2, pp. 18–24, 1976.

13.5 Chapter 7 References

1. J. R. Searle, "Minds, brains, and programs," Behavioral and brain sciences, vol. 3, no. 03, pp. 417–424, 1980.

13.6 Chapter 9 References

1. I. J. Good, "Speculations concerning the first ultraintelligent machine," Advances in computers, vol. 6, no. 99, pp. 31–83, 1965.

2. R. I. Blackwell, "8 Galileo Galilei," Science and religion: A historical introduction, p. 105, 2002.

3. F. Golden, "The worst and the brightest. For a century, the Nobel Prizes have recognized achievement–the good, the bad and the crazy.," Time, vol. 156, no. 16, pp. 100–101, 2000.

4. P. Goodchild, Edward Teller: The Real Dr. Strangelove. Harvard University Press, 2004.

5. M. A. Finocchiaro, The Galileo affair: a documentary history, vol. 1. Univ of California Press, 1989.

www.ingramcontent.com/pod-product-compliance
Lightning Source LLC
Chambersburg PA
CBHW071405050326
40689CB00010B/1759